THE SECRET LIFE OF

MUSICAL
NOTATION

THE SECRET LIFE OF
MUSICAL
NOTATION

DEFYING INTERPRETIVE TRADITIONS

Roberto Poli

Amadeus Press
An Imprint of Hal Leonard Corporation

Published in 2010 by Amadeus Press
An Imprint of Hal Leonard Corporation
7777 West Bluemound Road
Milwaukee, WI 53213

Trade Book Division Editorial Offices
33 Plymouth St., Montclair, NJ 07042

Printed in the United States of America

Book design by Kristina Rolander

Library of Congress Cataloging-in-Publication Data is available upon request.

ISBN 978-1-57467-184-1

Contents

Acknowledgments   vii

Prelude   ix

1 . . . Of Hairpins   1

2 . . . Of *Sforzandi*   69

3 . . . Of *Rinforzandi*   103

4 . . . Of Pedals   139

5 . . . Of *Stretti*   181

6 . . . Of Rhythmic Values   207

Notes   239

Index of Musical Works   249

Acknowledgments

Shortly after I made the United States my home, I felt that something was changing the way I observed music. I owe this in many ways to the rare opportunity of studying with Russell Sherman. The four short years I spent under his guidance were seminal to my evolution as a musician, and their long-range influence continues years after my studies with him came to an end. It is the inquisitive nature of Sherman's teaching that stimulated me to find my own voice and to search indefatigably for the truth. The simple but essential question that he often posed during my lessons—"What is the character of the piece?"—was one that Sherman's own teacher, Eduard Steuermann, had asked him in his teens. In time, that question became an important tool in my own teaching philosophy and generated a necessity—that of examining the role of musical notation to reveal the meaning of what Steuermann and Sherman had appropriately identified as a vital instrument of exploration. The investigation led to unforeseen outcomes, and these pages are their natural consequence.

I could not have predicted this journey: some eighteen months, many late nights, early mornings, and every available scrap of time spent with fervor in front of a computer screen, assembling writings and ideas from years past and new ones that emerged during the process. The task seemed insurmountable at first, but I was encouraged by the support with which my friends endowed me once this book started to appear in different forms in their lives. This is the product of years of lively conversations with Angel Ramón Rivera, whose friendship and support have been extraordinary; my inspiring exchanges with Ian Lindsey, which have joyfully accompanied the last decade of my life; and years of teaching, which have provided me with irreplaceable experiences and lessons. Without my exceptional pupils, this book would not exist.

I am grateful to Susan Gula for her unwavering support during the early months, for not laughing at me when I told her that I was going to write a book, and for always smiling in regard to any adversity I might have encountered; to John Bell Young, for believing in me, and for convincing me to pursue these writings without knowing it; to James Johnson, for his fundamental role in this project, for his encouraging words and gentlemanly ability in pointing out redundancies and linguistic flaws without changing my voice in the early stages of this book; to Ramona Leeman, whose positive outlook and stylistic elegance have been essential to the completion of the manuscript, and for her noble effort in tirelessly reviewing it over the months; to Toni Rosenberg, for her unparalleled contributions in the world of language during the arduous task she faced while editing the book, and for the important suggestions she offered; to Iris Bass at

Amadeus Press, for her contributions in the final copyedited version of the book, and for pointing out oversights that had escaped me for years; to Jessica Burr at Amadeus Press, for her infinite patience, her support, and her dedication to the project, and for guiding me through the process of getting the book published; to Mattia Ometto, for predicting how my ideas might be received in Europe (and for losing the manuscript twice); to Andi Zhou, for his wizardry with Sibelius and contagious joie de vivre; to Christopher Staknys, for providing double dots; to David Kim, for his passion, and for helping me with hairpins at the last minute; to Annette Oppermann at the Haydn Institut in Cologne, for knowing just about every single marking in Haydn's works; to Aldo Ciccolini, for welcoming my discoveries so enthusiastically; to Robert Levin, for his infinite knowledge and precious input; to John Rink, for our conversations, his invaluable help and friendly spirit; to Jeffrey Kallberg, for his heartening response to my writings and our illuminating exchanges, and for helping me understand the direction I wanted to take; to Selimir Prodanović, for his tireless support, his astonishing musical intuitions and inspiring presence in my life; to Artur Szklener at the Fryderyk Chopin Institute in Warsaw, for granting permission to use photographic excerpts from the manuscripts of Chopin's Opp. 28, 47, 58, and 61; to Sylwia Heinrich, for her infinite kindness, for being instrumental in obtaining a photograph of the manuscript of Chopin's Barcarolle, Op. 60, in possession of the Jagiellonian Library in Kraków, and for allowing its appearance in the book.

And then there is my great teacher, Russell Sherman, whose presence in my life has been fundamental. To him I owe who I am as a musician today. To him I dedicate these pages.

Prelude

Several years ago, the thought of my creating a book about music would have seemed farfetched to me: I had jotted down a few ideas, some better articulated than others, but that something more significant would begin to emerge from my little traveling diaries and the various notepads I had disseminated around the house was not what I anticipated. Scattered as they were, though, my writings were drawn together by a reoccurring motif: the notion that the long-standing interpretation of several commonly encountered musical signs and symbols may be in conflict with what the composers originally intended. This position stemmed from my inability to come to terms with certain interpretive instructions that seemed awkward or, indeed, infeasible in their execution but that most musicians deem intentional. In my teenage years I had already sensed that various indications in the scores were musically inconclusive, but as my studies continued I felt that their conventional interpretation profoundly compromised what I construed as the intent and meaning of the music I played. Ignoring them was not the answer, but a limitation that deprived me of the appropriate musical grammar. Eventually, I understood that the contradictions prompted by these markings reside partly in the way we read musical notation.

The analytical approach encouraged by contemporary scholarship has not only generated a new curiosity in regard to original manuscripts and early editions, but resurrected a clarity that was obfuscated by some of the overly edited revisions of the late nineteenth and early twentieth centuries. Seeing a piece of music in its original form is a legitimate expectation, and we all derive pleasure from opening the uncluttered pages of recent authoritative editions of Mozart's sonatas or Bach's *Well-Tempered Clavier*, in which articulatory gestures and notational symbols become visually available, alive, compliant. Without question, the purified and informative urtext editions are an asset. It is their very nature that implicitly calls us to adhere to the composer's instructions, and therein is found a dilemma: For many musicians the text is sacrosanct, and its strict observance is the means of drawing closer to its secrets and complexities; yet the belief that a musician should execute precisely what is on the printed page rather than interpret it was an element that emerged insistently in the playing of the last century, as no performer before that time would have considered the rigid approach to reading the score that is professed today. As I acquainted myself with the more transparent incarnations proposed by the urtext editions, I sensed that some of the markings that I found inexplicable seemed to arise even more persistently in the roles imposed so forcefully by interpretive dogma. In the process of investigating the original functions and historical applications of the unyielding indications, how artists from an earlier era creatively translated what they saw in the score and how we might do so today became pressing questions. It was increasingly apparent to me that what modern musicians dismiss as the excesses of a past era may have been at the center of an aesthetic approach that guided artists in the communication of their individuality.

An unexpected revelation was the turning point in what was to be a lengthy evolution, and along the way, doubt was an inevitable and not unwelcome presence. Much of what I apprehended about notation emerged as I deepened my analysis of original manuscripts, early editions, and subsequent versions and revisions; worked through a variety of miscalculations; and applied and tested my ideas in hundreds of scores. Forming a persuasive correlation between the sounds I produce and the printed page in front of me has not always been easy: I had to be willing to set aside some of the interpretive principles that accompanied my youth and that had become unreliable though customary accessories to my musical intuition. I also had to accept, as the evidence mounted, that I was confronting traditions and canons that seem to be received knowledge.

My hope is that in providing alternatives to interpretive traditions, this book will bring us closer to practices that have been forcefully removed from our vocabulary, and that it will reopen creative possibilities that have been lost to us for some time. In the process of discovery, signs and symbols in the score have turned from hostile elements to friendly companions—a gift I certainly had not envisioned. In retrospect, the contemplation of the ideas that these writings contain has bestowed a greater interpretive insight than had my long hours spent at the piano.

◄◆►

It was during the final editing stages of *The Secret Life of Musical Notation* that Jessica Burr, project editor at Amadeus Press, enthusiastically shared an idea: the creation of audio clips as parallel contributions to the musical examples found in the book. As Burr pointed out, what these pages propose is a dramatic shift from the conventional understanding of the signs and symbols I discuss, and imagining their implications without hearing their transformation might be problematic. This idea had been suggested early on by several friends, though in the form of an accompanying compact disc. Offering the brief excerpts as permanent audio files hosted on the Internet seemed to be a more practical way of reaching the reader. The examples represented by audio clips are marked throughout the book with the download icon ⬇, and they can be heard at www.roberto-poli.com/secretlife.

ONE

...OF HAIRPINS

Why hurry over beautiful things?
Why not linger and enjoy them?

— CLARA WIECK SCHUMANN

Frédéric Chopin's Polonaise-Fantaisie, Op. 61 has been in my repertoire for well over a decade, appearing frequently in my recitals next to other late works of the composer, or in programs exclusively devoted to fantasies, from John Bull's Fantasia in D to Liszt's *Réminiscences de Don Juan*. Repeated performances solidified an intimacy with the piece that only time can grant. And yet, even after several years, I sensed that my vision failed to persuade my audiences, often eliciting a tepid response. What was it that made my performance unconvincing? Was an answer to this question perhaps lying within the course of time?

In his *Vie de Chopin*, written shortly after the composer's death, Franz Liszt gave a description of the Polonaise-Fantaisie—a portrayal with which we are all too familiar:

> Pictures largely unfavorable to art like all these of extreme moments, of agonies, of death rattles and the contractions in which the muscles lose all elasticity and the nerves, ceasing to be organs of will power, reduce men to the passive prey of pain. Deplorable aspects, which the artist should admit to his domain only with an extreme circumspection.[1]

As overstated as it may seem, this depiction is not too distant from other contemporaneous accounts. Chopin's final creations were considered morbid, enigmatic, the outcome of his ailing condition—a perception no doubt supported by the rich vocabulary of his late style, which engaged in contrapuntal experimentation and remote chromatic implications. Liszt eventually conceded to the greatness of the Polonaise-Fantaisie and Chopin's compelling intuitions. As for me, I came to the realization that what inhibited my performances might not have been the piece's ineffable message or the complexity of its language, but something practical: the intertwinement of seemingly incongruous dynamic indications. Much as I tried to interpret them, the discontinuity posed by the interaction between symbols was such that I felt at a loss. Why would Chopin be so specific to the extent of being at times contradictory? Was I being overly analytical? I felt a profound devotion to Chopin's art, yet sensed that following his instructions as I understood them was not bringing me any closer to it.

Chopin made use of an abundance of symbols that conventionally indicate short dynamic changes over several beats, and which have commonly been identified as hairpins, or crescendo and diminuendo forks (⎯⎯⎯⎯, ⎯⎯⎯⎯). While learning the Polonaise-Fantaisie, I began to notice that in many of the recorded interpretations of the piece that I considered significant points of reference, some of those directions were frequently ignored. In other cases, the eagerness to follow them in a literal manner led pianists to choices that were musically unconvincing. Consider the following passage, where the rather elaborate way of notating dynamic nuances leads to a seeming contradiction:

EXAMPLE 1.1. F. Chopin: Polonaise-Fantaisie in A-flat Major, Op. 61, mm. 103–108.

Why did Chopin instruct us with indications that seem so directly at odds? I tried to do justice to the hairpin marked in measure 104 by decreasing the volume in the thematic motif of the left hand, but the outcome seemed contrived. Curiously, most editions of the past did not include this hairpin—the rationale possibly being that, had Chopin desired a decrease in sound, he would probably have started the crescendo a measure later.

Perhaps not as inconclusive but equally puzzling, a few measures earlier the markings for crescendo and diminuendo are accompanied by hairpins that suggest exactly the same increase and decrease in sound, making the presence of both directions a redundancy:

EXAMPLE 1.2. F. Chopin: Polonaise-Fantaisie in A-flat Major, Op. 61, mm. 87–92.

Why did Chopin feel the need to use two sets of instructions simultaneously to express exactly the same concept?

Comparable occurrences in the Polonaise-Fantaisie appear equally enigmatic, but this is not the only work of Chopin's in which these interpretive conundrums present themselves. Throughout his life, the composer marked his scores with redundancies and with contradictions in which reconciliation seems unattainable. In the opening measures of the Barcarolle in F-sharp Major, Op. 60, for instance, a long diminuendo has a very slim opportunity of coexisting with the hairpin that precedes it, because the hairpin already determines a reduction in volume, as does the decay of sound that is caused by the sustained chord on the second beat. According to the Henle edition, which I used while learning the Barcarolle, the diminuendo starts before the hairpin even comes to a close:

EXAMPLE 1.3. F. Chopin: Barcarolle in F-sharp Major, Op. 60, mm. 1–5 (Henle edition).

Not only did Chopin use two indications that propose exactly the same concept; in this case, they actually cross paths. Why did he choose not to mark a longer diminuendo starting from the second beat of measure 1, if diminuendo alone was his intention?

In other works, Chopin's notation is even more cryptic. Consider measures 577–79 of the Scherzo in E Major, Op. 54 as reported in the Breitkopf & Härtel edition of 1843:

EXAMPLE 1.4. F. Chopin: Scherzo in E Major, Op. 54, mm. 576–583 (Breitkopf & Härtel edition, 1843).

In the Schlesinger edition, also of 1843, the hairpin ends a measure earlier, and the *p* completely vanishes. Were these well-intended "touch-ups" made by a puzzled editor, or afterthoughts introduced by Chopin himself? Or could it be that the German edition reported what had been an inadvertent writing slip on Chopin's part? The Schlesinger version unquestionably made the passage more reasonable. Still, in light of the other peculiar instances that we just analyzed, I wondered whether the version published by Breitkopf & Härtel was truly an oversight.

Over the years, I found myself engaged in endless conversations with other musicians in regard to these unusual cases. None of our dialogues succeeded in providing consistent explanations, mostly because the interpretations they yielded were based all too often on subjective preferences and intuitions. Chopin was not alone: the notation employed by other composers showed similar issues, posing the same questions. Franz Schubert used hairpins in the same arbitrary way, in combination with other dynamic indications. For example, at the end of the development in the first movement of his Sonata in A Major, D. 959, I was surprised to find the marking *crescendo* immediately followed by a hairpin. The inclusion of both would seem to be superfluous:

EXAMPLE 1.5. F. Schubert: Sonata in A Major, D. 959, I. Allegro, mm. 95–98.

In the performances that I heard over the years, pianists simply played a sustained crescendo. This was probably done in the belief that the presence of both instructions intends to reinforce the concept of an increase in volume.

A most curious case emerged during a conversation with one of my former teachers. While discussing the cathartic conclusion of Franz Liszt's Sonata in B Minor, his attempt to find a rational explanation for the presence of the opening hairpin that starts in measure 755 seemed far from elucidating. He proposed that Liszt might have intended a choreographic instruction rather than a dynamic one, as it would be unfeasible to apply an increase in dynamic to a sustained chord:

EXAMPLE 1.6. F. Liszt: Sonata in B Minor, mm. 754–760.

He went on to suggest that the performer's torso slowly lean forward once the chord in measure 755 has been struck, abruptly leaning backward right before the following *ppp* chord is played in measure 756. These motions, he proposed, would give the listener the illusion of an inner crescendo that is "felt" rather than heard. I later discovered that imaginative solutions such as this one had already been illustrated by Alfred Brendel in his writings. If a composer marked an opening hairpin on a single note, Brendel explains, its mysterious meaning can be conveyed only through gesture—in other words, physical motion. I assume that the validity of this approach would apply exclusively to a live performance in which the audience is given the chance to be visually engaged. Alternatively, the gesture may become an opportunity for the performer to participate emotionally in the intensity of a specific passage—an element that could become a crucial component of its interpretation.

A few years ago, while reviewing some works of Chopin, Schubert, and Liszt in preparation for a recital, I was once again faced with the challenge of assigning such contradictions and redundancies a meaning. I decided to omit all the hairpins so as to obtain a clear representation of the dynamic skeleton of each piece. By doing so, I realized that the hairpins were not as critical to the dynamic structure as I had thought they were. Further, I could see that the hairpins often interfered with logical shaping: in some cases they proposed an increase in intensity when one would expect the phrase to end; in others, a closing hairpin was placed in the middle of a phrase apparently to indicate a decrease in sound, just when one would anticipate an opening gesture. This held true in the principal theme of the Barcarolle, Op. 60, where the slurs outline two-bar phrases while the hairpins challenge the shape that these slurs suggest:

EXAMPLE 1.7. F. Chopin: Barcarolle in F-sharp Major, Op. 60, mm. 5–9.

Eliminating these hairpins allowed me to follow the phrasing that Chopin notated (increasing the intensity to the middle of the slurs and decreasing it as each phrase ended)—exactly the opposite of what those closing and opening hairpins seemed to be proposing.

Thanks to this approach, other instances began to make perfect sonic sense. For example, in measures 18–21 of the Largo from Chopin's Sonata in B Minor, Op. 58, the dynamic swells that I deemed unacceptable were now inert, innocuous symbols:

EXAMPLE 1.8. F. Chopin: Sonata in B Minor, Op. 58, III. Largo, mm. 18–21.

Not only did this reorganization embody what I had envisioned for these brief gestures; it also corroborated a fundamental principle of musical inflection, tirelessly communicated by Chopin in his teaching—that the end of a slur should be dynamically tapered. Whereas the slurs clearly determined the shape of phrases, the hairpins often implied the opposite of those basic principles of dynamic inflection, hindering the natural flow of the musical discourse. I reluctantly decided to ignore the hairpins in general, at least for the time being. This strategy did not resolve the nagging belief that I was missing Chopin's intentions, but it did remove one source of my unease. As weeks went by, my plan still seemed to work. Yet I felt that I could not quite overlook the reality that Chopin had painstakingly marked all those hairpins in his manuscripts. Above all, did I have the authority to disregard the dynamic shapes that they seemed to designate?

Several months later, during a long train ride on my way to Rome, I was again examining the score of the Polonaise-Fantaisie. In the quiet of an unusually empty compartment, I pored over each measure, singing the piece in my head. It was in those moments that I was led to the greatest musical revelation of my life: when I inflected a phrase with the flexibility of pulse that is usually prescribed for expressive playing, I often found that there were opening or closing hairpins that followed these gestures. As I gently slowed down, sometimes an opening hairpin would outline that modification of speed. Likewise, after I took time and returned to the previous speed, a closing hairpin appeared in the score. Was this merely a coincidence? In some instances, the normal dynamic curve of a phrase was indeed underlined by an opening and a closing hairpin (⟨ ⟩). In many cases, though, the placement of hairpins set them in opposition to regular, predictable inflection, as we just saw in the main theme of Chopin's Barcarolle or in the Largo from his Sonata in B Minor. Could it be, I wondered, that hairpins were contributing to a broader, more detailed description of what was illustrated for the first time in the late nineteenth century by German musicologist Hugo Riemann (1849–1919) as *agogics*—the fluctuation of tempo given by slight variations of pulse? Might these hairpins not be dynamic markings at all, but indications for what we describe as *rubato*—the flexibility imparted to the fundamental pulse of a piece, which in most cases is crucial to the conveyance of its expression? While still in its germinal stage, this intuition was structurally and musically credible. I immediately sensed its magnitude and understood that my new reading of the symbol signified a radical departure from the way I conventionally interpreted the printed page. I also realized that my earlier decision to set aside temporarily the dynamic role of hairpins had helped me perceive their agogic significance. Whatever accounted for it, the insight made sense and seemed to solve a quandary that had perplexed me for years.

As the train approached the Roma Termini station, I quickly formulated three basic principles to illustrate my theory:

1. ◁ indicates taking time as the end of the symbol approaches, slightly slowing down.

2. ▷ indicates lingering on the note or group of notes at the beginning of the symbol, gradually returning to the former speed.

3. As a result, ◁ ▷ combines both elements, the phrase or group of notes being affected by some elasticity in the middle.

My new approach succeeded perfectly as I applied it to the repertoire that I had been playing, from Beethoven and Haydn through the romantics. Perhaps inevitably, the thought that such an important concept is unknown to musicians today made me question some aspects of my training. As I examined the works of composers from the mid-eighteenth century to the second half of the nineteenth century, my intuition was confirmed. At some point the use of hairpins as agogic markings had been discontinued—an event that perhaps took place in the late 1800s or in the early 1900s. But who was responsible for transforming their meaning? Could it have been Johannes Brahms? Although his late works display hairpins that seem to outline agogic freedom, in many cases their use could indeed imply an increase or decrease in volume, as they are placed between two diametrically opposite dynamics—a phenomenon that rarely occurs in Chopin's writing, for example. Was Claude Debussy to blame for changing the meaning of hairpins from agogic symbols into dynamic indications? I promptly consulted some of his works and noticed that there was no direct evidence that hairpins would have exclusive dynamic validity: in fact, in *L'isle joyeuse*, composed in 1904, Debussy employed hairpins that seem to outline agogic fluctuations. I was confused, but was reminded that I had done myself a good service by leaving out the hairpins a few months earlier. Now that they had become my main focus, I was determined to learn whether I could conclusively substantiate my theory.

Understanding how hairpins were going to revolutionize the way I played required a great amount of patience. Months elapsed before I achieved a certain degree of fluency in their delivery, and some instances remained enigmatic for quite some time. In many cases, as I eventually found out, the riddle was caused by the appearance of hairpins in print—that is, the ways in which most editions, even the most authoritative ones, had reinterpreted them. It was at a later stage that I came to an essential realization: out of necessity, my ability to understand their roles involved the correlation of intuition and deductive reasoning. In the past, what I had felt to be musically instinctive was often hindered by preconceived notions about symbols that I tended to interpret mechanically, usually by obediently reproducing what had become their conventional attributions. Unearthing what I thought were the real designations of hairpins brought me to a different cognitive level—a condition that, I felt, could be attained only by my transcending the rigid rules that had governed my musical upbringing. As I rid myself of interpretive dogmas that had compelled me to respond to hairpins as dynamic indications, I perceived that many of those hostile symbols became serviceable through the intuitive side of my musicianship. Phrases with which I had previously struggled suddenly made sense, because the effects that I had envisioned as viable solutions were taking shape in front of me, thanks to the new designations I had allowed to materialize in the music. While singing the Polonaise-Fantaisie in my head during a train ride to Rome, the visual, the aural, and the intuitive had for a moment crossed paths. A quote by Marcel Proust, which I found several days before that journey, almost prophetically described my experience: "The only real voyage of discovery consists not in seeking new landscapes but in having new eyes." Perhaps an agogic meaning, my initial discovery, was not the only direction I could take. Rather, I understood that looking at these symbols with "new eyes" might disclose them as responsive and pliable, with other possible connotations, and that electing this predisposition may have revealed alternative meanings for other symbols as well. It was then that I realized how predominant the faculty of listening should have been in the way I sought to understand the function of hairpins. The presence of a marking in a score should have not been taken at face value but explored in regard to the way it could serve the musical narrative. Having validated the association between the intuitive and cognitive aspects of my musical perception, I now found that hairpins seemed to adapt to the flexibility of phrasing that I had often felt necessary but that I frequently had held back for fear of violating rules of musical appropriateness. Could it be that if a hairpin were interpreted as meaning a sudden crescendo, thereby compromising the tenderness found in the lyrical opening section of a slow movement, for instance, the attribution given to it by tradition might have been at fault? As I imagined possible solutions for an opening hairpin in the context of a page whose only dynamic indication was *pianissimo*, it was clear that an agogic involvement seemed a more reasonable alternative than a clamorous intrusion. It soon became evident that discovering this side of notation had opened the door to other possibilities for which an agogic connotation was perhaps only a prologue. In time I came to the conclusion that in the ever increasing implementation of detailed notation in the printed scores that occurred at the end of the eighteenth and the beginning of the nineteenth centuries, there may have been a progressive abandonment of deductive reasoning on the part of musicians, perhaps even a loss of more profound attentiveness. Much had been based on intuition, reasoning, and listening until this transformation took place. Did the introduction of new notational tools and their steady growth limit active participation in the process of music making, initiating a neglect of older practices? Did the emergence and proliferation of these tools inexorably contribute to an increasing unawareness of the original designations of certain markings in favor of their mechanical reproduction? Perhaps, it occurred to me, at this early stage of my explorations these thoughts were premature. For the time being, hairpins were there to liberate my imagination from the musical prison in which, until then, I had been held captive.

Hairpins appeared as early as 1712, in the *XII Sonate a violino solo e violoncello col cimbalo, opera prima* (Twelve Sonatas for Violin, Violoncello, and Harpsichord, Opus 1) by Giovanni Antonio Piani (1678–ca. 1760), published in Paris. These sonatas are the composer's only surviving creations, and establishing what his use of hairpins intended can only be based on speculation. Further, in Piani's hand the hairpins were closed and filled in, causing them to resemble thin isosceles triangles, which would hint at some sort of personal code. During the course of the eighteenth century, other composers used hairpins in an individual but noncommittal way, and the exact meaning they intended in most cases remains inexplicable to this day. The first composer to use hairpins with a degree of consistency was perhaps Franz Joseph Haydn, who began to evaluate the potential of the symbol during the last decade of the century. It is in some of his last keyboard sonatas, completed between 1789 and 1795, that we find a regular use of their notation, although hairpins were already sparingly introduced in works such as his String Quartets, Op. 50 (Hob. III/44–49), composed in 1787.

When the German composer Daniel Gottlob Türk (1750–1813) set out to describe his personal symbols to indicate agogic fluctuations in his *Clavierschule* (School of Piano Playing), compiled in 1789, he did not anticipate that his notation would not set a precedent:

I have already made use of some signs in my easy clavichord sonatas by means of which the passages where a quickening or slowing of the tempo should take place are made known. Here are the signs with the added explanation.

Complete passages which are to be played gradually slower I have indicated as follows:

a. The slower passages must not be too prolonged, however; rather they are to be played only gradually and imperceptibly a little slower than is required by the tempo.

b. Certain thoughts which can be played somewhat slower (dragging, haltingly, lingering, *tardando*) have this sign:

c. What has already been said in (a) applies here as well, except that in this (second) case, the tempo is not taken gradually slower, but where the sign begins, the tempo should immediately be taken a little slower, although again imperceptibly.

d. For the places which can be played somewhat quickly (accelerated) I will choose these signs:

Since my signs were introduced, several composers have made use of them in their works. Many players also observe these signs very carefully, only they make mistakes by not following the explanation (a). Thus they go from Allegro almost into an Adagio which often has a very bad effect.[2]

Even though these symbols did not make history, Türk should be credited with being the first composer to write explicitly about the notational codification of interpretive elements that previously had been left to the discretion of the performer. Unfortunately, we do not have proof that his system (which he had admittedly used prior to writing his *Clavierschule*) prompted others to employ hairpins as agogic markings to evoke the same principles. What is relevant, though, is that hairpins appeared in the works of Haydn and in those of some of his contemporaries around that time, showing that an interest in codifying the notation of flexibility of pulse had collectively begun to surface.

A productive late-night e-mail exchange with Annette Oppermann of the Haydn Institut in Cologne proved to be a starting point for my research. While discussing Haydn's Sonata in C Major, Hob. XVI:48, which the German firm Breitkopf & Härtel published in 1789, Oppermann confirmed that it was in this two-movement work that the composer began to use hairpins with a degree of consistency. No autograph or any other authentic source of the sonata is known, challenging the notion that 1789 was the year of its composition, and that the symbols may have appeared before its first printed version. At this early stage, nevertheless, establishing a precise date was outside the scope of my research: although learning about the circumstances that led Haydn to write or publish the piece was undoubtedly of great interest, my goal was to discover his motivations for using hairpins so abundantly. Analyzing the score validated Oppermann's assertion that these symbols were used more profusely here than in any of the works Haydn had written prior to 1789. It also revealed that their use was confined primarily to the lyrical first movement—a fact that may corroborate their agogic intentions. Two examples stood out as significant, and are both found in the recapitulation of the opening movement:

EXAMPLE 1.9. F. J. Haydn: Sonata in C Major Hob. XVI:48, I. Andante con espressione, mm. 55–59.

The opening hairpin that accompanies the ascending gesture in measure 55 may ideally introduce the recapitulation with a ritenuto; and the opening and closing gesture in measure 58 seems to express agogic fluctuation involving the sinuous melodic line in the upper register.

———————— •◄●►• ————————

In the last two decades of the eighteenth century, musical notation became increasingly detailed as printed music began to catalog more meticulous instructions about articulation and dynamics. Composers understood that being more specific about dynamic and agogic fluctuations would be crucial to imposing their interpretive conception. Consequently, we encounter a variety of explicit directions, such as *sempre più Adagio* in the Moderato from Haydn's Sonata in G Minor, Hob. XVI:44; *mancando* in the closing measures of the Adagio in Mozart's Sonata in C Minor, K. 457; *perdendosi* in the Adagio in Haydn's Sonata in G Major, Hob. XVI:40; and *a suo piacere* at the beginning of the short cadenza that precedes the recapitulation in the first movement of Haydn's Sonata in E-flat Major, Hob. XVI:49.

This evolution, however, generated a paradox: although musicians in the eighteenth century underwent a rigorous training that emphasized freedom of inflection in addition to agogic and dynamic variety as improvisatory elements of a performance, over the decades this knowledge was supplanted by a growing dependence on notational symbols and signs, which a performer could not ignore. With such wealth of explicit notation, certainly a decline of understanding and awareness of early, more flexible practices must have slowly crept onto the musical landscape. This shift in thinking evolved to such an extent that by the turn of the nineteenth century, Ludwig van Beethoven had replaced most figurations that previously had appeared in small print in the scores (appoggiaturas, turns, etc.) with standard values, such as eighth- or sixteenth-notes—this in an attempt to show their literal execution, by default excluding any alternative interpretation or omission.

The placement of hairpins between two opposite dynamic markings, from the works of Haydn to those of the late-nineteenth-century composers, has supported and encouraged the belief that hairpins were used to indicate an increase or decrease in volume. Consider the hairpin found in measure 28 from the opening movement of Beethoven's Sonata in C Minor, Op. 111, published in 1822—a piece that I have chosen because it represents the crucial transition between what we define as classical and romantic eras. Some might argue that the hairpin intends to signal a diminuendo between the *forte* at the beginning of the descending gesture and the *piano* that follows:

EXAMPLE 1.10. L. van Beethoven: Sonata in C Minor, Op. 111, I. Maestoso-Allegro con brio ed appassionato, mm. 26–30.

The belief that the hairpin indicates a diminuendo seems plausible, and we have all been instructed to treat hairpins in this manner. I discussed this general belief with friends and colleagues on many occasions, proposing that a closing hairpin positioned between a *forte* and a *piano*, visually conveying a decrease in volume, may not always be intended to serve that purpose. My argument against the notion that hairpins denote dynamic fluctuations is corroborated by a performance practice that was common knowledge in the second half of the eighteenth century and that was taken for granted, whether or not the composer added explicit instructions: that ascending figurations are supposed to be played in crescendo and descending ones in diminuendo. Indeed, this assignment of intent was supported well into the nineteenth century by authorities such as Carl Czerny, who wrote about it in his *Vollständige theoretisch-practische Pianoforte-Schule* (Complete Theoretical and Practical Pianoforte School), Op. 500, of 1839:

> As a rule, crescendo is used for ascending passages and diminuendo for descending ones [...]. This rule shall be observed as well when the composer did not indicate such way of execution. Where else he wishes the opposite effect, the composer shall undoubtedly indicate that.[3]

Czerny's remark goes to the core of a significant element that I observed in the first work that Beethoven published—the Trio in E-flat Major, Op. 1, No. 1. Although hairpins appear consistently throughout the piece, the composer never used the terms *crescendo* and *diminuendo*, with the exception of three *crescendi* in the Scherzo movement. These three occurrences are confined within eight measures, and the context seems to confirm that they were marked to signal anomalous increases in volume that would not be intuitively placed by the performer. Is it reasonable to conclude that Beethoven intended dynamic fluctuation to be determined in accordance with the context, especially when the only indications he provided were placed at opposite ends of the dynamic spectrum, such as *f* and *p*? Further, in the Trio in E-flat Major hairpins as dynamic markings often seem to contradict logical shaping, while their purpose as agogic inflections seems to support a more coherent interpretive design. Yet an even more substantial consideration needs to be made: had Beethoven used hairpins as a tool to signal dynamic fluctuation, why would their employment be so inconsistent and relatively limited, given the potential they yielded? This holds true in the late keyboard works of Haydn: his Sonata in E-flat Major, Hob. XVI:52 is a perfect candidate to demonstrate that hairpins would often compromise the musical discourse if employed as dynamic indications. When Haydn wrote this ambitiously virtuosic sonata on a new and more powerful instrument lent to him by Jan Ladislav Dussek (1760–1812), Beethoven had just interrupted his brief apprenticeship with him on account of Haydn's extensive travel to the English capital, and his teaching (he did not seem to appreciate the strictness with which the master imparted notions of counterpoint). However brief and problematic their relationship, Beethoven's extensive use of hairpins throughout his life was a practice he most likely learned from Haydn, who had begun to use the symbols consistently only several years before the two composers met. Beethoven's early works make use of the hairpin in such variety that one is left to wonder how influential a concept it must have been for the young composer.

It was shortly after Haydn's return from his last trip to England that the Viennese firm Artaria published Beethoven's three Piano Sonatas, Op. 2, which the composer dedicated to his teacher as a sign of deference. These substantial compositions show an unprecedented originality and display great inventiveness in the employment of new symbols. The opening movement of the first sonata, for example, features a notation quite extravagant for the time: the symbols ⬚ and ⬚ are combined in very close proximity, in most cases presented over three-note gestures. Hairpins seem to have been the object of a growing interest in Beethoven's evolving language during the period following the publication of Opp. 1 and 2. In the Largo from the Sonata in E-flat Major, Op. 7, published by Artaria in 1797, measure 9 and its analogous repetition in measure 11 show a set of hairpins placed in the middle of two chords—a gesture that perhaps does not intend an inexplicable and unachievable crescendo:

EXAMPLE 1.11. L. van Beethoven: Sonata in E-flat Major, Op. 7, II. Largo, con gran espressione, mm. 8–12.

As Beethoven entered the new century, his writing tended to display a more economical use of hairpins, usually confined to melodic contexts and slow movements, thereby attesting to the more limited agogic flexibility that fast-paced passages may have been meant to display. For example, the entire first movement of the Sonata in C Major, Op. 53 features only one hairpin, in the second thematic group (measure 38 and analogous passage in the recapitulation):

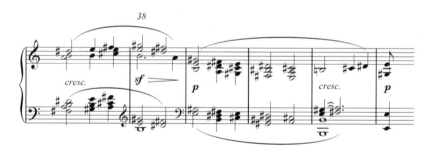

EXAMPLE 1.12. L. van Beethoven: Sonata in C Major, Op. 53, I. Allegro con brio, mm. 37–42.

In the opening section of the more peripatetic first movement of the Sonata in F Major, Op. 54, opening and closing hairpins appear quite frequently. Conversely, in the *sempre forte e staccato* section (anacrusis of measure 29 and following), the bolder character contrasts with the dancelike material of the beginning, and fluctuation is less serviceable; hence it may not be surprising that Beethoven omitted the use of hairpins in this passage:

EXAMPLE 1.13. L. van Beethoven: Sonata in F Major, Op. 54, I. In tempo d'un menuetto, mm. 20–32.

In his late years, Beethoven's language remained unvaried in this respect: hairpins were meant to suggest interpretive nuances in more melodic contexts, not dynamic variations within a passage or phrase. The Sonata in A-flat Major, Op. 110 offers a significant example: the fast-paced second movement and the two fugues present virtually no hairpins, in contrast with the opening Moderato cantabile or the Adagio and the Arioso sections of the closing movement, where they are generously used, specifying the inflection of individual beats, climaxes, arrival points or cadences. Opening hairpins are found less frequently in Beethoven's music: especially when in conjunction with the arrival of a new section, the composer probably found it easier to notate a decrease in speed by using the terms *rallentando*, *ritardando*, *ritenente*, and *ritenuto*, usually followed by the indication *a tempo*—even when a brief episode was involved. In fact, opening hairpins virtually disappeared from his language once these terms became more habitual occurrences. Beethoven's decision to replace hairpins as opening gestures with terms that provided greater specificity in regard to pace may confirm the extent to which he viewed hairpins as accessories to interpretive flexibility rather than signals of dynamic shift.

As the nineteenth century began, Beethoven's imposing figure began to affect the musical life of Vienna. The time in which Franz Schubert received his formal training coincided with this pivotal moment in music history. The two composers had officially met only in 1822, but from his youth, Schubert manifested a profound veneration toward the master. It was therefore predictable that the use of hairpins in the music of the young composer would fall into the designations classified by an already well-established tradition in the Austrian capital, most likely initiated as early as the 1790s by composers such as Haydn and Beethoven. In Schubert's works, nonetheless, the roles of hairpins became more specific and elaborate: especially in his last period, they appeared profusely either in the middle of the system or assigned to one hand (often being marked above the upper staff or beneath the lower, but sometimes below the right hand as well). It is these singular placements that seem to perplex many. For example, measures 39 and 41 of the first movement from his late Sonata in A Major, D. 959 (1828), show a curious use of short hairpins:

EXAMPLE 1.14. F. Schubert: Sonata in A Major, D. 959, I. Allegro, mm. 39–43.

Most pianists submit to the notion that these hairpins intend a diminuendo at the beginning of each gesture of descending triplets. Considering the context, the effect that derives from this approach seems unnatural. Did the composer intend to signal slight agogic nuances? Or is there a further meaning?

Concurrently with these short closing hairpins, Schubert frequently employed opening hairpins in the middle of the system. Interpreting these symbols as agogic inflections would validate some of the interpretive eighteenth- and early nineteenth-century practices. In the context of a piece in sonata form, these symbols may be found at the onset of significant sections such as the second thematic block, the development, or the recapitulation to imply a slight ritenuto. We mentioned that, at the turn of the nineteenth century, Beethoven chose to indicate such instances with greater accuracy by using *ritardando—a tempo*, even when a short transition was involved. Before that time, these agogic concessions had been implicit components of musical rhetoric, but a growing concern about the imposition of an interpretive design persuaded composers to implement opening hairpins to specify some of these cases. On page 5, we mentioned the concluding measures of the development section in the first movement of the Sonata in A Major, D. 959. Along with a crescendo in measure 96 to the *fortissimo* in measure 98, the hairpin perhaps indicates a slight broadening of tempo to announce the recapitulation:

EXAMPLE 1.15. F. Schubert: Sonata in A Major, D. 959, I. Allegro, mm. 95–98.

Schubert also employed the term *diminuendo* when a rallentando of substantial length was in sight, establishing an unambiguous distinction between *decrescendo* and *diminuendo*, which were used interchangeably by other composers. Schubert typically used *diminuendo* before the recapitulation, before a new section, or at the end of a movement. In some cases, it appears concomitantly with the marking *decrescendo*. We find one occasion in the celebrated Impromptu in E-flat Major, D. 899, No. 2:

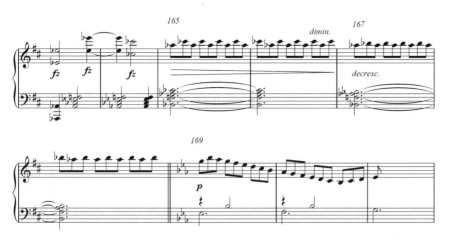

EXAMPLE 1.16. F. Schubert: Impromptu in E-flat Major, D. 899, No. 2, mm. 163–171.

What did Schubert intend the performer to understand when he combined a closing hairpin and the instructions *diminuendo* and *decrescendo* within just three measures—and, even more perplexing, when the confluence of the three written notations occurs between the very end of one measure and the beginning of the next? The explanation, it seems to me, must involve separate meanings, with distinct functions that together create a justifiable musical logic: the hairpin beginning in measure 165 and extending for two measures may indicate a slight agogic concession as the figuration in triplets begins; the *diminuendo* marked at the end of measure 165 suggests a rallentando that ends with the recapitulation in measure 169; and the *decrescendo* that starts in measure 167 asks the performer to decrease the volume from the ideal *forte* or *fortissimo* still present at the beginning of the measure, reaching the *piano* marked as the main theme returns. We also encounter the simultaneous appearance of *decrescendo* and *diminuendo* in the Impromptu in B-flat Major, D. 935, No. 3, at the end of the theme and of each variation, which allow each section to conclude with a decrease in both volume and speed.

We can only begin to imagine the puzzlement of early-twentieth-century scholars and editors as they rearranged some of these inconclusive instances to achieve what they must have considered a more coherent notation. To illustrate the degree of revision that printed music underwent during that time, when functionality played a more prominent role than preservation, I would like to return briefly to Schubert's Sonata in A Major, D. 959, and show how the redundancy incurred by the hairpin and the crescendo that we discussed in example 1.15 caused the editors at Breitkopf & Härtel to propose a rather awkward adaptation:

Example 1.17. F. Schubert: Sonata in A Major, D. 959, I. Allegro, mm. 95–98 (Breitkopf & Härtel edition).

In editions that were subject to this kind of revision, it is the short hairpins that are especially misconstrued. The most substantial flaw lies in their visual reinterpretation as what we intend today as dynamic accents—a reading that emerged in hopes of resolving the many anomalies of the original manuscripts or early editions. Example 1.17 shows that the last beat of measure 95 is affected by an accent for the left hand. Compare this accent with the short hairpin in example 1.15 and the considerable difference in the inflection of this passage that derives from compressing the short hairpin into an accent. The decision behind this adjustment may have been practical: as the marking had been placed in the middle of the system, it probably seemed unlikely that it would have referred to the right hand (had this been the case, Schubert would in all probability have written it above the upper staff); and a symbol meant to instruct the playing of both hands was narrowed to an indication for the left hand only, being further modified in the process. In editions that appeared before more authoritative publications brought back the original notation, this erroneous reading may have caused many short hairpins to become accents, thus blurring the distinction between the two symbols.

⎯⎯⎯⎯⎯ ◂◆▸ ⎯⎯⎯⎯⎯

Finding trustworthy editions of Chopin's works is a task challenged by considerations that are as diverse as the available sources and their dependability. Chopin relied on three countries for the circulation of his compositions: France, Germany (on several occasions, Austria represented an alternative), and England. These three covered the needs of other countries as well. For instance, Chopin's family in Warsaw purchased his newly published works through distribution provided by Breitkopf & Härtel, located in Leipzig. His dealing with publishers was a laborious process that accompanied Chopin throughout his days in Paris. It came with a price, as composing was for him a relentless quest for perfection, a continuous process of refinement. One of the most problematic aspects of evaluating the discrepancies among these early editions stems from that very process: the different versions that Chopin sent to the publishers rarely agreed with one another—an extraordinary fact if we consider that the three manuscripts (to which we refer with the German term *Stichvorlagen*—"engraver's copies") were generally prepared at the same time. When Chopin decided to include a variant to a second or third Stichvorlage, he did not always amend the previous versions. The three manuscripts would then be sent out, in most cases on the same day to avoid copyright piracy in any of the three countries of publication. This was the beginning of a fairly long procedure that involved the engraving of proofs and their correction. Even at this stage, Chopin's process of revision was evolutionary: new versions, most of the time simply modifying small details, were added to the copies prepared by the engravers, incurring alternative readings. Chopin did not always have the opportunity to correct the preparatory plates: although the French publisher in many cases offered more accurate readings because it had access to the composer, who eventually made corrections, the German and English publishers could not consistently rely on that assistance to ensure the accuracy of their printed proofs (time-consuming exchanges between the firm and the composer would have delayed the date of publication). For some of Chopin's works, Wessel & Co. of London reprinted the preparatory plate or the final version of the French edition. In a few isolated instances, Breitkopf & Härtel used the proofs from the French edition as the basis for its printings as well, with minor differences sometimes making their way into these versions notwithstanding. One infamous example, of which Chopin was probably unaware, is the alteration made by Breitkopf & Härtel at the end of the introduction in the Ballade in G Minor, Op. 23. The rolled chord in measure 7 conventionally features an E-flat as its final destination, as seen in the Schlesinger edition of 1836:

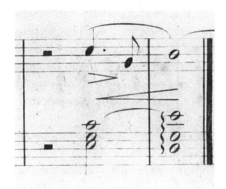

EXAMPLE 1.18a. F. Chopin: Ballade in G Minor, Op. 23, mm. 6–7 (Schlesinger edition, 1836).

But Breitkopf & Härtel turned this E-flat into a D:

EXAMPLE 1.18b. F. Chopin: Ballade in G Minor, Op. 23, mm. 6–7 (Breitkopf & Härtel edition, 1836).

To the contemporary ear, the E-flat seems perfectly appropriate in light of its implied harmonic resolution to D in the next measure, but to the engravers in Leipzig it must have sounded like an unspeakable cacophony, unaccustomed as they were to Chopin's harmonic inventiveness.[4]

Even though such editorial corrections were not often encountered, unintentional inaccuracies abounded. For instance, Chopin must have responded with indignation at the sight of the first French edition of his Mazurka in G-sharp Minor, Op. 33, No. 1, published by Schlesinger, which bore the marking *Presto* instead of *Mesto*—"mournful." Was the cause an inadvertent misreading by the engraver, or by Chopin's friend and factotum Julian Fontana (1810–1869), who prepared the final Stichvorlage? This episode may indicate that Chopin either was somewhat inattentive while proofreading the manuscripts that served as the basis for printed proofs, or was not concerned that an associate might copy his manuscripts inaccurately. He was quite perturbed, however, by misprints in the works of other composers: in Bach's *Well-Tempered Clavier*, he found it especially entertaining to correct what in some cases might have been simple cases of false relations. Chopin frequently delegated Fontana and other associates to proofread the preparatory plates for his own pieces, as he very often lacked the time or the desire, or both, to do so himself. Some publishers requested the assistance of other composers to face that task: at times Ignaz Moscheles was hired for Wessel, and Clara Schumann for Breitkopf & Härtel. Chopin, himself, also entrusted various people with making fair copies of his works—copies based on manuscripts that he considered definitive versions but which may have still presented some inaccuracies. He often proofread the copies that were sent to the publishers, but in some cases trusted that the manuscripts prepared by the copyists would be in order. Some of these fair copies show that the copyists were requested to limit themselves to writing the notes, and at some point later Chopin would add other relevant notation—from articulation to dynamics, from pedal markings to slurs.

As we survey these original sources, therefore, we observe several reasons to question the dependability of Chopin's scores that were published during his lifetime:

1. Not being consistently accurate, Chopin himself may have been responsible for some oversights in his own manuscripts.

2. Copyists may have been at fault for incorrectly reproducing the drafts that Chopin submitted.

3. Publishers may have been unable to have the plates proofread by Chopin or his affiliates, thus allowing misprints to make their way into the final published version.

4. Believing that they understood Chopin's intentions, publishers made changes of their own.

Besides the information that generated from these four levels of activity, further layers emerged from modern revisions. Over the last several decades, new editions have aimed to provide more authoritative versions based on a comparison of all the surviving sources—from sketches to Stichvorlagen, from fair copies to first editions. Although these revisions are commendable, their outcome is not always successful, because many details are still the subject of speculation. Rather than presenting faithful reproductions of the sources, their analysis has often led to adaptations of particular notational symbols that, to those editors, seemed misconstruing. The recapitulation in the Etude in D-flat Major, Op. 25, No. 8 perfectly illustrates how modern editions tend to differ in very small yet misleading details, as a result of this maze of documentation. In measure 21, the accent that the Paderewski edition proposes for the left hand appears instead as an accent for the right hand in the Wiener Urtext edition:

EXAMPLE 1.19. F. Chopin: Etude in D-flat Major, Op. 25, No. 8, m. 21 (Left: Paderewski edition; Right: Wiener Urtext edition).

In the critical notes of either edition there is no mention of possible alternatives. It is the Breitkopf & Härtel edition of 1837 that seems to provide a more plausible version: a short hairpin is notated in the middle of the system, not as an accent for either the right or the left hand:

EXAMPLE 1.20. F. Chopin: Etude in D-flat Major, Op. 25, No. 8, m. 21 (Breitkopf & Härtel edition, 1837).

The Etude in F Minor from *Trois Nouvelles Etudes* shows a rather curious incident—a contradiction caused by the presence of an opening hairpin placed between two diminuendi:

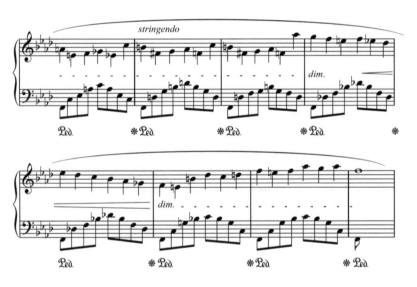

EXAMPLE 1.21. F. Chopin: Etude in F Minor for the *Méthode des Méthodes*, mm. 50–57.

In the Wiener Urtext edition, the editor Paul Badura-Skoda states in a footnote regarding this hairpin,

The cresc.-fork which contradicts the preceding dim. might be a writing slip by Chopin.[5]

Although this comment was surely prompted by the widespread conviction that hairpins indicate dynamic variations, I wondered why so many peculiarities of this sort would appear in Chopin's scores. Is it reasonable to presume that all these instances were writing slips? In some editions some of the markings that were construed as contradictory were simply deleted; in others they were altered to conform to the notion that hairpins are dynamic markings. In its revision of the Etude in F Minor illustrated above, the Paderewski edition proposed that the hairpin be reversed, thereby indicating a redundancy:

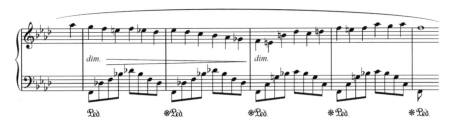

EXAMPLE 1.22. F. Chopin: Etude in F Minor for the *Méthode des Méthodes*, mm. 52–57 (Paderewski edition).

While evaluating the puzzling outcomes of some of these revisions, I came across a summary from Charles Rosen's monumental volume *The Romantic Generation* concerning the main theme of the Ballade in F Minor, Op. 52:

> The harmonic climax is always on the last of these four repeated notes, and is so marked by a crescendo, but paradoxically, before the end of the crescendo is reached, a diminuendo is indicated in the melody for the last two notes. It is clear from manuscript and edition that Chopin intended the diminuendo to commence in the middle of the crescendo and to coexist with it briefly although almost all editors, pulled by the anomaly, remove it.[6]

Here is the passage in question:

EXAMPLE 1.23. F. Chopin: Ballade in F Minor, Op. 52, mm. 8–13.

The perplexity caused by the overlapping of these markings led the editors of the Paderewski edition to delete the hairpins above the right hand in all analogous cases found in the ballade. Their position is illustrated in this excerpt from the extensive commentary:

> Chopin often wrote accents so large that they look like decrescendo signs. As this problem is insoluble, we have left out the signs.[7]

Badura-Skoda's preface to his 1973 revision of Chopin's etudes agrees with that conclusion, and confirms what we have already observed about ill-informed alterations made to Schubert's music:

> Like Schubert, Chopin often wrote his accents so big that they look like short diminuendo wedges.[8]

I remember the feeling of discomfort I experienced as a teenager when trying to find a musically practical solution for the accents featured in the opening theme (measure 8 and following) of Chopin's Ballade in G Minor, Op. 23 in a mainstream edition:

EXAMPLE 1.24. F. Chopin: Ballade in G Minor, Op. 23, mm. 8–16.

Upon close examination of the manuscript and the first French edition of 1836 (Schlesinger), accurately reproduced by Jan Ekier in the Wiener Urtext edition, it appears that these accents in the opening theme were notated as short hairpins:

EXAMPLE 1.25. F. Chopin: Ballade in G Minor, Op. 23, mm. 16–17 (Schlesinger edition, 1836).

While comparing the three early editions of the Ballade in G Minor, I discovered to my great surprise that in the 1836 Breitkopf & Härtel edition almost all the short hairpins were already converted into accents. I contemplated the possibility that the difference between short hairpins and accents had eluded the German publishers, until it occurred to me that perhaps short hairpins were retained only if they encompassed more than one note. In other words, if a hairpin was placed on a single pitch, in many cases it may have been converted into what we now regard as an accent. I had already encountered similar cases in Haydn's and Beethoven's works, but scrutinizing this early version of the Ballade in G Minor caused me to realize how this conversion practice held true for the romantics as well. The master class that the nonagenarian Artur Rubinstein (1887–1982) conducted in Jerusalem confirmed this interpretive intuition. While reviewing the opening theme of the ballade with one of the performers, Rubinstein instructed the student by saying, "Not accent there!" and proceeded to demonstrate the passage with an almost imperceptible inflection on the first note of each group, but with no accent. Nearly blind at the time, Rubinstein was relying on an instinctive insight about the passage, indirectly telling us that what is *behind* the notes is in many ways more vital to the music than what we read on the printed page.

Hairpin or accent? The mystery extends to additional notations. One of these is *sforzando*, the subject of chapter 2. The opening page of Chopin's Sonata in B

Minor, Op. 58, may confirm that what we view as an accent may also need to be differentiated from the *sforzando* that the composer marked on the same note:

EXAMPLE 1.26. F. Chopin: Sonata in B Minor, Op. 58, I. Allegro maestoso, mm. 7–9.

Is it then possible that Chopin employed what we view today as an accent to designate a coordinate other than a dynamic stress? By the time he published his Ballade Op. 23, Chopin had already introduced accents, as distinguished from his use of longer hairpins, but how are we to know what significance these accents bore at the time? Cases found in Chopin's etudes, for instance, cannot be considered agogic markings for definite reasons. In the Etude in C Major, Op. 10, No. 1, accents are proposed only for the first two measures, outlining a model to follow for the duration of the piece:

EXAMPLE 1.27. F. Chopin: Etude in C Major, Op. 10, No. 1, mm. 1–2.

These accents are often the subject of conversation among pianists, yet are generally ignored by most of them, because a performance of this etude in which the accents are deliberately afforded a dynamic role would be impracticable—the effort to play them with consistency would become a challenge at the metronome marking indicated, as well as a source of unevenness. I suspect that this approach would also do the music an injustice: Chopin expected his students to practice the broken arpeggios of this etude with a supple approach, requiring a quiet hand and an execution that eliminated any stiffness of wrist.[9] By placing accents on the first note of each quadruplet in measure 1, Chopin may have intended to indicate the avoidance of a strong emphasis of the thumb, which would cause a displacement of the metric pulse on the second sixteenth-note of each group in this measure and in measures throughout the etude that bear the same or similar fingering. These accents do not serve as dynamic emphases; rather, they outline a metric order that differs from the organization that the thumb may dictate if used as a customary point of reference on each ascending gesture.

Other etudes from Op. 10 evoke the same insight. In No. 8 in F Major, for example, accents seem to counter any displacement of the meter that could be caused by the lateral attack of the thumb on the last note of each quadruplet in the descending gestures, and the possible dynamic stress caused by the thumb passage in the ascending ones:

EXAMPLE 1.28. F. Chopin: Etude in F Major, Op. 10, No. 8, mm. 1–3

In No. 12 from the same set, the accents establish an unmistakable metric order that denies an otherwise misleading placement of beats:

EXAMPLE 1.29. F. Chopin: Etude in C Minor, Op. 10, No. 12, mm. 1–3.

In the first version of the Etudes Op. 10 that was made available on the European market, published in Leipzig in 1833 by Kistner, we can observe that the accents are slightly longer than those notated in modern times. Is this perhaps proof, or even a strong indication, that Kistner had to adapt a short hairpin to indicate what Chopin chose to use so frequently to specify these metric placements? The accents that we just observed in the Etude No. 12 in C Minor, for example, indeed appear in the Kistner edition as very short hairpins, most of the time encompassing the space of two notes:

EXAMPLE 1.30. F. Chopin: Etude in C Minor, Op. 10, No. 12, excerpt of m. 5 (Fr. Kistner edition, 1833).

We find another significant example of metric validity of short hairpins in the first movement of the Sonata in B-flat Minor, Op. 35. In the extended coda of the exposition, Chopin signaled the observance of a regular metric system, which could otherwise be incorrectly interpreted as starting from the first chord of each group of three quarter-notes, marked by the slurs:

EXAMPLE 1.31a. F. Chopin: Sonata in B-flat Minor, Op. 35, I. Grave, Doppio movimento, mm. 81–85.

The intended metric organization seems to have completely escaped the notice of the editors at Breitkopf & Härtel in their first version of the sonata:

EXAMPLE 1.31b. F. Chopin: Sonata in B-flat Minor, Op. 35, I. Grave, Doppio movimento, mm. 77–91 (Breitkopf & Härtel edition, 1840).

The German editors, in their somewhat casual placement of these short hairpins, did not designate a specific alignment—an indispensable element when considering metric guidelines. Rather, they interpreted the notations (albeit inconsistently) as markings that encompassed each slur. Had Chopin had the chance to proofread Breitkopf & Härtel's initial plate, he probably would have applied the correction by rewriting the accents above the right hand, as they were printed by the Troupenas and Wessel editions. The Stichvorlage for the first Breitkopf & Härtel edition was prepared by Chopin's pupil Adolph Gutmann, but includes corrections in the composer's hand. The passage in question shows that most accents have the size of short hairpins placed under two or three beats, possibly providing an explanation for the increased width of those accents in the printed version.

Other Chopin manuscripts substantiate the same tendency to notate accents in a rather large fashion. In the 1844 Stichvorlage of the Scherzo from the Sonata in B Minor, Op. 58, the conclusion of the A section features a sequence of accents (measures 51–54) that outline an independent voice in the bass register in the context of a perpetual-motion eighth-note figuration. Note how the lighter ink used for the accents may indicate that Chopin did not add relevant notational markings and symbols as he completed the main body of the music, but after he drafted the notes of an entire line, passage, or page:

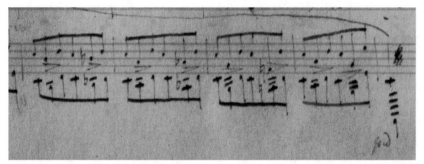

EXAMPLE 1.32. F. Chopin: Sonata in B Minor, Op. 58, II. Scherzo, mm. 51–55 (Breitkopf & Härtel Stichvorlage, 1844).

Likewise, in the opening measures of the development in the first movement from the Stichvorlage of the same sonata, what seem to be short hairpins are placed on specific pitches:

EXAMPLE 1.33. F. Chopin: Sonata in B Minor, Op. 58, I. Allegro maestoso, mm. 92–96 (Breitkopf & Härtel Stichvorlage, 1844).

In these two examples, hairpins are unlikely to represent short diminuendi or agogic inflection on the considered notes. Rather, in example 1.32 they may suggest a compound line that, in their absence, might not emerge as a feature of the passage; and in example 1.33, they may signal each entrance of the thematic material in the context of contrapuntal writing. This latter strategy had already been used by Schubert in his Sonata in A Major, D. 959:

EXAMPLE 1.34. F. Schubert: Sonata in A Major, D. 959, I. Allegro, mm. 82–85.

These short hairpins, in print often reduced to the size of an accent, seem to specify what in our time we call *voicing*—the emergence of a particular line in the context of polyphonic writing. By the beginning of the nineteenth century this practice was widespread, and composers also seem to have used long hairpins with the same purpose when the writing featured a multivoiced texture. The Bohemian pianist Vaclav Jan Tomášek (1774–1850) may have employed long hairpins to signal the predominance of one voice over another in a two-voice dialogue, or simply to indicate the presence of polyphony, as he seems to have suggested with opening hairpins in his *Variationen über ein bekanntes Thema*, Op. 16:

EXAMPLE 1.35. V. J. Tomášek: *Variationen über ein bekanntes Thema*, Op. 16, Var. VI, mm. 1–2.

The passage from Schubert's Sonata in A Major that we viewed in example 1.34 led me to contemplate the possibility that certain hairpins in the works of Chopin may indicate the same concept. For years I had been struggling with the contradictions caused by some hairpins that Chopin placed above or below the system, whose designation escaped me: sometimes an agogic role was a reasonable solution, but this explanation seemed frequently inconclusive. Viewing these hairpins as markings that help us identify lines whose presence would not be intuitively brought out clarified their role. Chopin had devised a sophisticated system, I realized, that allows us to recognize contrapuntal exchanges, for extended phrases or for simple fragments introduced by the alto, tenor, or bass voice. The composer's placement of the symbol is central to their meaning: hairpins that are positioned in the middle of the system can be construed as indicating that the entire passage is to be affected agogically; hairpins above the upper staff or beneath the lower staff can be understood to indicate voicing. In measure 25 of the Mazurka in A Minor, Op. 59, No. 1, both coordinates were specified: the hairpin in the middle of the system indicates agogic flexibility, whereas the hairpin under the lower staff signals that the left hand should be the relevant melodic feature:

EXAMPLE 1.36. F. Chopin: Mazurka in A Minor, Op. 59, No. 1, mm. 23–28.

In the Ballade in F Major, Op. 38, these different designations for hairpins occur simultaneously; if they are viewed dynamically, they appear to cross paths in a perplexing manner, consistently determining incongruous shapes:

EXAMPLE 1.37. F. Chopin: Ballade in F Major, Op. 38, mm. 141–144.

Modern traditions have led performers to believe that the intensity in this turbulent section should decrease in the right hand, while the intensity in the left hand should increase—a plan that would defy the shape that the slurs connote. On the other hand, were we to follow the same criterion I suggested for the Mazurka in A Minor, Op. 59, No. 1, the hairpin in the middle of the system would indicate agogic inflection whereas the one beneath the lower staff would indicate that the left hand should be melodically predominant.

This layered strategy seems to have been adopted by Chopin throughout his life, and it became conspicuously employed in passages whose layout involves chordal writing, which implies a higher incidence of compound lines and possible contrapuntal exchanges. Consider a common occurrence, demonstrated by measures 22 and 23 of the Mazurka in G Minor, Op. 24, No. 1:

EXAMPLE 1.38. F. Chopin: Mazurka in G Minor, Op. 24, No. 1, mm. 17–25.

The hairpin that begins in measure 22 beneath the lower staff indicates that the tenor line (G–F–E–E-flat) should interact with the melody in the right hand, creating the effect of a duet between the soprano and the tenor registers. Its shape, however, should be subject to the slur above it, not to a reduction in volume that a conventional attribution of a diminuendo to the close of this hairpin would cause.

As I took the time to become more familiar with Chopin's use of hairpins to signal contrapuntal relationships, another layer in the composer's notational strategy revealed itself. I began to notice that some of the hairpins I had thought designated agogic fluctuations because they were positioned in the middle of the system were actually referring to the voicing of inner lines. Their placement, I realized, was determined not by the composer's intentions, necessarily, but primarily by limitations in the space available in the manuscript. Depending on the registers used, the writing may not have allowed enough space: the downward stems in the right hand or a chordal accompaniment in the tenor register in the left hand might have forced certain hairpins to be notated in a rather constrained space. Yet comparing the original sources to modern editions disclosed a shocking truth: the placement of these symbols was often reassigned to the middle of the system by zealous editors who could not make out the original designation.

In light of these considerations, perhaps we could look again at examples I used earlier, and verify whether some of those puzzling hairpins were indeed meant to signal the occurrence and import of specific voices in the context of contrapuntal writing. Could the hairpin that we first viewed in example 1.1, in measure 104 of Chopin's Polonaise-Fantaisie, be signaling the presence of a compound line, rather than agogic flexibility?

EXAMPLE 1.39. F. Chopin: Polonaise-Fantaisie in A-flat Major, Op. 61, mm. 103–108.

If so, could it be that the objective of this hairpin was to outline the thematic motif in the left hand? It may be the presence of the symbol in the middle of the system that leads us to interpret it erroneously—a placement that was specified in Chopin's own Stichvorlage for Breitkopf & Härtel but that might have been dictated by the limited space caused by the pedal markings beneath the system, shown clearly in the left portion of the following illustration:

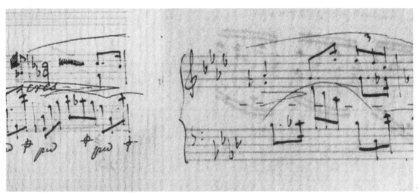

EXAMPLE 1.40. F. Chopin: Polonaise-Fantaisie in A-flat Major, Op. 61, mm. 103–105 (Breitkopf & Härtel Stichvorlage, 1846).

Further, I had originally interpreted the shorter hairpin in measure 105 as indicating metric order, as the third beat of measure 104 could have possibly been misconstrued as a strong beat if enunciated with emphasis. Until recently I believed that my inference was plausible, but when I revisited the passage in the German Stichvorlage I came to an astonishing realization: the page turn (measure

104 concludes a right-hand folio) may have prevented Chopin from extending a single, longer hairpin to both measures 104 and 105! Could it have been the alto line (G-flat–F–F-flat–E-flat) that Chopin meant to delineate? If so, he did not seem particularly concerned about its intelligibility. Some of the simplest clues, I then understood, can be withheld for reasons we would not dream of.

The notion that hairpins in the nineteenth century were understood in part as signaling the voicing of a compound line may find confirmation in the revision of Chopin's Etude in C Minor, Op. 10, No. 12 that was made in 1880 by Karl Klindworth (1830–1916). The coda of the etude shows that Klindworth inserted a hairpin for the alto voice in measure 80, in response to the hairpin marked by Chopin in the original version for the soprano voice in measure 78:

EXAMPLE 1.41. F. Chopin: Etude in C Minor, Op. 10, No. 12, mm. 77–84 (revision by Karl Klindworth).

If viewed dynamically, the hairpin that Klindworth added would cause a redundancy with the crescendo, which he also implemented in the original version (the *fortissimo* on the downbeat of measure 81 is editorial as well); should the added hairpin be viewed agogically, it would also create a redundancy with the *poco rallentando* that Chopin notated in the same measure. Rather, Klindworth intended to delineate the voicing of the alto line (G–F–E) in measures 80–81 as a mirrorlike response to the soprano line's C–D–E in measures 78–79.

While delving into the maze of information provided by Chopin's Stichvorlagen, I wondered why he chose to use hairpins of different sizes to outline various aspects of voicing or to delineate displacement of the rhythmic order. The answer may be found in the limited number of notational symbols that existed at that time. Chopin did not have other signs to indicate these instances and resorted to using a notational device that, decades later, came to relate specifically to dynamic fluctuations as new forms of notation arose to designate voicing and rhythmic organization. In some editions, through the years, short hairpins devolved into accents, and modern performers instinctively respond to them by placing dynamic emphases on the pitches they govern. This is the case in passages such as the ending of the outer sections of the Scherzo from Chopin's Sonata in B Minor, Op. 58, which we viewed in example 1.32. Rare are the performances in which these accents are interpreted as indicating a shaped melodic line, carved out of the thick texture of the closing statement. Were the accents not included, an intuitive interpreter might be able to identify the concealed melodic design, and bring out its profile with adequate inflection and without excessive dynamic stress. But just as we react instinctively to a symbol, we also feel compelled to charge it with excessive significance. We assume that its presence in the score must require an effort on our part to justify its purpose, in most cases by impulsively overstating it. Interpretations of the Fantasie in C Major, Op. 17, by Robert Schumann frequently reveal this predisposition: in the lyrical middle section of the marchlike second movement, accents are commonly interpreted as signaling substantial dynamic stresses. However, the intention to outline exclusively a rhythmic order seems all too plausible:

EXAMPLE 1.42. R. Schumann: Fantasie in C Major, Op. 17, II. Mäßig, mm. 114–118.

By using these accents, Schumann delineated two different sets of downbeats—one for the main body of the phrase and one for its penultimate measure (117). The accent placed above the second beat of measure 117 signifies the return to the predominant metric system. For Schumann, this was the only known way to signal the presence of interacting metric shifts within an episode, because the practice of alternating time signatures in contiguous measures was not yet common. The double stems for the alto voice suffice to identify it as the melody, which need not be signaled in a second manner with the use of accents.

When Sergei Rachmaninoff (1873–1943) intended to signal voicing and voice leading in the context of a multilayered texture, he employed an easy alternative—a short horizontal line—above or below the notes to be considered:

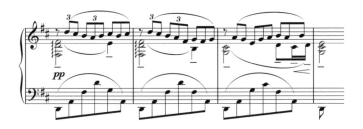

EXAMPLE 1.43. S. Rachmaninoff: Prelude in D Major, Op. 23, No. 4, mm. 19–22.

While perusing the German Stichvorlage of Chopin's Sonata in B Minor, Op. 58, I found an occurrence of metric displacement that, when viewed away from the piano, seemed to signal a more complex shift of the rhythmic system but that, when applied, revealed a simpler organization of the material and reduced its technical oddity. In the first movement, the section that leads to the second thematic block features patterned material based on sixteenth-note figurations:

EXAMPLE 1.44a. F. Chopin: Sonata in B Minor, Op. 58, I. Allegro maestoso, mm. 33–34 (Breitkopf & Härtel Stichvorlage, 1844).

In these transitional measures, the accents placed above the system seem to emphasize the syncopations caused by the quarter-notes.[10] Modern interpretive tradition has proposed that these accents are of the dynamic kind. Yet an approach that outlines their metric validity, which I have indicated in example 1.44b by inserting intermittent vertical lines where the Breitkopf & Härtel edition shows the accents, reveals that they may have been intended as a momentary reorganization of the downbeats:

EXAMPLE 1.44b. F. Chopin: Sonata in B Minor, Op. 58, I. Allegro maestoso, mm. 33–34 showing a displacement of strong beats (the intermittent vertical lines become the new bar lines).

Experimenting with this interpretive ambiguity enabled me to observe the technical challenges posed by these measures in a different light: shifting the metric focus temporarily to the accented beats disclosed a less knotted progression of the episode. The physical approach to these measures changes because the displacements caused by the accents are not understood as oppositions to the strong beats but rather as new pillars of the fundamental pulse—a departure from the primary rhythmic order but more of a referential diversion than a contrary one. Pianists fiercely accent the notes affected by these short hairpins; they fight against the regular pulse, creating an angularity that is rather unnatural. Although we cannot deny that a performer might have to place some dynamic emphases on the subsidiary pillars of a digressive metric order for it to be conveyed, I wonder whether the prominence that we commonly assign to them may be overemphasized.

Another relevant instance in which contemporary interpretation favors accents as forceful dynamic emphases is found in the opening of the first movement of Chopin's Sonata in B-flat Minor, Op. 35:

EXAMPLE 1.45. F. Chopin: Sonata in B-flat Minor, Op. 35, I. Grave, Doppio movimento, mm. 25–28.

For decades, these accents have been the subject of many a discussion among pianists. In the early twentieth century, the Italian pedagogue Attilio Brugnoli proposed a revision that attempted to justify their placement, interpreting them as diminuendo signs. According to Brugnoli, the accents in question were misread from the original sources, having been erroneously attributed to the eighth-note directly following the one that should have received the emphasis.[11] This position is easily disproved by the Breitkopf & Härtel Stichvorlage of the sonata, to which Brugnoli is unlikely to have had access. Today, some performers give these accents so much relevance that a sense of brutality, which could be modulated successfully, instead infuses the entire passage.

As I contemplated the intended scope of these disputed accents, I thought about their specificity and importance: I tried out the idea that the accents were meant to displace the downbeats to create a sense of unsettling angst, but this solution soon felt counterintuitive, making me doubt that this was Chopin's intention. It was during several ensuing months, in which I studied the meaning of hairpins placed above or below the system (as illustrated in examples 1.35–1.38 and 1.41), that I became aware of an alternative, more likely import. The episode is a textural variation of the first theme as it appears in the opening of the sonata. The melodic line is literally preserved, although several of the pitches are here woven into a thick chordal writing. Chopin might have been concerned that these chords could detract from the clarity with which the main theme in the upper line is enunciated, which in turn would create an imbalance in the voice leading of the different parts. It would seem credible that to avoid this potential distortion, he placed an accent above such pitches to ensure their importance. The opening hairpin in the second half of measure 27 and in analogous instances in the first movement shows the continuation of that line, which has to be extricated from the chordal writing to reproduce faithfully the theme from the opening page. Corroborating this assumption is another significance that can be aptly attributed to the positioning of these accents: the pitches over which they preside consistently conclude slurred gestures, and we already mentioned that Chopin adamantly expected the conclusion of slurs to be dynamically tapered.

After all these considerations, the reader might wonder what the difference is between short hairpins and accents. One of the leading Chopin scholars today, John Rink has considered this issue for years, and has summarized the distinction between short hairpins and regular accents, labeling the former as *long accents*—a classification that perhaps serves its purpose more than my description of these symbols as *short hairpins*, particularly when it pertains to metric organization. We examined how, during Chopin's lifetime, published scores were often inconsistent in reporting the long accents that the composer marked so clearly in his Stichvorlagen. We also saw how their application might even affect our perception of melodic inflection in a work such as the Ballade in G Minor, Op. 23 (examples 1.24 and 1.25). It is in his article *Les concertos de Chopin et la notation de l'exécution* (The Notation of Performance in the Concerti of Chopin) that Rink exhaustively expounds on his approach regarding these two symbols:

> Close scrutiny of the manuscript and printed sources for the two concertos indicates that Chopin's long accents had a multiplicity of functions reflecting both instrumental performance practice in general and *bel canto* practice as described in singing treatises such as Manuel García's. Their various roles in performance were determined by context but, in most cases, probably involved dynamic and/or temporal "spreading." [...] The four principal usages are for long rhythms (for the sake of dynamic reinforcement, expressive stress and proportional prolongation of a more conventional accent); to convey a sense of "leaning," or directional impulse, to appoggiaturas, suspensions and syncopations; to emphasise groups of notes (trills, acciaccaturas, grace notes and appoggiaturas/suspensions/syncopations comprising several notes, as well as lines to "bring out"); and finally to stress two or more tied notes. Needless to say, previous editions—including the first editions—have habitually transformed long accents into diminuendo hairpins or conventional "short accents" (i.e., >), to the music's detriment in performance. Even a cursory sample of recordings of the concertos, especially the *bel canto*–inspired slow movements, reveals that many pianists play certain notes with a sharp attack instead of the more spread one indicated by a long accent in the autograph or early printed sources; alternatively, the dynamic level sags when long accents are wrongly interpreted as diminuendos.[12]

The different categories that Rink recorded in the Concerti in E Minor, Op. 11 and F Minor, Op. 21 offer indeed a wealth of possibilities—a rich variety that appeared more conspicuously at the early stages of Chopin's career and that diminished over time, as his language became more refined, or explicit.

It is in considering one milieu in particular—the world of the opera—that we can perceive the inspiration that seems to have given rise, from the start of his career, to Chopin's layered use of accents and hairpins. His attendance at the opera was habitual after his arrival in Paris in 1831, but the influence of bel canto on the young composer stemmed from a much earlier involvement. As an adolescent, Chopin witnessed some remarkable performances of the most celebrated operas of the time. In 1826, when he was sixteen, his admiration for Gioachino Rossini led him to quote the aria "Vieni fra queste braccia" from *La gazza ladra* in the Trio of the early Polonaise in B-flat Minor, which he dedicated to Wilhelm Kolberg, one of his schoolmates at the Lyceum. When he was seventeen he wrote the Variations on "Là ci darem la mano" from Mozart's *Don Giovanni* for Piano and Orchestra, Op. 2. In Warsaw, in 1828, he witnessed the Polish premiere of Rossini's *Otello*, and during his stay in Vienna in 1829, *La Cenerentola* was one of the operas that captured his imagination. During the same sojourn, at the end of his debut in the Austrian capital, Chopin is reported to have improvised on themes from *La dame blanche* by Adrien Boieldieu, two days after attending one of its performances.

Once in Paris, Chopin was increasingly led by his absorption with the operatic milieu to research the expressive qualities of the human voice in the creation of his melodic lines. In 1999, conductor Will Crutchfield referred to this source of inspiration as "the trail of the vocalists," in an article he wrote for the *New York Times*:

> In Chopin's letters, and in the memoirs of his pupils [...], the names of those composers [Bellini, Rossini, and Donizetti] figure scarcely at all. But other names are prominent: Pasta, Rubini, Cinti, Malibran. In Chopin's mind, the style was coming from the singers. And as this was a period in which the singer was responsible for an enormous amount of the surface detail, the ornamentation and coloration, of the music he or she sang, we can get far closer to an understanding of what Chopin heard and how he transformed it by following the trail of the vocalists than by reading the scores they sang from. "His playing is entirely based on the vocal style of Rubini, Malibran, and Grisi, etc.: he says so himself," recalled Emilie Gretsch, a favorite pupil in the early 1840s who described her lessons in detailed letters to her father.[13]

In Chopin's early twenties and even in his late teenage years he seems to have used accents, mainly the long kind, to indicate some of the subtle nuances that are emblematic of the vocal tradition. John Rink points out that Chopin's long accents reflect interpretive elements that were formally explicated in treatises such as the *École de García: traité complet de l'art du chant*, written by Manuel Patricio Rodríguez García[14] (1805–1906) and first published in 1840.

Chopin's two piano concerti particularly illustrate this use of accents: positioned above or below the melody line, they seem to signal slight agogic prolongations or dynamic emphases involving appoggiaturas, syncopations, and tied notes—practices that were already familiar to Chopin because they were derived from baroque and classical aesthetic principles of vocal inflection. During the period when Chopin composed the piano concerti, the rather neutral meaning of the accent seems to have made it a well-suited candidate for investigations of notational aptitude. That this approach remained experimental, gradually mutating over the years, is evident in works such as the nocturnes—a form that comfortably allows us to trace the evolution of Chopin's melodic invention. The transformation in his use of accents ostensibly manifested itself at the same time that his rising reputation in Paris encouraged him to have his compositions published and distributed in other countries. In the three Nocturnes, Op. 9, written between 1830 and 1831 and published only in 1833, we find a profusion of accents, but in the opening section of the Nocturne in C Minor, Op. 48, No. 1 of a decade later—a page whose lyrical qualities would openly lend themselves to this type of notation—they are rare. Had the writing in the Nocturne in C Minor followed the notational criteria applied to the early nocturnes, the affecting line of the opening section would have been interspersed with accents, short and long, outlining appoggiaturas and tied notes, signaling the inflections of this fervent vocal line. Instead, very little of that experimental phase remains: long accents are placed under only two of the tied notes and under the two quarter-notes of the closing measure. In the last set of nocturnes, published in 1846 as Op. 62, accents are obsolete in melodic contexts. The abundance of accents as they are found in the early sources of the piano concerti indeed reveals a propensity to overcharge the score with instructions, a characteristic not uncommon among composers in their earlier years. It seems that as Chopin acquired experience as a composer, and as he was introduced to the more cosmopolitan Parisian world, his notation became progressively trimmed of dispensable details. Perhaps this evolution would have occurred inevitably, alongside the refinement of his notational language, but we cannot dismiss the exposures that are likely to have molded his language in Paris, where he had the opportunity to meet composers and hear performers whom he would have not had the chance to get to know while he was in Warsaw.

Recently, upon analyzing the original sources of Chopin's Concerto in E Minor, it occurred to me that some of the accents employed not only outline elements of vocal inflection, but also signal metric displacements or their avoidance. We saw this practice in examples 1.27–1.31, 1.40, and 1.42. Consider the opening tutti of the concerto in Chopin's own arrangement, in which, in measures 4 through 6, the long accents seem to be signaling a transitory adjustment to a duple meter. The accented dotted eighth-note in measure 3 also begins a displacement of the metric system because it functions as a downbeat:

EXAMPLE 1.46. F. Chopin: Concerto for Piano and Orchestra in E Minor, Op. 11, I. Riso-luto, mm. 1–6 (the intermittent vertical lines signal the new metric order caused by the accents).

A few measures later, long accents seem to determine another kind of irregularity, this time that of a hemiola that changes the meter from 3/4 to 6/8:

EXAMPLE 1.47. F. Chopin: Concerto for Piano and Orchestra in E Minor, Op. 11, I. Risoluto, mm. 37–39.

The examination of accents and hairpins that are responsible for metric anomalies in Chopin's manuscripts and first editions led me to a discovery involving the second episode from the Mazurka in G Minor, Op. 24, No. 1, which we briefly mentioned, on page xxx, regarding the voicing in the left hand. This passage, showing accents of different sizes, received the attention of Jean-Jacques Eigeldinger in *Chopin: Pianist and Teacher as Seen by His Pupils*:

> Chopin's notation includes here and there alternating agogic accents, making an undisguised duple meter pattern. [...] The coupling here of triplets with the following crotchets is significant: the dot under the crotchet shortens its value while the accent on the first quaver of the triplet lengthens it, following a compensatory system. Notated so precisely, this example gives a graphic idea of the deliberate rhythmic ambiguities which Chopin implanted in his Mazurkas.[15]

Here is the passage in question as it is illustrated by Eigeldinger:

EXAMPLE 1.48. F. Chopin: Mazurka in G Minor, Op. 24, No. 1, mm. 17–21 as illustrated in Eigeldinger's *Chopin: Pianist and Teacher as Seen by His Pupils*.

Hinging on a purely musical intuition, Eigeldinger's argument is at first persuasive because it confirms Chopin's sense of freedom that was described in the several accounts concerning his performances of his own mazurkas.[16] Yet Eigeldinger's hypothesis does not explain the specific roles of long and short accents in the preceding excerpt. The first German edition, which was published by Breitkopf & Härtel (and whose preparatory plate provided the basis for the first French edition, by Schlesinger), positions long accents above the triplets but shows that the accents in the analogous passage in measures 25 and 26 are of the short kind:

EXAMPLE 1.49a. F. Chopin: Mazurka in G Minor, Op. 24, No. 1, mm. 20–26 (Breitkopf & Härtel edition, 1835).

In the first English edition, published by Wessel—an exact reproduction of the first printing of the Schlesinger edition—no apparent distinction was made between long and short accents:

EXAMPLE 1.49b. F. Chopin: Mazurka in G Minor, Op. 24, No. 1, mm. 20–26 (Wessel edition, 1836).

Considering that the French and English editions were both based on the German edition, could these discrepancies prove that the publishers of the time did not give much weight to the length of accents? Rather than indicating rubato, are the accents in this passage signaling merely a duple-meter organization in the right hand while the left hand continues undisturbed in its triple-meter accompaniment? Is it also reasonable to surmise that, in Chopin's hand, the substantial differences in size of accents within scores and from one piece to another could have had to do simply with the space available and the immediacy of writing, more than with the intention of creating what to our modern eyes appears to be an obscure personal system?

                               ◄●►

The notion that accents in Chopin's works are not dynamic stresses would illumine several passages in which a sequence of accents may suggest agogic rather than dynamic emphasis on each note. One of my students cleverly pointed out that the accents on the second and third beats of measure 22 in the Nocturne in G Minor, Op. 37, No. 1 might intend an ideal recitato (recited) expressed by the descending gesture, rather than a series of louder (and brasher) sounds in the context of the already prescribed *fortissimo:*

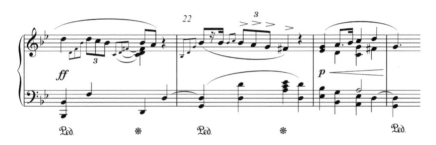

EXAMPLE 1.50. F. Chopin: Nocturne in G Minor, Op. 37, No. 1, mm. 21–24.

Despite the remarkable differences offered by the early sources of this nocturne, the idea of a recitato-like approach for these accents might be corroborated by their appearance in an earlier, analogous passage in measure 6, where the indicated dynamic is a *forte* rather than a *fortissimo.*[17] Moreover, Chopin marked the same notes in both passages with a rather original fingering—an addition that, by suggesting a portato-like attack of the key, may well support the approach I am proposing:

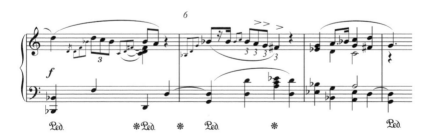

EXAMPLE 1.51. F. Chopin: Nocturne in G Minor, Op. 37, No. 1, mm. 5–8 (Breitkopf & Härtel edition, 1840).

In the first movement of the Sonata in B Minor, Op. 58, measure 30 offers another sequence of accents that are executed dynamically by most pianists. These accents seem to indicate that the descending sequence of chords based on the harmony of E-flat major should not be considered as mere passagework, but that the soprano line should be prominent against the other voices:

EXAMPLE 1.52. F. Chopin: Sonata in B Minor, Op. 58, I. Allegro maestoso, mm. 28–31.

Recently, one of my pupils came to a lesson having prepared the Mazurka in C Major, Op. 24, No. 2. Working on it helped to clarify the manner in which accents reveal Chopin's sense of freedom in this piece:

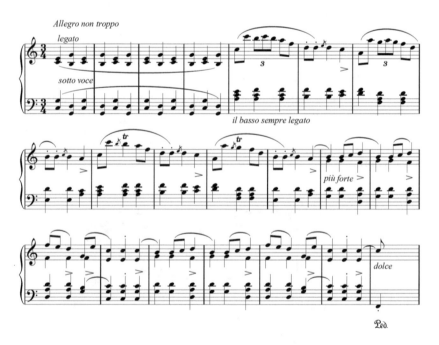

EXAMPLE 1.53. F. Chopin: Mazurka in C Major, Op. 24, No. 2, mm. 1–21.

Throughout the outer sections of this mazurka, Chopin marked accents on single pitches in several different patterned formulas, sometimes under a slur (at the beginning, middle, or end), sometimes on unslurred notes. It occurred to me that when an accent is positioned on unslurred notes or at the beginning of a slur, the entrance of the beat can be delayed; when an accent is positioned in the middle of a slur or at its end, the beat can be slightly prolonged. This simple procedure created a variety of attacks and a lilting, rustic quality that is endemic to the Polish folk dance. It dramatically changed the way I perceived these passages and other similar instances in Chopin's mazurkas, and I felt encouraged to apply the approach to my own performances.

The Ballade in F Minor Op. 52, presents us with a curious example of modern interpretation in regard to hairpins and accents. A comprehensive selection of recordings of the piece shows that almost every performer places an accent above the right-hand C, the last eighth-note of measure 7—an approach that reflects what we find in mainstream editions, such as the Paderewski:

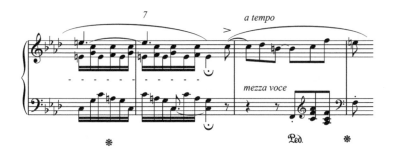

EXAMPLE 1.54a. F. Chopin: Ballade in F Minor, Op. 52, mm. 6–9 (Paderewski edition).

In the first version offered by Breitkopf & Härtel in 1843, the accent on the anacrusis was printed as a fairly long hairpin placed in the middle of the system (this modification was later reported in editions such as the Wiener Urtext):

EXAMPLE 1.54b. F. Chopin: Ballade in F Minor, Op. 52, mm. 7–8 (Breitkopf & Härtel edition, 1843).

In an attempt to understand why the length of the hairpin in question had changed, I consulted alternative early sources and discovered that the Schlesinger edition of 1843 was already proposing it as an accent, thus possibly being the source responsible for the misunderstanding:

EXAMPLE 1.54c. F. Chopin: Ballade in F Minor, Op. 52, mm. 7–8 (Schlesinger edition, 1843).

It is also interesting to note that the marking *in tempo* here is positioned on the anacrusis, rather than on the downbeat of measure 8. The Wiener Urtext edition "borrowed" it to compensate for its absence in Breitkopf & Härtel's first edition and to present this version with a full complement of markings.

I speculated on the identity and meaning of this accent, or hairpin, for quite some time. In my initial response I envisioned an agogic concession: slightly holding back the C would add hesitance, an unsettled air, to the transitional moment between the introduction and the main theme. Prolonging the note, rather than accenting it, would also circumvent the instinctive breaking of the two sections, and would consign the C to the prolonged tonicization of the C major heard in the introduction. Further consideration of this patter speculation, however, gave rise to a meaning that is quite practical: the C should be attributed an enunciation that implies its melodic nature, and it should not be woven into the texture of the concluding beats of the introduction. What is a poor pianist to do, then? Should this C be dynamically emphasized? And if so, how loud should that accent be? Is the approach that is conventionally heard in performance perhaps overly emphatic?

As published by Breitkopf & Härtel, the passage could take us even further in our consideration: the hairpin that begins from the anacrusis at the end of measure 7 looks longer than the one reported in the Wiener Urtext edition, and extends to the previous C major chord. I shared this point with a few of my colleagues, and most of them agreed that, on the basis of this original version, they would read the hairpin as starting from the chord, not from the anacrusis. My goal was not to prove that the hairpin should start from the chord; after comparing the Breitkopf & Härtel and the Wiener Urtext versions, I could see that the proximity of the C major chord and the C can lend ambiguity to the position of the marking. Rather, I wanted to show that the different placement of symbols can have far-reaching consequences.

This long excursion into the works of Chopin and their notational complexities provided much material for exploring the roles of hairpins and their interpretations. I was compelled to identify the meaning of each instance, either in the pieces I learned or in those that my students brought to their lessons, but it was not always an easy task: my eagerness to attribute a meaning to each hairpin in the formative stages of my knowledge of the symbols led me to commit oversights that, in retrospect, were not only necessary elements of my learning process, but also crucial steps that led to further discoveries concerning musical notation.

Despite the greater understanding I had acquired, there were many occurrences of hairpins that, for years, still remained doubtful or unresolved. I would like to illustrate some of these interpretive perplexities by returning for a moment to the early works of Beethoven. The opening movement of the Sonata in F Minor, Op. 2, No. 1 as it appears in the Henle edition (possibly the version of Beethoven's sonatas, among those readily available on the market, that most of us consider the most reliable) features a rather unusual notation: in measures 15 and 17, the symbols < and > are combined and positioned below a B-flat which, in this context, represents the release from an appoggiatura:

EXAMPLE 1.55. L. van Beethoven: Sonata in F Minor, Op. 2, No. 1, I. Allegro, mm. 15–18 (Henle edition).

Perhaps Beethoven was experimenting with a relatively new notational device, but these occasional interpretive nuances seem excessive. Every pianist who has encountered this passage has surely wondered what the composer had in mind. Most performers feel obliged to stress the B-flat with an accent, as they assume that the marking represents an opening and closing gesture that affects the note dynamically. I originally conceived these short opening and closing gestures as indicating a slight delay of the B-flat, so that the C would be emphasized agogically. Reacquainting myself with the precepts transmitted by an authority such as Carl Philipp Emanuel Bach in his influential *Versuch über die wahre Art das Clavier zu spielen* (Essay on the True Art of Playing Keyboard Instruments), published in 1753 and in its third acclaimed edition in 1787,[18] confirmed that placing an accent on that second beat would in fact go against any logic of musical inflection:

> With regard to the execution, we learn from this figure that appoggiaturas are louder than the following tone […] and that they are joined to it in the absence as well as presence of a slur […]. An undecorated, light tone which follows an appoggiatura is called the release.[19]

It was my recent work on this sonata with one of my students that offered a new, unforeseen perspective. The young pianist began to learn the piece from the revision made by Artur Schnabel, which his father had owned for years. Here is how Schnabel reported the puzzling double hairpin:

EXAMPLE 1.56. L. van Beethoven: Sonata in F Minor, Op. 2, No. 1, I. Allegro, mm. 15–18 (Artur Schnabel's revision).

The first edition of this sonata, published by Artaria in 1796, reveals that Schnabel reinterpreted these hairpins—a decision that he explained in the introduction to his revision as a necessary step in clarifying the composer's intentions. Although this hardly qualifies as a scholarly approach, Schnabel had a wisdom that the editors of the Henle edition may have not possessed: it is possible that these opening and closing gestures might have referred to the left hand in the long-lost manuscript, and that Artaria may have approximated their placement in the score. My impression is that they might originally have indicated that the left hand's chromatic ascent should have melodic relevance, succeeding a chordal accompaniment in the previous measures. Having learned that Chopin used hairpins to indicate voicing, I became open to the possibility that this instance in Beethoven's Sonata in F Minor might have been intended in the same manner. Although I could only speculate on the actual role of these symbols, this experience confirmed that my understanding of notation was limited by the editions on which I depended—versions that present what I believed to be faithful reproductions of the sources, and that I tried to render with accuracy in the hopes that doing so would represent what the composer had intended.

We viewed another curious case from the works of Beethoven in example 1.11—the unachievable dynamic inflection that the composer marked in the Largo from his Sonata in E-flat Major, Op. 7:

EXAMPLE 1.57. L. van Beethoven: Sonata in E-flat Major, Op. 7, II. Largo, con gran espressione, mm. 8–12.

Might these hairpins signal the prevalence of a melodic line in the context of the thick chordal texture? Should a performer consider the right-hand F-sharp in beats 2 and 3 the continuation of the melody, rather than proposing the top-oriented approach that most of the time is instinctively favored?

It is in the opening pages of a long letter to his friend Tytus Wojciechowski, dated October 5, 1830, that we may find especially valuable evidence concerning what

Chopin, then twenty years old, might have intended to express with hairpins. Among several interesting accounts of Warsaw's operatic life, a narrative of soprano Konstancja Gładkowska's rendition of the turns in one of the arias from *La gazza ladra* (1817) by Rossini (1792–1868) may reveal more than it first appears to:

It is admirable when she sings this:

She does not take it off short, like Mayer, but sings:

so that it is not a quick *gruppetto*, but eight clearly sung notes.[20]

Chopin explained that rather than rushing, as Mayer seems to have done, Gładkowska sang each *gruppetto* with an enunciation that rendered each note intelligible. Did the hairpins he sketched hint at the clarity of Gładkowska's version, implying that only slight agogic inflections at the beginning of each quadruplet could have made them musically meaningful? Were this considered a direct testimony of Chopin's intentions, it would prove that the use of hairpins to determine agogic freedom was a characteristic of his language before the composer's Parisian days.

The different degrees of inflection determined by Chopin's hairpins show an interest in codifying a freedom that was very much a characteristic of the composer's own playing. But how did Chopin use hairpins extemporaneously? For instance, how did they become an integral part of his pedagogical tools? Much of Chopin's teaching was documented by his students through accounts that, while not always detailed, give us an idea of the composer's expectations and his ability to convey elements of technique and interpretation. After his death, his pupils' scores also became a primary tool for understanding his approach, as the composer frequently notated in them fingering, articulation, dynamics, pedaling, and original or alternative embellishments. In 1919 and again in 1923 to 1925, through the agency of Louis Diémer, Chopin's pupil Camille Dubois O'Meara bequeathed a conspicuous quantity of scores to the Bibliothèque Nationale in Paris. Some of these invaluable documents served at her lessons, thereby showing annotations in the composer's hand. In addition to some fascinating fingering suggestions, the first page of the Nocturne in C Minor, Op. 48, No. 1 from this collection contains one precious detail that might support our thesis. The ending of the first phrase, in measure 4, shows an opening hairpin written in pencil. Its traits are uncertain, as if they were formed while their author was standing by the piano—possibly proving that they are Chopin's:

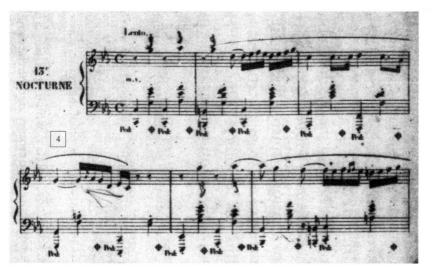

EXAMPLE 1.58. F. Chopin: Nocturne in C Minor, Op. 48, No. 1, mm. 1–6 (Schlesinger edition—score belonging to Camille O'Meara Dubois, including pencil annotations possibly in Chopin's hand). Bibliothèque nationale de France.

Is it possible that Chopin suggested to Mme. Dubois that she broaden the end of this phrase because she played it strictly in time, or even rushed through it? It seems to me unlikely that Chopin would have recommended a crescendo at the end of a phrase. A singer among my acquaintances who is also an accomplished pianist proposed what at first seemed an intriguing conjecture: the timbre of the register directly below the written-in notation, she said, could be evoking what is conventionally described as "chest voice"—a technique that allows the lower vocal range to be particularly resonant, thus justifying the presence of an increase in volume added in pencil by the composer. The idea, though engaging, felt somewhat convoluted. Is it likely that Chopin, who frequently alluded to the great singers of his time as a paradigm while inflecting melodic lines on the piano, would have been so literal in transcribing a vocal idiom? Further, several colleagues of mine—trying to justify what they viewed as the illogical placement of some of these opening and closing gestures—have proposed the position that a crescendo, by allowing the end of a phrase to flow into the one that ensues, would prevent the earlier phrase from dying out prematurely. This notion was advanced while a few of us were discussing cases such as the opening hairpins found in measures 6 and 8 of the Barcarolle, Op. 60 (example 1.7). But if that was the case, why did not Chopin use this practice systematically? Why would it have been relevant, or necessary, to mark such a concept in the opening theme of the Barcarolle but not in musically comparable phrases in the same piece, or in any other work?

I alluded earlier to uses of hairpins in Chopin's music that seem to suggest vocal elements derived from principles of bel canto. Such passages abound, including episodes in which trills may be evocative of an intense, expressive vibrato. The intricate, shimmering chain of trills in the recapitulation of the Nocturne in B Major, Op. 62, No. 1 is a marvelous example. Nevertheless, in the hands of many performers the vocal quality of some of these passages is overlooked. The closing hairpin on the trill in measure 81 of the Barcarolle, Op. 60 is one such case, being usually construed as a reduction of the dynamic level—a solution that leaves little room for the expressive projection of the ensuing episode:

EXAMPLE 1.59. F. Chopin: Barcarolle in F-sharp Major, Op. 60, mm. 80–82.

I originally viewed this hairpin as indicating metric order, thinking that the anacrusis could be aurally misconstrued as a downbeat. A slight dynamic or agogic inflection on the downbeat (or a combination of both) would be implied to clarify the metric organization, I thought, without necessarily entailing a subsequent diminuendo. Then, a closer inspection of Chopin's notation in the French Stichvorlage led me to notice that the hairpin extends to the small-print figuration at the end of the measure, and that its role could have pertained exclusively to agogic inflection: the trill could begin from the auxiliary note (F-sharp) and dwell momentarily at the speed of the eighth-note written as its anacrusis. Lingering at first and increasing the speed as it nears the small-print figuration at the end of the measure is a solution that may better reveal the vocal nature of this passage— indeed a true example of lyrical inflection.

Other cases involving trills show how interpretive traditions that commonly lead to questionable outcomes could be superseded by more reasonable approaches.

The end of the exposition in the first movement of the Sonata in B Minor, Op. 58, has often left pianists too tepid to include its repetition:

EXAMPLE 1.60. F. Chopin: Sonata in B Minor, Op. 58, I. Allegro maestoso, mm. 88–91a (Meissonier edition, 1845).

On three different occasions, when asked why the repeat sign was not observed in their performances, pianists responded that they did not accept the increase in dynamic proposed by the hairpin, that it was unappealing and that they had chosen to avoid such an abrupt conclusion. Is this hairpin instead suggesting a broadening of pace in these concluding measures … or is it perhaps suggesting the prevalence of the tenor line? Both solutions exclude the crescendo that so much displeased these pianists.

If agogic flexibility or voicing could manage to circumvent a crescendo that pianists may find unappealing, I wondered whether the opening hairpin in measures 11 and 12 of Chopin's celebrated Prelude in A Major, Op. 28, No. 7 could evade the same convention. A tradition seems to have informed the playing of generations of pianists who at times exaggerate the application of the crescendo by reaching a *forte*. As the only dynamic indication is the *piano* marked at the beginning of the piece, this hairpin may simply intend an agogic concession in order to outline the jarring harmonic shift to F-sharp major:

EXAMPLE 1.61. F. Chopin: Prelude in A Major, Op. 28, No. 7.

EXAMPLE 1.61 (continued)

The opening hairpin in the concluding measures of Chopin's Mazurka in C-sharp Minor, Op. 63, No. 3 usually receives a similar treatment. Were it intended instead as a progressive rallentando, the *forte* in the last two measures would receive a more assertive enunciation, without the preparation of a crescendo:

EXAMPLE 1.62. F. Chopin: Mazurka in C-sharp Minor, Op. 63, No. 3, mm. 65–76.

Alternatively, could this hairpin signal that the lower voice in the right hand should be melodically in charge? The disappearance of the only Stichvorlage, prepared for the French publisher Brandus, will forever make it impossible to determine whether the hairpin may have been notated in close proximity to the right hand, rather than being placed in the middle of the system.

That hairpins were a convenient notational tool to signal voicing may be confirmed by the opening page of the first movement in Chopin's Sonata in B Minor, Op. 58. Comparing its original sources revealed that the composer employed three alternative notational devices to indicate the same concept—a rare circumstance that allowed me to disclose an illuminating correlation between symbols, but also to suggest that the analysis of more recent decades may be at odds with Chopin's extemporaneous approach in the use of numerous variables.

In the first page of the 1844 Stichvorlage that Chopin sent to Breitkopf & Härtel, measures 13 and 14 show the marking *ten.* (*tenuto*, in Italian "held") above the half-notes C and C-sharp, respectively:

EXAMPLE 1.63a. F. Chopin: Sonata in B Minor, Op. 58, I. Allegro maestoso, mm. 12–14 (Breitkopf & Härtel edition, 1845).

These tenuti were faithfully reproduced in the first edition of 1845 and in subsequent reprints of the work that the German firm published during the nineteenth century. They are also reported by all modern editions, which for the most part base their sources on the Breitkopf & Härtel version. In the Meissonier edition, which was published in the same year in Paris but used a different manuscript as a source, the two tenuti are replaced by accents:

EXAMPLE 1.63b. F. Chopin: Sonata in B Minor, Op. 58, I. Allegro maestoso, mm. 12–14 (Meissonier edition, 1845).

Published in London about a month and a half before the Meissonier edition, the Wessel edition used a third manuscript and shows lengthened accents, one of which encompasses two beats:

EXAMPLE 1.63c. F. Chopin: Sonata in B Minor, Op. 58, I. Allegro maestoso, mm. 12–15 (Wessel edition, 1845). © The British Library Board, h.472.(30.).

Observing the different lengths of the two accents in the Wessel edition may lead us to one likely conclusion: in cases where our credible efforts fail to rationalize two differing intentions, the conjecture that accents of different sizes designated the same function is not unreasonable. In addition, if these three different notations were meant to express the same idea, it would imply that Chopin used *tenuto*, a short accent, and a long accent interchangeably.

What remained, then, in regard to the apparently compatible notational symbols on the opening page of Chopin's Sonata in B Minor, Op. 58 was the question of meaning. At first, I considered that the short hairpins and accents were indeed signaling agogic flexibility (in this case, a slight prolongation of the notes in question), and I reasoned that *tenuto* expressed exactly the same idea (*tenuto* in Italian also means "prolonged"; hence the agogic implications). This might have satisfied my deliberations on the subject, but the works of Haydn offered a different perspective.

The presence of tenuti in some of Haydn's sonatas from the early 1770s conveys a rather explicit role, according to modern conventions: it indicates legato (in some cases marked after a passage that is written in staccato); a decrease in speed (appearing at the end of episodes, especially in slow movements, as a primitive form of ritenuto); or it implies that a note or chord should not be released. These were attributions that I had grown to accept as universal and that I did not question. Yet, while I was perusing the works of Haydn, my attention was called to several occurrences of the marking in the first movement of the Sonata in C minor, Hob. XVI:20. It seemed newly possible, even likely, that these tenuti meant to indicate voicing for the upper line in the right hand. Whether or not this application was suitable (the *tenuto* in these cases may simply have indicated legato), my speculation encouraged me to examine uses of the marking in other composers' notation. What emerged from my analysis of the works of Chopin was compelling: the infrequent markings of *tenuto* seem to signal the presence of a main line whose predominance, in the absence of this instruction, might be compromised by active inner lines, or voices, in the context of a multilayered texture. It seems to be the case in the opening page of Chopin's Sonata in B Minor, which we just mentioned: without the use of *tenuto* to indicate voicing (example 1.63a), the right-hand chords in measures 13 and 14 might deceptively encourage a continuation of the melodic material (C–B-flat–A and C-sharp–B–A-sharp). Hairpins or accents of different sizes, as we saw in examples 1.63b and 1.63c, yielded the same potential as the *tenuto* indication in example 1.63a, thus justifying the conjecture that Chopin used *tenuto* as well as hairpins and accents to signal voicing and that, indeed, the three instructions corroborated and supported one another. If the election of three different ways of signaling the same concept indicates the degree of flexibility with which Chopin used notation, I wondered whether this elasticity could have been caused by an immediacy of writing that he took for granted. And, if this was the case, is it possible that the spontaneous variations that ensued in the composer's notation have more recently been read with too literal an eye?

In considering the difference between long and short accents as they appear in Chopin's manuscripts and scores, we encounter a significantly delicate issue concerning our reading of musical notation. Thanks to the gradual introduction of detailed interpretive instructions, composers brought the performer closer to their conceptions. But this evolution toward explicit notational expression had a paradoxical aspect: printing errors, inconsistencies in manuscripts, improvisatory use of notation, and reliance on guesswork in attributing specific meanings to some symbols all may be assumed to have contributed to a diminished awareness of intended practices and a reduction in their use. The intent of a marking, especially if used with various purposes—some newer than others—may not have been immediately discernible. Indeed, it could be helpful to imagine how a musician might have experienced this ambiguity in the years in which Chopin was experimenting with a range of notational approaches.

How did pianists react to the sight of accents of differing size, or to hairpins placed in the middle of the system, or above or under it, in the first part of the nineteenth century? Were these arrangements perceived to emanate from the personal prerogatives of each composer? Let us envision a pianist living in the 1840s in Berlin, who pays a visit to the local music store to see whether there are any interesting new arrivals. Some scores of Chopin's compositions, published by Breitkopf & Härtel, have just come in from Leipzig. The pianist purchases them, goes home, and sits at the piano to play them for the first time. The composer included symbols the pianist has never before encountered, and gave neither instructions for their use nor any consistency in the notation that might allow their role to be intuitively understood. The pianist reacts to them instinctively, guessing their meaning, most likely without being overly concerned. Every pianist who purchased the same scores was left with the task of devising a means of interpreting the new symbols on the basis of their context or the character of a specific passage. Very likely, this was only one of a number of interpretive conundrums that a pianist would have had to face when encountering hairpins in a piece of music. For example, would a performer have been aware that the way in which the symbol was used may have differed greatly even among contemporaneous composers? Or that the same symbol within a piece may have concomitantly addressed several interpretive aspects? Or that a specific piece of instruction over time may have begun to refer to completely different elements or to one definite attribution among the older given meanings? We will see in the next two chapters how the neutralizing of this complexity, through a slow but certain process of reductive interpretation of older notational formulas, has affected our perception, and how the assumption that there must be a universal language of notation to which performers submitted seems to have taken hold.

One further layer of information concerns the wealth of details found in the original sources: although musicians tried to make sense of what they saw in the scores, most of them may have been unaware that what they had at their disposal were versions presenting misprints caused by editors, copyists or the composer himself. This was an issue that applied quite generally to most music published in the first half of the nineteenth century. In Chopin's music, this problem must have been exacerbated by the substantial discrepancies offered by the different versions that were published during his lifetime—inconsistencies that derived from the composer's habitual practice of changing small details in the manuscripts he sent to the publishers and in the plates that he proofread. This progression did not end with the publication of a piece: Chopin kept revising his music incessantly, as is confirmed by the slight modifications added to his works in the scores that his pupils used during their lessons. In our time, these inconsistencies have gained recognition owing to decades of acoustical recordings and detailed scholarship, but it is unlikely that in Chopin's time even the most cultivated audience member would have been aware of the differences presented by the French, German, and English editions. A pianist who was learning the Ballade in G Minor, Op. 23 from the first printed version by Breitkopf & Härtel would never have suspected that Chopin had not intended a simplified 6/4 harmony in measure 7 (see examples 1.18a and 1.18b); nor is it likely that a performer in the 1830s, when learning the Mazurka in G Minor, Op. 24, No. 1, would have speculated on the differences between short and long accents (examples 1.48–1.49a). In the case of the Wessel edition of this mazurka, it is highly unlikely that a pianist would have known that other editions proposed accents of different sizes (example 1.49b). When performers tried to assign meanings to these symbols, we can only imagine how Chopin may have reacted to their playing if the pianists' misunderstanding of a particular marking in one of his compositions occurred in his presence. As his career unfolded, Chopin may have perceived that his abundant use of accents might be confusing or misleading. Was this also one of the reasons that accents of different sizes gradually disappeared from Chopin's works, especially in melodic contexts? Did he come to understand that what he had thought at first to be a powerful expressive tool might have turned into a source of misconstruction?

⋅◂●▸⋅

These considerations may stimulate our imagination, but we still lack an explanation as to why, according to some methods written by relevant pianistic figures of the late eighteenth and early nineteenth centuries, hairpins did not explicitly have any agogic connotation. Rather, they were quite consistently invested with dynamic validity. This is the case in the *Méthode complète théorique et pratique pour le piano-forte* by Johann Nepomuk Hummel (1778–1837), which was published in 1828 and sold thousands of copies within days of its debut appearance. A pupil of Mozart in his childhood and of Muzio Clementi after Mozart's death, Hummel may not have been directly exposed to the possible functions of hairpins by his teachers during his youth. Considering his education, perhaps the agogic utility was too peripheral a practice for him to absorb as part of his vocabulary at that time, especially as he spent four years in England—a region of Europe that may have not been reached in the short term by the more recent innovations in the field of notation. It is possible that in evaluating hairpins as they began to appear in the music of other composers, Hummel may have determined that they had dynamic significance. It is also possible that he deliberately chose to view hairpins as dynamic indications from a pedagogical viewpoint, since he tried to transmit the concept through his *Méthode*. In his own works, hairpins seem to be used to indicate an increase or decrease in volume, often between two diametrically opposed dynamic markings; yet they occasionally seem to indicate the prevalence of specific voices in the context of polyphonic writing. Some performers trained in the tradition established by Hummel must have been as puzzled as we are in front of certain inconclusive markings in printed music. Clementi, Dussek, Moscheles—all composers educated in a period in which late baroque principles were still predominant—regarded hairpins as indicating dynamic fluctuations. Some of the piano methods published during the first half of the 1800s were written by luminaries who had been trained in the latter part of the eighteenth century. As these composers and pedagogues were highly popular and influential, their methods, and those of other well-known teachers, writers, and performers of the era, molded generations of musicians and may be responsible for early instilling the idea that hairpins belong to the notation of dynamic variation alone.

When considering hairpins from an agogic point of view, it is tempting to hypothesize that this practice had relied on some sort of secret code familiar only to composers and their associates, but this idea can be easily dismissed: the agogic legitimacy of hairpins was confirmed by Hugo Riemann in his *Die Elemente der musikalischen Ästhetik* (The Elements of Musical Aesthetic), written in 1900. In this comprehensive publication, hairpins are described as affecting both dynamic and agogic coordinates. Riemann explained that the symbol might serve different purposes, its agogic function only strengthening the dynamic one and vice versa. He formulated that, should the context in which the hairpin is found convey the necessity, one or the other function can be abandoned, as long as this would not incur a great loss of either parameter.[21] Riemann also went beyond the agogic or dynamic validity of hairpins to assert a policy that is rather foreign to modern interpreters and that, with some irony, poses a counter to the notion of agogic flexibility: speed, he said, is directly proportional to dynamics—as the volume of a passage increases, the tempo is also supposed to quicken, and vice versa.[22]

Riemann's evaluation of the uses of hairpins at the turn of the twentieth century may explain why, in some of the more mature works of Brahms, the symbols were positioned between two diametrically opposed dynamic markings (a practice that Chopin and his contemporaries adopted in extremely rare occurrences). Although this placement did not exclude an agogic function, especially in light of Riemann's exposition on the relationship between dynamics and speed, most interpreters felt led to consider hairpins so placed exclusively for their dynamic implications. By the end of the nineteenth century, these opening and closing symbols seem to have assumed a more prominent dynamic role. Composers had begun to indicate agogic fluctuation with different markings that were able to define the degree of flexibility with even greater accuracy, which likely explains why the agogic purpose of hairpins diminished. The Sonata, Op. 1 by Alban Berg comes to mind, a work in which the rubato is stylized by frequent employment of indications such as *accel.* and *ritard.* In some cases, hairpins in this one-movement composition still seem to designate agogic freedom; in others their dynamic role seems quite explicit; and occasionally, either role could be considered.

Discrepancies and variations in the use of hairpins and accents throughout the nineteenth century are such that no rule can apply strictly to every composer, or to the entire canon of any one composer. Thus our vantage point is *scholarship*— not with the intent of analyzing music aridly, but with the goal of revealing a composer's real intentions through an accurate assessment of the sources. Being aware of the differences between dynamic, agogic, and metric legitimacies of the marking is no small issue, as this knowledge profoundly redefines music by giving us greater insight about a composer's intentions and an interpretive freedom that we might not have regarded as possible. The research is fascinating because it leads to conclusions that, in the process of simply viewing or even studying individual scores, would not be drawn. Uncovering the potential of these symbols may clarify extremely complex contradictions to which performers have been heir for decades, not only in and among scores, but also over the historical continuum from one era or composer to another—circumstances that, out of convenience, or lacking an alternative, a musician often resolves to ignore.

TWO

...OF SFORZANDI

*As beautiful as simplicity is, it can become
a tradition that stands in the way of exploration.*

— LAURA NYRO

The extent to which hairpins achieved recognition in the nineteenth century as a versatile notational tool led me to wonder why Wolfgang Amadeus Mozart discontinued their use after they appeared in three significant works written between 1781 and 1782. In the String Quartet in G Major, K. 387, a solitary hairpin seems to signal agogic freedom during a cadenza-like passage played by the first violin; in the Serenade for Winds in E-flat Major, K. 361 and his first mature opera, *Idomeneo, Re di Creta*, K. 366, hairpins seem to have dynamic connotation. Had he found it superfluous to bring notation to such a level, and was therefore unable to foresee the relevance that the symbol would gain in ensuing decades? Yet he did welcome and continue to employ some of the innovative markings that composers had begun to use with increasing frequency throughout Europe as of the late 1770s, and whose function affected and expanded relevant aspects of articulation, dynamics, and agogic freedom. As a testimony to his growing interest in notating detailed interpretive elements, it will suffice to mention that, beginning in 1784, Mozart added substantial dynamic and agogic instructions while revising some of the pieces that he had published in the mid-1770s. This degree of specificity would have been unimaginable just ten years earlier, and perhaps hardly a necessity, but he was submitting both to common trends of the time and to the appealing notion that various symbols would more explicitly indicate his interpretive concepts.

Around 1778 he introduced the term *sforzando*, which he abbreviated with the symbol *sf*. The marking appeared often as part of the thorough revisions he undertook only several years later, and remained a prominent notational device in his language until he left the world in 1791.

⸻

The introduction of interpretive notation in printed music during the last two decades of the eighteenth century was endorsed enthusiastically by most composers. Haydn himself did not reject the inclination, and his initiation to newly invented symbols may have occurred during his interactions with visiting performers while he served at the extravagant court of Prince Nikolaus Esterházy (1714–1790). The exchanges with other composers during his brief trips to Vienna, which must have provided some solace from thirty years spent in seclusion at Esterháza, might have stimulated the introduction of more complex notation. After leaving his post at court in 1790, the year of Esterházy's death, he made repeated trips to England, where he gained contacts with celebrated composers and performers—opportunities that may also have given him new perspectives on notational markings. Concurrently with Mozart, at the end of the 1770s Haydn began to use *sforzando*, notating it with the symbol *fz*—in some cases omitting the *s* and spelling it *forzando*. At first he used the marking discreetly, but his belief in its utility eventually led him to exceed Mozart in the frequency and creativity with which he employed it.

Working with one of my students on the middle movement of Haydn's Sonata in E-flat Major, Hob. XVI:49 brought back memories of the time in which I learned the piece, during my teenage years. I was now looking at the Adagio with new eyes, thanks to a greater concern about the complexities of musical notation, but I clearly remembered how its opening measures proposed interpretive elements that I had not completely understood at an earlier stage. Essays written in the eighteenth century, including Leopold Mozart's *Gründliche Violinschule* (Complete School of Violin Playing), published in 1756, assert that two-note slurs should follow a principle of stress and release—the latter being always softer.[1] This concept found the same application in keyboard playing, and was still at the core of interpretive principles as the century neared its end—Daniel Gottlob Türk, for example, wrote about it in his *Clavierschule* of 1789, only months before Haydn composed the sonata in question. In light of these precedents, several instances in the middle movement appeared quite enigmatic:

⬇ **EXAMPLE 2.1.** F. J. Haydn: Sonata in E-flat Major, Hob. XVI:49, II. Adagio e cantabile, mm. 1–9.

What emerges from the melodic line of these measures is rather unusual: the placement of the symbol *fz* on the resolving notes of the two-note slurs in measures 3 and 7 seems to contradict what some of the eminent musicians of the time had affirmed in their writings about such instances. In my youth, I had found great pleasure in learning this movement, but I recall distinctly the uncomfortable feeling that had derived from placing dynamic stresses on notes that I knew were supposed to sound softer than the ones that preceded them. In view of this apparent contradiction, I remember wondering whether I had the moral authority to ignore either the *sforzandi* or the slurs, but submitted to the notion that Haydn must have had a valid reason to include such strong gestures in the contemplative, lyrical opening page of the Adagio. At that time, the mechanical reproduction of notation was such a relevant interpretive aspect of my musical life that the idea of finding alternative meanings for *sforzandi* did not even cross my mind. According tacit assent to interpretive traditions, as I had been trained to do, I applied the emphases.

The *sforzandi* in the Adagio from the Sonata, Hob. XVI:49 were not an oversight on Haydn's part: other works that the composer completed during the same period feature similar cases, however perplexing. We find an example in the opening page of the middle movement of his Sonata in C Major, Hob. XVI:50—another piece of Haydn that I had begun to study with interest during my teenage years. The symbol *fz* is displayed above or beneath some of the pitches during an exchange of sixteenth-note figurations as the second episode gets under way:

EXAMPLE 2.2. F. J. Haydn: Sonata in C Major, Hob. XVI:50, II. Adagio, mm. 8–11.

While observing a parallel between the *sforzandi* in the middle movements of the two sonatas we just considered, I wondered whether it was appropriate to disrupt the inspired poignancy of these passages by placing accents as they were indicated. Most pianists whose recordings I listened to as points of reference for both sonatas seemed to reject the notion, but with a sense of unease: while not entirely dismissing the *sforzandi*, they tried to undermine their presence by dramatically reducing their dynamic impact. This was probably done in the belief that, if the peculiar presence of a symbol needed to be represented faithfully, it should have been done at least with discretion. I thought that the outcome of these solutions was contrived and unconvincing, but felt that I would not have been able to provide an alternative.

In the same movement of the Sonata in C Major, Hob. XVI:50, the *sforzandi* prescribed in measures 18 and 19 have puzzled generations of performers:

EXAMPLE 2.3. F. J. Haydn: Sonata in C Major, Hob. XVI:50, II. Adagio, mm. 18–19.

I once heard a prominent pianist assert that in the absence of a logical explanation for these *sforzandi*, we can safely assume that they were displaced, possibly even by Haydn himself, and that they should be attributed to the pitches that precede them. Indeed, a dynamic emphasis on the F-sharp or D-sharp in the first and second measures, respectively, would make sense only on account of the appoggiatura role that they fulfill,[2] in anticipation of a melodic resolution that agrees with the harmonic context. The pianist's conclusion impressed me as an easy way out in the face of a mystery that, while not yet a cold case, may have been on its way to becoming one.

More recently, a passage from another major work by Haydn posed a similar enigma: while learning the Sonata in E-flat Major, Hob. XVI:52, I felt that the chords affected by the *sforzandi* in measures 22 and 23 of the first movement sounded rather out of place if approached from a dynamic standpoint:

EXAMPLE 2.4. F. J. Haydn: Sonata in E-flat Major, Hob. XVI:52, I. Allegro, mm. 22–24.

My instinct led me to delay the entrance of these chords, and to gently prolong them with a slight roll—a solution that seemed to suit the grace and elegance of the passage. Yet for a while I wavered: this interpretation was perhaps doing justice to the music, but it was not reproducing what I thought Haydn had prescribed. My quest for accuracy drew me to incorporate those emphases, despite my reluctance to accept them as coherent elements of the musical rhetoric. For years, this remained my position: in the repertoire that I was so fortunate and eager to play, many markings that suggested dynamic emphases continued to puzzle me, and, obliged to choose one solution or another, I espoused the belief that composers truly desired sharp accents and incongruous stresses, regardless of how much they halted the flow of the music or compromised its beauty.

The Italian word *sforzando* is the gerundive of the verb *sforzare*—from the noun *sforzo*, "effort." Although it derives from *forza* (strength or force), *sforzando* means "with effort" or "applying effort." An authoritative Italian dictionary gives the meaning of *sforzo* as "*impiego di forze e di risorse superiori al normale, spec. allo scopo di ottenere un determinato risultato*"[3] (the employment of resources or energies that are considered above normal, especially with the goal of obtaining a specific result).[4] Tradition had instructed me that *sforzando* signifies the placement of a dynamic stress over a note or chord with an emphasis of varying degree, generally based on the dynamic level indicated by the score. Yet the verb *sforzare* does not necessarily suggest force or loudness. As I pondered this matter, I also realized that the term was introduced by composers living in German-speaking countries, which may legitimate asking whether the nuances of its authentic meaning had escaped them. Were there alternative designations for *sforzando*? The etymology of the term gave me much to contemplate. My delving into the meaning of hairpins and accents had begun to change my perception of musical notation, and now I felt that perhaps I should reconsider the connotation of *sforzando*: what if it were not an indication of dynamic stress at all?

A few months ago, discussing the Adagio that we viewed in Haydn's Sonata in E-flat Major, Hob. XVI:49 with one of my students provided another opportunity to perceive the music with new eyes. The manner in which the young pianist was inflecting the melody while playing the lyrical opening page brought to mind the evolution that we observed in chapter 1: thanks to the advent of elaborate new symbols, composers were able to specify minute interpretive details, which compelled performers to reproduce a musical concept with greater precision. As I listened to my student play, I comprehended that what Haydn might have envisioned for these *sforzandi* perhaps pertained more to expression than dynamics. Could the intention here have been of the agogic kind? Delaying or slightly lingering on the pitches in question seemed to produce a more emotional rendition of the melodic material, very persuasively conveying its tenderness and improvisational qualities.

The process of contemplating alternative meanings for *sforzandi* in eighteenth-century music began to confirm my intuition that strong emotional inflections may not have been an exclusive prerogative of the romantics. Although I understood that any significant degree of agogic freedom in music that directly preceded what we call the romantic era would be regarded as inappropriate by modern standards of interpretation, over time I came to the conclusion that the widespread notion that eighteenth-century music should be played somewhat strictly may be responsible for hindering its expressive potential. Decades of traditions have inclined us to dismiss any idea that the music of composers who lived in the baroque and classical eras should be played with abandon, or that the agogic fluctuations found in works from the nineteenth century should also apply to those that preceded them. It occurred to me that *romantic* is a label that was posthumously attached to the nineteenth century to refer to a specific period of time. But artists in that period did not describe themselves "romantics," any more than people in the era that we call Victorian referred to themselves as "Victorians." They thought of themselves as "modern," as we likewise think of ourselves today. The term *romantic era* aptly alludes to a time in which emotion and intuition achieved full recognition in their centrality in the aesthetic experience and fruition of art. The contemporary connotation has more to do with love, passion, fervor, and other sentiments that can be communicated in music with extroverted effect. I sensed that this more recent categorization perhaps lies at the base of a modern misunderstanding: if these most ardent feelings were conveyed through art during the romantic era, then one might conceive anything that preceded that period, by default, as being subject to a lesser degree of freedom and bound to be emotionally more contained. Some modern commentators have even advanced the idea that the sparer interpretive notation in music from the 1700s corroborates a greater objectivity. One of their claims, for example, is that the rare appearance of agogic markings in the works of composers such as Haydn or Mozart would confirm that tempo changes in these pieces should be treated with circumspection. Were the same interpretive criterion valid in the performance of baroque music, I thought, Bach's music should then be subject to no inflection whatsoever. Quite to the contrary, it was none other than Carl Philipp Emanuel Bach who disproved this supposition in his *Essay on the True Art of Keyboard Playing*, a major portion of which he devoted to the illustration of what constitutes a convincing premise: from the appropriate mood of a piece to the inflection suited to conveying it, he attested that inflective freedom and tempo fluctuations are fundamental principles of interpretation.

As Carl Philipp Emanuel Bach defined it, the degree of expression necessary to convey emotions through music was based on parameters that our modern ears would deem objectionable. Inflective freedom and tempo fluctuations comprise some of the most powerful means of expression available—whether we apply them to the inherent dichotomies between sections within musical structures or as slight, localized modulations to produce what today we define as "musicality." I wondered how Chopin must have played Bach, Haydn, or Mozart. Although their works were written for harpsichord or fortepiano, this is unlikely to have informed a different approach to expression in his music making. His interpretive insight probably stemmed from principles of inflection that applied generally to music as a language. The notion that Bach, Haydn, and Mozart were not romantic composers must have never occurred to Chopin: he probably played their music with abandon, unaware that within a century from his death, demarcations of style would restrain the interpreter's inspiration.

Soon after I reflected on these issues, comparing different editions of Haydn's sonatas led me to discover the introductory notes for the Wiener Urtext edition, written by Christa Landon in 1963. A short paragraph in which she describes the use of *sforzando* particularly caught my attention:

> The *sforzato* sign so frequently used by Haydn—and often falsified in print as an *f* or even *ff*—has a varied significance which may even include emphasizing the formal structure of a particular passage. The manifold possibilities for performing this sign comprise not only the execution of a sharp rhythmic accent—especially in fast movements—but also that of a highly expressive, hesitating, or even soft attack of the key. Not only in slow movements but even in fast movements as well, this sign may often indicate the application of *rubato*.[5]

Landon's interpretation indeed offers possibilities that go beyond the common dynamic application of *sforzando* that late-nineteenth-century treatises support as the only possible reading, a simplification that twentieth-century interpretive traditions have perpetuated. Further, Landon's observation that some editions have turned *fz* into *ff* or a simple *f* is a revelation that forever changed my perception of certain passages in Haydn's compositions: in the first movement of the Sonata in C Major, Hob. XVI:50, for instance, the placement of the marking *fz* in lieu of two *ff*s that are found in the development would dynamically turn upside down most of the section, at last disclosing a logical reading of these pages.

Were we to apply the notion that *sforzandi* indicate rubato, could the instances illustrated in example 2.3, from the Adagio in Haydn's Sonata in C Major, Hob. XVI:50, signal inflective freedom by delaying the notes that resolve from the appoggiaturas? And were we to entertain the same interpretive solution for the *sforzandi* illustrated in example 2.4, was my idea of broadening the chords affected by the symbol intuitively correct? Or were there alternatives of which I was not yet aware?

I mentioned that as of the late 1770s, Mozart consistently began to employ *sforzandi* as part of his vocabulary. In the mid-1780s he introduced various dynamics and other markings in reprints of earlier pieces, which originally had presented only very little articulation and basic dynamic indications. As a result, many instances of *sforzandi* are later additions, like those in the ambitious Sonata in D Major,

K. 284, written in 1775 and published again nearly ten years later by Christoph Torricella in Vienna after it underwent a thorough revision. While investigating the occurrences of *sforzandi* in the final movement of this sonata, I noticed that they appear exclusively in Variations VII and IX—the only portions of the movement to feature material of an explicitly melodic nature.[6] Consider, for example, the placement of the *sforzandi* in the concluding measures of Variation VII:

EXAMPLE 2.5. W. A. Mozart: Sonata in D Major, K. 284, III. Andante, Var. VII, mm. 14–17.

The right-hand articulation in beats 1 and 2 of measure 16 would suggest that A, the resolving note, be softer than the G-sharp, as a slur connects the two. Rather than being dynamically stressed, should the 6/4 harmony in the second beat perhaps be gently prolonged, emphasizing the suspension before the perfect cadence brings the variation to a close? With this *sforzando*, did Mozart propose the prolongation of the chord beyond its intended duration—what we would describe as a fermata?[7]

A different case, this time in the Sonata in B-flat Major, K. 333, also published by Christoph Torricella in 1784, shows an intriguing utilization:

EXAMPLE 2.6. W. A. Mozart: Sonata in B-flat Major, K. 333, II. Andante cantabile, mm. 20–22.

Following the logic discussed in example 2.5, I initially concluded that the note affected by the *sforzando* in measure 21 of example 2.6 and in analogous instances in this Andante could be delayed. As a solution, it would have reasonably outlined the ending of one phrase and the beginning of a new one. But I suddenly remembered that soon after, composers had begun to indicate the emergence of a particular line in the context of polyphonic writing by using hairpins. I thought about whether Mozart might have intended this *sforzando* to signal that the left hand should be melodically relevant. Rather than being confined to the role of Alberti-bass accompaniment, should this sequence of sixteenth-notes be treated as an interacting compound line against the material in the right hand, which is marked with a *forte*? Could the "effort" intended by the term *sforzando* indicate the importance of a line that might otherwise go unnoticed?

These considerations led me to investigate the possible meaning of *sforzandi* in Mozart's late period. The solutions that I had formulated in his earlier works did not seem to apply with ease, for example, to the *sforzandi* in the opening measures of the Adagio in B Minor, K. 540:

🔊 EXAMPLE 2.7. W. A. Mozart: Adagio in B Minor, K. 540, mm. 1–2.

I first considered agogic fluctuation, but it seemed an awkward proposition; then voicing, but this intention seemed inconclusive as well. I felt at a loss until I recollected an earlier insight into notation in the nineteenth century: hairpins served, among other purposes, to clarify metric displacements, or to outline the presence of a specific meter that would not have been intuitively perceivable. Was this strategy adopted by Mozart when he chose to use *sforzandi* in the Adagio in B Minor? And if so, was the marking used to avoid the deceptive metric order that the weak beats could have implied?

If the *sforzando* was employed to designate agogic fluctuation, metric order and voicing, its resemblance to the functions of hairpins seemed all too coincidental. Perhaps predictably, I began to understand that Mozart may have considered *sforzandi* as a notational tool to indicate interpretive elements that composers later began to specify more consistently with hairpins. It occurred to me that the reason he may have discontinued hairpins from his vocabulary is that *sforzando* already provided their interpretive purposes. Had he lived into the nineteenth century, how would his notation have evolved? Can we infer that he would have eventually adapted to standardized notation to conform to various necessities—from the publication of his music to the simplicity of its fruition?

––––––––––––– ‣●‣ –––––––––––––

The marking *sforzando* emerged significantly in Mozart's writing after his visit to the musically stimulating city of Mannheim, which he left in mid-March 1778, arriving in Paris after a nine-day trip. It was probably in the month of April that he wrote the Concerto for Flute, Harp and Orchestra, K. 299, allegedly the first of his compositions in which *sforzandi* appear, perhaps suggesting that it may have been during the end of his time spent in Mannheim that Mozart became acquainted with the marking. Early in his career the composer had used *fp*, and he continued its use after he introduced *sf* and *sfp*. While in Mannheim, Mozart had the opportunity to study for a brief time under the tutelage of Christian Cannabich (1731–1798), the director of the Mannheim Court Orchestra. Mozart described this inspiring experience in correspondence to his father, Leopold, who, despite his son's enthusiasm, did not miss a chance to disapprove of the innovative compositional procedures proposed by the Mannheim school. Still, Leopold only marginally criticized his son for the vague influences that one of his recently composed keyboard sonatas displayed:

> Your Sonata is a strange composition. It has something in it of the *rather artificial* Mannheim style, but so very little that your own good style is not spoilt thereby.[8]

Mozart's works from that period indeed display an artistic evolution that confirms the influence of his experience in Mannheim. Under Cannabich's guidance, he refined his skills in orchestration, and through his participation in the city's cultural events, he had the privilege of meeting some of its leading composers, who were also members of the court orchestra. These encounters provided unique opportunities to gain insight into some of the precepts that these composers advocated. The Mannheim school was known for its progressive compositional methods and for abandoning baroque performance archetypes in favor of novel ideas—for example, the introduction of crescendi and diminuendi in orchestral playing. It was also known for espousing the *Affektenlehre* (theory of affections), a doctrine of aesthetics of music whose proposition was to attribute specific emotions to musical contexts, and to provide interpretive and compositional tools to assist in achieving that goal. In this regard, *sforzando* as an agogic marking may have been devised for that purpose by one of the composers of the Mannheim school. We do not know whether Mozart was introduced to *sforzando* by Cannabich or by any of the new acquaintances among the orchestral players, but it would seem all too coincidental that he began to use the marking consistently only after his immersion in this very productive and stimulating environment. It was also at this stage that his interest in interpretive instructions became more prominent, as is confirmed by the increasing employment of articulatory and dynamic markings that he implemented in his works over the following years.

My aim of discovering the various implications of *sforzando* in the works of Haydn and Mozart prompted enlightening conversations with other musicians. These exchanges substantiated a common ground: in modern times, *sforzando* universally designates a dynamic accent.[9] The musicians interviewed were asked to form an opinion about the role of certain *sforzandi* in Mozart—instances that I believed would not make sonic sense were they interpreted strictly as dynamic emphases. From their responses and the discussions that generated from them, the consensus was that *fp*, *sf*, and *sfp* all would fall into the category of dynamic accents, distinguished by different degrees of loudness in the attack of the key: *fp* would indicate a loud sound (*f*) followed by a sudden return to a soft dynamic range (*p*); *sf* would signal a sharper attack than the one intended by *fp*; and *sfp* would imply a reduction in volume after a sharp accent. *Mfp*, occasionally used by Mozart, would indicate a milder accent than the regular *fp*. Although these responses conformed to basic rules that seemed to be generally accepted, I found such rationalization not completely convincing: if the introduction of notation was still at its early stages, would it not be unreasonable to believe that Mozart used more symbols to specify dynamic nuances pertaining to accents than those he used to indicate the contextual dynamic level? Put another way, since *p* and *f* are the two basic dynamic symbols we find in his works, and *pp* and *mf* occur with infrequency, I thought the idea peculiar that *fp*, *mfp*, *sf*, and *sfp* would denote four individual degrees of dynamic stress. Over time, in an effort to disentangle what I believed to be an otherwise inexplicable matter, I arrived at some interpretive possibilities of my own:

1. *fp* is simply a dynamic stress, namely, an accent.

2. *sf* represents several interpretive elements:

   a. agogic inflection

b. the voicing of a line that might not otherwise be considered melodically relevant

c. the signaling of metric order

3. *sfp* indicates a soft dynamic level in combination with any of the alternatives described in point 2.

This would allow us to view *fp* and *mfp* as the two markings that assume the role of a dynamic stress, whereas *sf* (and derivatively *sfp*) would refer to interpretive coordinates that only indirectly involve dynamics (voicing, as it implies dynamic relevance against a softer background; and metric order, with its potential reliance on dynamic emphasis). As I began to apply these connotations to *sf* in Mozart's music and to *fz* in Haydn's, I realized that the etymology of *sforzando* very aptly relates—we apply "effort" to delay the entrance of a note or chord; to bring out a compound line by voicing it over the general texture; or to stress a note or chord agogically or dynamically, or both, in order to confirm a metric distribution or establish a new one.

When were the various implications of *sforzando* reduced exclusively to dynamic emphasis? Was Beethoven responsible for diminishing its connotations? The manner in which he used *sforzando* from an early age seems reliably to indicate this intention. Unlike Mozart, Beethoven did not use *fp* to determine an accent; instead, he employed it to indicate a sudden decrease in dynamic level after a passage in *forte*. An episode from the Rondo of the Sonata in B-flat Major, Op. 22 demonstrates this treatment:

EXAMPLE 2.8. L. van Beethoven: Sonata in B-flat Major, Op. 22, IV. Allegretto, mm. 39–42.

A few measures earlier, in the same movement, *fp* is used to determine the arrival point of a crescendo as well as a sudden change in sonority:

EXAMPLE 2.9. L. van Beethoven: Sonata in B-flat Major, Op. 22, IV. Allegretto, mm. 30–34.

Beginning with the appearance of his Op. 1 in 1795, Beethoven's notation displayed such sophistication that the prior roles of *sf* may have been already superseded by other markings. The necessity of finding a symbol that could replace *fp* to indicate a dynamic stress may have led Beethoven to "recycle" *sf*, which was becoming obsolete in its original connotations. Of the markings that were conventionally used in the eighteenth century, he may have retained *fp* to represent conveniently the notation of *piano subito*, which he was the first to introduce prominently and consistently as an effect.[10] *Sfp* may have been used to indicate the placement of an accent combined with a *piano subito* or an accent in the context of a soft dynamic level.

In chapter 1 we saw that accents in some of the works of Chopin may determine a specific organization of the metric system when the writing could induce a misleading placement of strong and weak beats. We already identified that Mozart may have used *sforzandi* with that intention in his Adagio in B Minor, K. 540 (example 2.7). The absence of a notational device that specified metric order may have led composers to use a symbol that, while being employed for other purposes, at that time must have been one of the few viable options—especially if we consider that, to clarify a displacement of the meter, a performer may have to rely on dynamic stresses. In that respect, I began to suspect that the marking *fp*, more frequently encountered at an earlier stage in Mozart's keyboard works, may have specified metric order rather than dynamic emphasis. Especially in slow movements, I found it curious that entire passages would be affected by accents, which most interpreters tend to place with substantial weight. I noticed that Mozart often placed *fp* on strong beats when the writing could suggest an inaccurate deviation from the fundamental metric order. In doing so, he warned the performer that such metric inaccuracies should be avoided. Although Mozart's notational evolution may show that *sforzandi* began to indicate such instances more conspicuously, the central task in his early pieces in regard to this marking is to establish contextually where and when metric validity is truly intended—a process that involves deductive reasoning as much as musical intuition.

An analysis of *sforzandi* in the works of Beethoven seems to indicate that the composer often used the marking with the metric purpose that we just mentioned. A convincing example appears in the third movement of his Sonata in D Minor, Op. 31, No. 2, where the placement of the regular meter in measures 87 through 90 is specified to avoid the hemiolas that would instinctively result from the writing itself:

EXAMPLE 2.10. L. van Beethoven: Sonata in D Minor, Op. 31, No. 2, III. Allegretto, mm. 83–94.

An analogous instance is found nearly two decades later in the first movement of the Sonata in C Minor, Op. 111. The sequence of *sforzandi* marked in measures 26 through 28 is commonly interpreted as signaling strong emphases that are prescribed by the rhythmic drive of the passage. Rather, the *sforzandi* in this ascending figuration would seem to impose an organization of the pulse that counteracts the erroneous stressing of the groups of three sixteenth-notes:

EXAMPLE 2.11. L. van Beethoven: Sonata in C Minor, Op. 111, I. Maestoso-Allegro con brio ed appassionato, mm. 26–30.

EXAMPLE 2.11 (*continued*)

In the first movement of the Sonata in E Major, Op. 109, *sforzandi* seem to outline a diminution of the metric pulse, signaling groups of two beats instead of the preceding four-beat gestures that derive naturally from the harmonic organization of the phrases (the dotted slurs, in my hand, show the groups):

EXAMPLE 2.12. L. van Beethoven: Sonata in E Major, Op. 109, I. Vivace, ma non troppo, mm. 25–46.

EXAMPLE 2.12 (*continued*)

The regular four-beat pattern resumes once the use of *sforzandi* comes to an end.

Other relevant cases in Beethoven show that he placed the marking in a sequence to initiate a metric order in which weak beats become the new points of reference. This organization might appear in conjunction with a metric diminution, also caused by *sforzandi*. Here is an instance found in the closing movement of the Sonata in A Major, Op. 101:

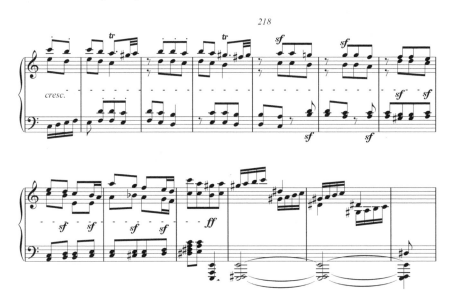

EXAMPLE 2.13. L. van Beethoven: Sonata in A Major, Op. 101, IV. Allegro, mm. 214–226.

The *sforzandi* in measures 218 through 222 may not signal a mere syncopation, but might imply a metric modification that incurs a deliberate switch to a new order. With the *fortissimo* in measure 223, both the regular two-beat pattern and the regular metric scheme would resume. Besides the rhythmic coding that these two coordinates contain, the passage may reveal a further layer of information: placed above or below either hand, the *sforzandi* signal an active voicing exchange between the two parts—a dialogue that, starting in measure 220, is interrupted by a more vertical organization, indicated by *sforzandi* in the middle of the system.

My study of Haydn's late sonatas revealed that the use of *sforzando* to outline metric displacements may have been a practice that Beethoven learned from his teacher. A case in point is represented by the shift of meter between the initial 3/4 and the 6/8 in measures 20 through 22 of the opening movement of Haydn's Sonata in E-flat Major, Hob. XVI:49, written shortly before Beethoven began to study under the master's guidance:

EXAMPLE 2.14. F. J. Haydn: Sonata in E-flat Major Hob. XVI:49, I. Allegro, mm. 12–24.

In light of these observations concerning metric organization, could we regard the *sforzandi* found in measures 22 and 23 of the first movement of Haydn's Sonata in E-flat Major, Hob. XVI:52, illustrated in example 2.4, as signaling a new, temporary set of downbeats?

Beethoven held the sonatas of Muzio Clementi (1752–1832) in the highest regard, ranking them as better than those of Mozart. In his youth, as he ambitiously explored the technical possibilities of the piano, he must have invested a great deal of time in studying the works of the Italian composer, and probably found their technical challenges and compositional procedures immensely inspiring. Evident references to Clementi's extensive employment of scales, arpeggios, and chordal passages are brought forth in Beethoven's early style, such as the Sonata in C Major, Op. 2, No. 3 and the Piano Concerto in C Major, Op. 15. As with other composers of the time, Clementi's writing shows that *sforzandi* (notated with *fz*) were used to signal diverse interpretive aspects, from dynamic to metric accentuation. The latter is well exemplified in an excerpt from the first movement of the Sonata in G Minor, Op. 34, No. 2, written in 1797. After the hemiola in measures 106 through 108, Clementi used *sforzandi* to reestablish the original meter in measure 109:

EXAMPLE 2.15. M. Clementi: Sonata in G Minor, Op. 34, No. 2, I. Largo e sostenuto, Allegro con fuoco, mm. 101–112.

Although late in his career Clementi also used the marking to call attention to the presence of different voices in the context of contrapuntal writing. In the Adagio from the Sonata in A Major, Op. 50, No. 1, published in London in 1821, *sforzandi* seem to signal the imitations that occur in the midst of the rather elaborate four- and five-voice texture, rather than an accent on the first note of each group:

EXAMPLE 2.16. M. Clementi: Sonata in A Major, Op. 50, No. 1, II. Adagio sostenuto e patetico, mm. 16–19.

The excerpt from the final movement of Beethoven's Sonata in A Major, Op. 101 that I illustrated in example 2.13 shows an analogous intention, with *sforzandi* signaling the exchanges between the two hands. A few years later, Schubert chose to indicate similar occurrences with the use of accents, and Chopin followed suit by using long accents or hairpins placed above or below the voices in question (see chapter 1, examples 1.33 and 1.36–1.40).

In the Adagio in example 2.16, our notion of *sforzando* would conventionally lead us to apply forceful angularity to the notes or chords in question. Although it is conceivable that we might choose to rely in part on dynamic inflections in instances that prescribe a change of meter, I have frequently wondered whether those emphases, particularly when they are strong, are appropriate, and whether they contribute to revealing what a composer intended. I often pose that question to my pupils, inviting them to disregard the more predictable dynamic placements of *sforzandi*—especially if their role defines metric order—and to consider agogic accents as a substitute. This experiment invariably leads to captivating alternatives.

Why is our musical instinct superseded by mechanical responses to *sforzandi*? Throughout the years, I observed that a strong emphasis applied to a *sforzando* in my own playing and in that of my students seemed to derive from habit—a reaction that has more to do with a visual attribution acquired from the score in front of us than with the necessity to make the notation a purposeful element of musical rhetoric. Identifying the different functions of the marking is no easy task, as an essential prerogative of the way notation comes to life in the music we play is the interaction between intuition and deductive reasoning during the process of codification. In particular, I recognized a further level of comprehension that I now deem as a vital element of this cognitive and intrinsic transformation: I understood that the different designations that notation provides represent a path to interpretive freedom. It was not about the unsuspected agogic nuances provided by hairpins or by *sforzandi*, but a higher degree of freedom that comes from behavioral and intellectual perspectives. If certain symbols that I reproduced mechanically did not originally have the same connotations, I wondered whether there were other interpretive coordinates that suffered a comparable rigidity. I became increasingly aware that the labels that have been affixed to eras as well as the appropriateness of sound that is deemed necessary to categorize these periods of music history may all have been pieces of information that derailed my ability to discover my own voice, preventing me from setting myself apart as an interpreter. Being able to communicate the essence of a work may have been far from the all too familiar "this is how it goes" that informed my conceptions: a piece of music, I came to understand, does not reveal itself when a performer manages to reproduce faithfully the printed score, as it is often claimed, but when the work reemerges from decades of stifled conventions, regardless of preconceived stylistic appropriateness or classified aesthetics of sound. The degree of intensity of a melody or the agogic flexibility imparted to specific pitches, phrases, or sections should not be restrained or suppressed by a set of rules according to which the music of the classical era should be represented with purity and decorum. These traditions impeded my ability to reveal the true nature of the pieces I played, because I believed that proposing a performance that does not fall into predetermined stylistic and aesthetic categories was going to be received as improper and offensive. I now understood that these classifications were inconclusive: it was in my ability to extract its inherent communicative traits that a work of art would have been able to unveil itself.

⋯◆▸⋯

To what extent might Beethoven's approach to *sforzando* have affected the vocabulary of composers from his own time? While reading the book *Inside Beethoven's Quartets*, by Lewis Lockwood and the members of the Juilliard Quartet, I came across a statement that sums up our modern belief quite aptly:

> [Beethoven's] is a sforzando that we will then live with, more or less, for the rest of musical history.[11]

The mark that Beethoven left in the nineteenth century was perhaps indelible, and the notion that *sforzando* had different implications other than dynamic ones might have completely vanished in the following generations. The admiration that composers and performers in the German-speaking countries and abroad manifested for him during the first three decades of the nineteenth century was such that the manner in which Beethoven treated *sforzandi* may have ultimately developed into a universally accepted connotation for the marking. Schubert, twenty-seven years Beethoven's junior, may have gained knowledge of this well-established tradition during his formative years in Vienna. From his early works, the utilization of *fz* addressed all the interpretive aspects that the notational symbol *sf* seem to have intended for Beethoven, although a few exceptions can be identified—for instance, Schubert never used it to specify voicing in the context of contrapuntal exchanges, because hairpins had begun to represent those interpretive elements with greater precision. Throughout the younger composer's brief existence, *sforzandi* remained as convenient tools to indicate dynamic emphases and metric order. For example, the opening page of the Sonata in A Minor, D. 845, written in 1825, shows that *sforzandi* might signal both coordinates:

EXAMPLE 2.17. F. Schubert: Sonata in A Minor, D. 845, I. Moderato, mm. 18–26.

The rearrangement of the metric system in measures 20 through 23 is the natural outcome of an order that was tentatively introduced in the previous measures by the alternating half-notes between the two hands. The displacement caused by the *sforzandi* designs a new profile that outlines a dactylic figure (long-short-short), a rhythmic pattern that became an identifying trait in Schubert's language. The regular meter is brought back by the *sforzandi* in measures 24 and 25. This momentary displacement reminds us of a similar instance in a passage from the first movement of Chopin's Sonata in B Minor, Op. 58, which the composer signaled with long accents (see chapter 1, examples 1.44a and 1.44b). A cursory examination of Schubert's piano works, chamber music and lieder also revealed that the implementation of *sforzandi* grew significantly as his language matured over the course of the years 1818 and 1819, and that they were dramatically reduced in his late output a decade or so later. In these last struggling years of his life, Schubert seems to have used hairpins to designate metric order, relegating *sforzandi* to indicate strong dynamic placements and, speculatively, agogic emphases.

Schubert's limited use of *sforzandi* in his final years may have reflected a collective shift toward a type of notation that is represented by explicit interpretive directions, relying on worded instructions rather than symbols. This phenomenon led composers to apply progressively specific connotations for *sforzandi*, using them for the first time exclusively to signal dynamic emphases. The dynamic function became an established tradition over time, and a universally accepted meaning by twentieth-century standards, yet I was curious whether there were composers during the first half of the nineteenth century who went against this inclination, using *fz* or *sf* in alternative ways. In the works of Chopin, for example, I remained perplexed in front of what were supposed to be strong accents, which the composer marked with *fz* rather than *sf*, wondering whether they should affect passages that seemed more logical without them. Consider the closing measures of his Nocturne in C-sharp Minor, Op. 27, No. 1:

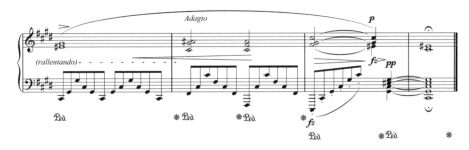

EXAMPLE 2.18. F. Chopin: Nocturne in C-sharp Minor, Op. 27, No. 1, mm. 98–101.

In the hands of many pianists, the two *sforzandi* in measure 100 are often deliberately ignored. Although the first instance could ostensibly signal a strong placement of the bass, the second one seems to be counterintuitive and musically incongruous if viewed as a dynamic stress. Was Chopin using the symbol *fz* to indicate a slight resistance in the placement of a note? Although it may easily resolve an interpretive conundrum, this way of indicating an agogic nuance might be construed as excessively elaborate. In their conventional dynamic role, we might try to imagine what kinds of emphases we should place on these *sforzandi*. Should they be strong? Or should they be subtle, since the dynamic prescribed is *pianissimo*? When we encounter these awkward instances, we often adapt their function by choosing the least offensive level of loudness. I once heard a well-known pianist explain that these two *sforzandi*—in particular the second one—do not indicate dynamic emphases, because they are clearly unreasonable from a musical perspective. He proposed that they suggest "emotional" inflections, which he illustrated by singing with a generous vibrato, subtly dynamic fluctuations, and slides between pitches. We know that these nuances are not possible on the piano, because its fixed tuning and acoustic nature exclude the possibility of a portamento or dynamic variation within a note. Singing might help a performer comprehend and appreciate the emotional content of a phrase, but I doubt that Chopin or any other composer of his time would have used *sforzando* to illustrate this degree of interpretive sophistication. Allowing these justifications to intrude, moreover, may create a double standard: not only does this approach succeed at minimizing the dynamic emphases that we find irrational; the interpretive surrogate permits us—consciously or unconsciously—to reject the notion that it is *we* who might be misinterpreting the printed page.

Finding an alternative role for *sforzandi* in Chopin may seem unrealistic to many, but his extremely rare use of the marking is a clue that intrigued me for years. An analysis of his works starting with the Warsaw period, including those that were not published during his lifetime, confirms such a sparing use of *sforzandi* that the notion of a possible dynamic implication would be easily challenged. Compare its use in the early Rondo à la Mazur in F Major, Op. 5—four instances in a piece whose length is approximately eight minutes—with its application in Beethoven or Schubert or even Haydn, and an inclination to reserve the marking to very special places is unquestionably detected. This careful use did not diminish over the years: in the Ballade in G Minor, Op. 23, Chopin applied only six instances, the first one rather late in the piece, in measure 100. Most occasions of *sforzandi* in this piece appear at the site of structurally relevant pillars, such as the return of the second thematic material in the abridged recapitulation, in measure 166. Here, the volume provided by the reiterated *fortissimo* would seem substantial enough to delineate the crucial arrival point, making the presence of *sforzando* somewhat redundant:

EXAMPLE 2.19. F. Chopin: Ballade in G Minor, Op. 23, mm. 162–169.

The presence of *sforzando* also supports the arrival of the coda in measure 208:

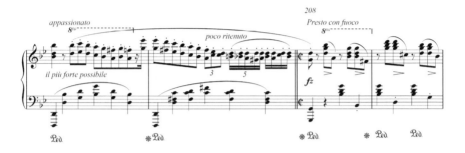

EXAMPLE 2.20. F. Chopin: Ballade in G Minor, Op. 23, mm. 206–209.

Fz further appears at an important modulating moment in the Ballade—the harmonically decisive shift to E-flat major in measure 158, before the recapitulation:

EXAMPLE 2.21. F. Chopin: Ballade in G Minor, Op. 23, mm. 154–162.

I suppose that the loudness entailed by their respective contexts suggests that these instances should be approached with due emphasis, but a comparison of a dozen recordings of the Ballade curiously demonstrated that only one of the selected pianists endorsed particularly strong dynamic placements as an interpretive element for these arrival points; in all the other interpretations the consideration of the musical context ultimately superseded the impact of notation. Although it is conceivable that dynamic emphases be applied to all these occurrences, the very limited use of *sforzandi* in this Ballade made me wonder whether Chopin intended for it to be almost completely devoid of strong accents. Might he have intended to imply that dynamic emphases were part of the musical rhetoric, therefore intentionally leaving them to the interpreter's intuition to discern? And if so, do these *sforzandi* request louder emphases than the ones already applied instinctively by the performer?

A *sforzando* that I was never quite able to accept as a dynamic emphasis is found in the first movement of Chopin's Sonata in B-flat Minor, Op. 35. The aggression with which most pianists execute the downbeat of measure 81 has always left me perplexed:

EXAMPLE 2.22. F. Chopin: Sonata in B-flat Minor, Op. 35, I. Grave, Doppio movimento, mm. 77–85.

The downbeat affected by the *sforzando* represents the end of the second thematic block and the beginning of an extensive coda, which may validate the notion that a strong accent should perhaps be avoided. After determining that all the early sources agree on the presence of this *sforzando*, I began to consider the options. In regard to the agogic solution that came immediately to mind, the first French edition is particularly tempting: the *fz* creeps back behind the bar line, rather than aligning with the chord in question:

EXAMPLE 2.23. F. Chopin: Sonata in B-flat Minor, Op. 35, I. Grave, Doppio movimento, mm. 80–81 (Troupenas edition).

Yet not only was it less than believable that Chopin would have used the marking so placed to imply that level of interpretive nuance; I also suspected that had he considered *fz* an efficient marking to represent very slight agogic concessions, he would have signaled comparable instances in a similar fashion throughout the sonata, and this was not the case. Discovering what this *sforzando* may have meant for Chopin was a revelation almost as remarkable as the one I had experienced while investigating the secret life of hairpins. It came to me as an unexpected illumination, while devising a set of physical motions that would establish the appropriate inflection for the end of the second theme and the correct metric subdivision of the ensuing episode. The *sforzando* on the downbeat of measure 81 could refer to an element that pertains to dynamics, though without an especially overt emphasis. Just as the role of a specific pitch or chord can be minimized in the context of a sudden textural modification, so can it also be augmented. Here, Chopin is giving relevance to the D-flat major chord by signaling its importance: it should still belong to the second theme, though it may be misconstrued as belonging to the athletic chordal sequence that opens the extended coda of the exposition, whose writing is melodically less relevant. As the chord in question functions as a hinge between the two sections, Chopin is cautioning the performer that it should not be absorbed in sound or articulation, or both, into the episode that follows.

An instance at the onset of the same movement confirmed this interpretive discovery and offered an unpredicted interpretation of a passage whose peculiar harmonic and melodic configurations have puzzled many pianists since it first appeared in print:

EXAMPLE 2.24a. F. Chopin: Sonata in B-flat Minor, Op. 35, I. Grave-Doppio movimento, mm. 1–6 (Breitkopf & Härtel edition, 1840).

A rather surprising contrapuntal imitation, which functions in the tenor register as a rhythmic diminution of the opening intervallic material, generally goes unnoticed:

EXAMPLE 2.24b. F. Chopin: Sonata in B-flat Minor, Op. 35, I. Grave, Doppio movimento, mm. 1–5 (Outline of the contrapuntal exchange between voices).

In light of this exchange, the *fz* on the downbeat of measure 5 could signal the melodic resolution of the tenor voice in measures 2 through 4. The B-flat in measure 5 would become a melodically relevant pitch, whereas it is generally disjointed from the opening measures, and functions exclusively as the elemental tone in a column intended for coloristic effect on the harmony of B-flat minor:

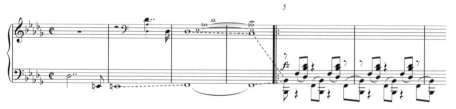

EXAMPLE 2.24c. F. Chopin: Sonata in B-flat Minor, Op. 35, I. Grave-Doppio movimento, mm. 1–7 (Outline of contrapuntal exchange and voice leading. The pitches in the right hand of measure 2 have been treated enharmonically).

The excitement caused by these discoveries in the first movement of the Sonata in B-flat Minor brought to mind the *sforzandi* in the Ballade in G Minor, Op. 23, which we considered earlier in this chapter. Shortly after I began to evaluate the symbol in this new light, it became apparent that Chopin had employed *fz* when a note or chord of a melodic passage might have been compromised by a sudden textural change. The passages from the Ballade illustrated in examples 2.19 through 2.21 seem to confirm that Chopin used these *sforzandi* to counteract a modification in the writing that could have minimized the melodic role of a specific chord or pitch. Soon it occurred to me that *sforzandi* also appeared in passages whose textural complexity may have prevented the melodic implications of a specific line from being easily detected, both from an aural and visual standpoint. An excerpt from the extended coda of the Barcarolle in F-sharp Major, Op. 60 provides an example:

EXAMPLE 2.25. F. Chopin: Barcarolle in F-sharp Major, Op. 60, mm. 109–111 (as notated in the Wessel edition, 1846).

The presence of *sforzandi* on the downbeats of measures 110 and 111 cautions the performer that the two chords have melodic relevance against the purely ornamental background. In this case the import may be intuitively grasped (the small-print notation may itself lead to a lighter execution, because it suggests a cadential hue for the material), but other works of Chopin show that this device was applied to more conventional, unassuming passages. The opening measures of the Polonaise in A-flat Major, Op. 53, for example, demonstrate the concept aptly. The *sforzandi* outline an ascending chromatic progression, which can be recognized melodically only if the background is dynamically removed from the imposing presence of these harmonic pillars. The material is in fact recurrently marked with *piano* until the marking *crescendo* in measure 10 preempts it— although very few pianists observe these directions:

⊕ **EXAMPLE 2.26.** F. Chopin: Polonaise in A-flat Major, Op. 53, mm. 1–13.

The Barcarolle, Op. 60 and the Polonaise, Op. 53 are mature creations, however, and I wondered whether Chopin used *sforzandi* with the same intention in earlier years. We saw how the marking had a rather different connotation in the ballade and in the sonata discussed earlier, where it indicated that the concluding note or chord of a phrase or gesture should not be undermined by being absorbed into the textural change that ensues. Did Chopin consider the marking to be versatile, intending to signal both interpretive elements, or was there an evolution? It was while learning the Polonaise in E-flat Minor, Op. 26, No. 2, that I realized how the notion that *sforzandi* indicated the emergence of a particular line from a more complex texture had been devised at an earlier stage, concomitantly with the Ballade in G Minor:

EXAMPLE 2.27. F. Chopin: Polonaise in E-flat Minor, Op. 26, No. 2, mm. 31–35.

The cascading arpeggio in the right hand of measure 33 is purely ornamental, reiterating the harmonic content rather than establishing a melodic descending line. The *sforzandi* in the same measure determine what pitches should be detected as melodically relevant.

Observing the role of the *sforzandi* in the Barcarolle and the Polonaise in E-flat Minor led me to a fundamental interpretive conclusion: the notes outlined by the marking could be considered as dynamically emphatic only to the extent that they do not emerge as strong accents against their background. In other words, although it is conceivable that a note or chord marked with a *sforzando* be played *forte* or *fortissimo* because of its dynamic context, it is the surrounding material that has to be played in a softer, more discreet dynamic range.

Despite these conclusions, at times a sequence of *sforzandi* may give the impression that Chopin used the marking to indicate dynamic emphases. One such moment appears in the middle section of the Nocturne in C-sharp Minor, Op. 27, No. 1, published in 1836 concurrently with the Polonaises, Op. 26, the second of which we viewed in the preceding example:

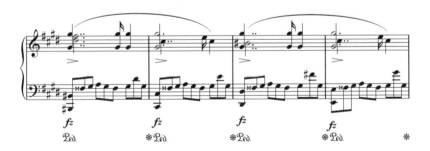

EXAMPLE 2.28. F. Chopin: Nocturne in C-sharp Minor, Op. 27, No. 1, mm. 37–44.

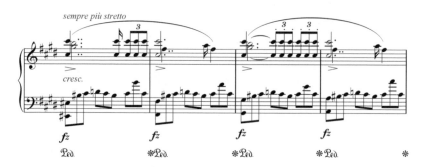

EXAMPLE 2.28 (*continued*)

These *sforzandi*, nonetheless, may signal that the compound line in the bass register should have its own melodic profile. Had Chopin notated his intent with accents instead of with *sforzandi*, a confusing homogenization of symbols with the accents in the upper staff could have arisen—especially if we take into account the context of an already heavy texture. These inferences occurred to me in light of the purpose expressed by the accents in the right hand, which seem to outline an exchange of voicing between the two lines—a dialogue that can be better understood if notated as follows:

EXAMPLE 2.29. F. Chopin: Nocturne in C-sharp Minor, Op. 27, No. 1, mm. 37–40 (accents showing the exchange of voicing between the two lines in the right hand).

In the coda of the Prelude in A-flat Major, Op. 28, No. 17, which features a long peroration on a pedal point of tonic, a sequence of *sforzandi* marked on each of the eleven A-flats in the bass register discloses the prevalence of the bass notes against the rather thick texture of the middle register:

EXAMPLE 2.30. F. Chopin: Prelude in A-flat Major, Op. 28, No. 17, mm. 61–69.

Chopin may have intended these *sforzandi* to pertain to timbre, rather than loudness—the *pianissimo* and *sotto voce* that are indicated for the entire passage most likely imply a veiled sonority, obtained by employing the left pedal. In this way, the chordal thematic material could float as an echolike effect on the bass notes, which would not require prominent accentuation.

Much of our discussion has focused on music written by composers who lived in German-speaking countries in the eighteenth and early nineteenth centuries. As we consider the output of composers who were born in the first part of the nineteenth century, we come to the realization that after the death of Beethoven, musicians perhaps overgeneralized his use of *sforzando* as simply a dynamic stress, and may have disseminated a tradition in this use that he was only partly responsible for initiating. Even though not all composers might have followed the same approach, the practice had such a strong impact on nineteenth-century music making that it was confirmed as a convention and was perpetuated well into the twentieth century. I mentioned that, although *sforzando* for Beethoven was an essential and ineffaceable marking for indicating dynamic emphasis, in today's approach to reading music the notion may be taken to an extreme. Perhaps this attitude has developed from his sometimes insufferable personality: we are all familiar with his proverbial outbursts of temper, and we easily infer that his deafness exacerbated both anger and isolation. These attributes, and the legends that have formed around them, have established the idea, without modulation, that *sforzando* is a fingerprint in Beethoven's music that enables it to be immediately recognizable. Yet we saw how he also employed *sforzandi* to indicate changes of meter—a characteristic that might have very little to do with angular dynamic stresses.

In the 1870s, Breitkopf & Härtel resolved to neutralize the difference between *sf* and *fz* in scores that they had been printing for decades. This modification, which eliminated any ostensible distinction between the two indications, affected the entire corpus of Chopin's works, and was evidently caused by the belief that the composer had indiscriminately chosen one marking over the other to signify a dynamic emphasis. Most mainstream publications of the twentieth century, including the Paderewski edition, propose Breitkopf & Härtel's preference, which remained unchallenged until the urtext editions made their appearance. This decision—which was nothing short of misleading—has likely caused substantial repercussions in the way *sforzando* has been perceived from the end of the nineteenth century to our time, thus preventing the appreciation of the marking's alternative implications. The scholarship of the last thirty years has brought back the original symbols, but the manifold implications of *fz* have still not been clarified. The modern notion of the marking does not prescribe alternative readings, because we have been persuaded that placing strong emphases on notes or chords that are affected by *sforzandi* is some sort of moral principle by which we must stand firm. At the same time, we are unaware, or deny, that force of habit based on interpretive traditions informs this practice more than a truthful representation of the musical material. Although in certain instances the application of a strong dynamic emphasis may be acceptable, the decision of how to treat each case can be favorably achieved only if a mechanical reproduction of the symbol is not the only possible reading.

I mentioned the puzzlement caused by many of the *fz*s in Haydn's music when they are treated exclusively as dynamic emphases. At the onset of his studying the Sonata in C Major, Hob. XVI:50, one of my most gifted young students instinctively eliminated almost all of the *sforzandi*, alleging that they went against musical logic. His refusal to apply the marking prevailed until he was persuaded by Christa Landon's commentary, which explains that the *sforzandi* that he had found unacceptable could be invested with different meanings—metric order, agogic freedom, and voicing, all of which should be determined by their context. The notion that the symbol *fz* might have also been misprinted as *f* or *ff* brought a smile to his face.

THREE

...OF RINFORZANDI

*All good things
are wild, and free.*

— HENRY DAVID THOREAU

When asked to describe the role of a *rinforzando* that has been placed at the end of a crescendo whose destination is an *fff*, quite a few musicians offered a predictable response: it demands a greater increase in volume. I had assigned the same connotation in my own musical vocabulary, but as I looked anew at the contexts in which *rinforzando* appears concurrently with *crescendo*, I began to question the logic of the redundancy: would not indicating a crescendo have sufficed? As to the degree of dynamic intensity, would the emotional charge of its context be more instructive than a generalized duplicative marking?

In *Musik-Lexikon*, compiled in 1882, Hugo Riemann attributed dynamic validity to *rinforzando*, stating that a strong crescendo—"ein starkes *Crescendo*"— is to be employed.[1] Other authoritative publications in the second half of the nineteenth century shared this position, relating the term to *sforzando, crescendo,* and even *forte*. Its interpretation did not change in the twentieth century: all the reliable encyclopedic sources I consulted agree that *rinforzando* indicates an increase in volume or a localized dynamic swell. Music theorists of the late eighteenth and early nineteenth centuries often referred to the marking's dynamic involvement, but the German composer Justin Heinrich Knecht (1752–1817) seems to have seen in the marking a broader scope. In *Knechts allgemeiner musikalischer Katechismus* (Knecht's General Musical Principles), published in 1803, his definition of what was then a term in its infancy reveals that *rinforzando* may have not referred exclusively to volume:

Rinforzando can only be applied to a group of several notes to which one should give a strong emphasis.[2]

Only a few years before Knecht's *Katechismus* began to circulate, Beethoven had published his Piano Trios, Op. 1 and Piano Sonatas, Op. 2—six works that contain a prolific amount of interpretive instructions and a profuse application of *rinforzando*. In my teenage years, when I approached the study of some of these pieces, the conventional treatment of the marking was often so perplexing that I questioned whether a dynamic role should have been regarded as its only feasible treatment. The presence of these irrational instances was often justified by the supposition that the composer had deliberately intended for certain anomalies to take place. But how could the dynamic abruptness of certain *rinforzandi*, which seemed to hinder and deform the expression of entire passages, be accepted as manifest truth? The musicians with whom I interacted or performed during those years did not seem too perturbed by these dynamic swells, though they occasionally recognized their peculiarity. I suspected that these unusual outcomes were perhaps the result of a system that assigns inalterable meanings to notational symbols, and that we had allowed these interpretive traditions to become part of our language, to be crucial elements of the way we faced the complex prosody of the music we played. Further, it seemed to me that the belief that the mechanical reproduction of these symbols and signs, aimed to reveal the composer's intentions, was often brought to an extreme and encouraged by teachers and performers alike—an approach that may have perpetuated erroneous convictions about a composer's language.

The idea that Beethoven was developing a personal vocabulary at a young age is not incorrect: his early style was governed by a prodigious originality and a forward-looking attitude. But these attributes have helped to legitimate the cultivation of stereotypes—"a typical Beethoven sound" or "a Beethovenian character." We all have heard statements such as, "The sound should be more robust, here: this is Beethoven, not Mozart!" or "More graceful: this is Mozart, not Beethoven!" Pianistically speaking, Beethoven's distinctive language may have stemmed from his ambitious and inquisitive nature, but we cannot dismiss the influence of the more sophisticated and powerful instruments with which he was provided; it is easy to believe that these may have further contributed to the development of a more vigorous pianism, and in any case they inevitably affected his perception of sound production and the manner in which he wrote. But he is also the composer who used the marking *dolce* the most, as Russell Sherman pointed out in a conversation we had several years ago. The claim that Beethoven's piano music should sound "thicker" than Mozart's is as historically correct, it seems to me, as the assertion that the music that preceded the romantics should not be as expansive and free because it was a prerogative of romanticism to be communicative. As I mentioned in chapter 2, musicians in the nineteenth century did not label themselves "romantic," nor did they establish that their music-making had suddenly parted with a stricter approach to pulse, rhythm, or expression. Their language was simply in evolution. Mozart's Adagio in B Minor, K. 540 is perhaps the perfect paradigm of this contradiction: it is possibly one of the most "romantic" pieces of the late eighteenth century, yet pianists play it with a kind of restraint. "It is, after all, a classical work," was the dismissive retort of a young pianist when I asked whether the piece should have been approached less rigidly.

———————◆———————

In chapters 1 and 2 I discussed how my understanding of what I saw in print had been based on dogmatic principles and traditions that had been instilled in me during my formative years. I took these conventions at face value, assuming that there must have been a truth to the manner in which the generations that preceded me had interpreted musical notation. The musicians with whom I interacted, the concerts I attended and the recordings to which I regularly returned all shaped the way in which I heard, read and understood music. I began to communicate those notions in my deliberations about how a piece should sound and in my early teaching experiences, perpetuating beliefs that, I thought, were respecting the composer's intentions. Yet the substantial conclusions to which I came over time concerning hairpins, accents and *sforzandi* made me reconsider many occurrences of *rinforzando* whose mechanical reproduction in its conventional dynamic attribution did not always seem to correspond to musically logical solutions. Was our perception of *rinforzando* also based on an interpretive misconstruction, I wondered.

An opportunity to address this question arose while I was working with a student on the opening page of the Adagio from Beethoven's first sonata from Op. 2. In this inspired slow movement, a *rinforzando* is encountered in measure 14, as the first sixteen-measure episode nears its close. A new phrase introduces the relative key of D minor, starting from the anacrusis of measure 17:

EXAMPLE 3.1. L. van Beethoven: Sonata in F Minor, Op. 2, No. 1, II. Adagio, mm. 13–18.

Beethoven's only dynamic indication for this tender, intimate episode is a *pianissimo* as the movement begins, yet the student applied an increase in volume in its concluding measures—quite an unusual choice, considering the poignant lyricism of the passage. If Beethoven had a particular effect in mind for this *rinforzando,* its meaning eluded me. Was my student's interpretation correct? Was he really supposed to apply a crescendo—a strong one, if Riemann's suggestion were to be followed—at the end of the opening phrase? Where would the increase end? Should it continue through the new phrase that starts in measure 17? Or should the emphasis be a localized dynamic one on the third beat of measure 14, as some performers interpret it? By comparison with a crescendo, a single stress seemed a more reasonable solution; nevertheless I wondered what would necessitate its odd presence in an opening section whose only dynamic marking is an initial *pianissimo.*

I then noticed a curious parallel between this *rinforzando* and the opening measures of the second movement of Haydn's Sonata in E-flat Major, Hob. XVI:49, written only a few years earlier. In measure 15, the application of the term *forzando* not to a single pitch but to a cluster of notes is the only such instance in the composer's entire output for keyboard:

EXAMPLE 3.2. F. J. Haydn: Sonata in E-flat Major, Hob. XVI:49, II. Adagio e cantabile, mm. 14–18.

My puzzlement only grew. The uncanny resemblance between this passage and the one we looked at in example 3.1, I thought, might not be just a fortuitous occurrence. Did Haydn also expect a crescendo, as I had been trained to believe that Beethoven did? And if so, how could I make sense of an interpretive instruction that parted with my musical instinct—indeed, that seemed incoherent? Further, as this instance in Haydn's adagio bears such a remarkable similarity to the passage in Beethoven's first sonata, was I permitted to assume that the markings *forzando* and *rinforzando* had comparable connotations?

As with *sforzando, rinforzando* owes its etymology to *forza,* "strength." It is generally believed that in Italian the verb *rinforzare* means "to apply extra force"—a reading that might conjure up a sudden accent or a swift increase in volume. Yet a more fitting translation may be "to provide additional support, to strengthen," which adds unforeseen nuances. This more compelling explanation gets to the core of what I have recently observed: investigating its role in the numerous instances found in Haydn, Beethoven, and Liszt helped me comprehend that *rinforzando* may be a marking whose connotations can be determined only by observing its context. Might then the passage we saw in example 3.2, from Haydn's adagio, be reasonably based on agogic premises? And if so, might the *forzando* suggest a gradual ritenuto to the end of measure 16, rather than an increase in volume that, for the conclusion of this phrase, may appear unconvincingly incongruous? Were this consideration plausible, would the parallel we drew with the *rinforzando* in example 3.2 allow us to attribute the same agogic prospects?

We just illustrated two moments in which slow tempi afford a greater degree of agogic freedom, but cases in which *rinforzandi* may serve as agogic indications can also be found in fast-paced movements. In Beethoven's Menuetto from the Trio in C Minor, Op. 1, No. 3, some performers observe the conventional dynamic function of *rinforzando* and interpret the occurrence in measure 19 as a crescendo. Rather, a progressive ritenuto lasting almost four measures could ideally end with the introduction of the *forte* in measure 22:

EXAMPLE 3.3a. L. van Beethoven: Trio in C Minor, Op. 1, No. 3, III. Menuetto: Quasi Allegro, mm. 12–23.

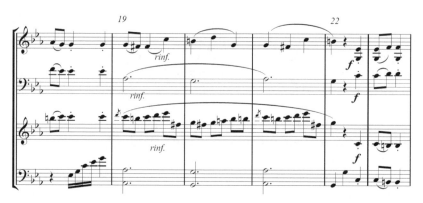

EXAMPLE 3.3a (*continued*)

In chapter 1 we observed that Beethoven dispensed with the marking *crescendo* in his Trio in E-flat Major, Op. 1, No. 1, apart from the Scherzo movement, in which three rare instances of *crescendo*, all placed within a brief eight-measure passage, seem to signal uncharacteristic dynamic swells. That *rinforzando* in the early Trios, Op. 1 may not indicate an increase in volume might be suggested by the complete absence of equivalent markings that would indicate diminuendi (one irregularity being a brief, solitary *diminuendo* in the third Trio). The only exception is the occurrence of *calando*, which for most composers of the time expressed a decrease in volume because of its etymology—the antithesis of *crescendo*.[3] Used rarely in the Trios, Op. 1, *calando* is always confined to the ending of a section or movement. The general absence of crescendi and diminuendi throughout the composition may validate the idea that the performer should extemporaneously add increases or decreases in volume while attending to the basic dynamic markings and their individual context, as well as the direction of the music (i.e., crescendo in an ascending sequence of pitches and decrescendo in a descending one; see Czerny's description in chapter 1, page 15).

In the passage from the Trio in C Minor in example 3.3a, the idea that *rinforzandi* indicate dynamic emphases led some editors to reinterpret their application as referring to individual pitches. In many instances, typographical limitations reduced the space allotted to the term, which was shortened by using the marking *rf*. It is this abbreviation that may have prompted the attribution of a loud dynamic level, because *f* visually became its predominant element. Ironically, although the shortened form made its reference to specific notes or chords more intelligible, it also increased the likelihood of arbitrary placements. In some cases, *rf* was replicated in analogous passages and printed parenthetically—with a goal of consistency, in the obvious attempt to interpret Beethoven's intentions.

Here is what the Henle edition proposes in measures 18–23 from the same passage:

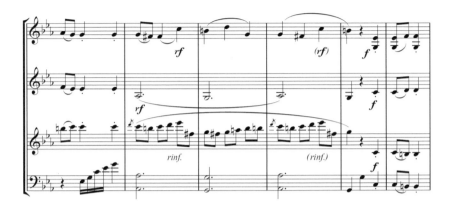

EXAMPLE 3.3b. L. van Beethoven: Trio in C Minor, Op. 1, No. 3, III. Menuetto: Quasi Allegro, mm. 18–23 (Henle edition).

The works of Beethoven that followed the rather successful publication of Opp. 1 and 2 show that *rinforzando* may have preserved its apparent agogic relevance. The opening *Allegro molto e con brio* from the Sonata in C Minor (1795–97), the first of a triptych of sonatas for piano that Beethoven published as Op. 10, provides an example. The introductory eight-measure period displays an exchange of tragic, violent statements, which alternate with pleading invocations. A new episode that begins in measure 9 features three attempts which lead, in measure 22, to the reappearance of the thematic material from the opening measures:

EXAMPLE 3.4a. L. van Beethoven: Sonata in C Minor, Op. 10, No. 1, I. Allegro molto e con brio, mm. 1–22.

🔊 EXAMPLE 3.4a (*continued*)

I would interpret the *rinforzando* at the beginning of the third proposal, in measure 13, as signaling a progressive rallentando that applies to the descending gesture. The regular tempo could ideally reemerge in measure 17, as the triplets introduce a new rhythmic and melodic element that hastens the thematic reentry in measure 22.

In Artur Schnabel's revision of this Sonata, editorial markings suggest that he interpreted the *rinforzando* as a crescendo for the entire descending gesture. His approach is adopted by most performers:

EXAMPLE 3.4b. L. van Beethoven: Sonata in C Minor, Op. 10, No. 1, I. Allegro molto e con brio, mm. 9–16 (Artur Schnabel's revision).

Schnabel envisioned the first of the three gestures (measures 9 and 10) as beginning in the *piano* range. Being a slight variation of the first, the second proposal (measures 11 and 12) is marked "un poco più *p* e tranquillo ma bene in tempo." At the beginning of the third attempt (measure 13), *rinforzando* is supported by three editorial markings: an opening hairpin that suggests a crescendo to the highest pitch of the rolled chord; an *energico* ("with energy"); and a *forte* placed on the third beat of the measure. Schnabel further added an accent for each hand on the last notes of the descending gesture (measure 16). Executing a crescendo and placing the accents prescribed by Schnabel would contradict two fundamental precepts of musical inflection that were advocated by theorists of the second half of the eighteenth century: a descending figuration should decrease in dynamic intensity; and the end of a slur should be dynamically tapered. Schnabel's interpretation is confirmed by the recording he made in 1935 of the sonata as part of his celebrated Beethoven cycle. Undeniably, this is a curious fact: Schnabel, born in 1882, was a pupil of Theodor Leschetizky's from the age of nine; Leschetizky (1830–1915) had studied with Czerny at an early age; and Beethoven became Czerny's mentor when the boy was ten. I doubt that Schnabel would have knowingly dismissed the original meaning of a marking whose presence is rather prominent in Beethoven's writing; or that Czerny, most likely aware of the different meanings of *rinforzando* in the music of his mentor, would have been responsible for breaking the legacy in his own teaching. Could Leschetizky be accountable? His tutelage with Czerny lasted only several years, and might have not provided Schnabel with an insight into the interpretation of *rinforzando* in the works of Beethoven.

As the humorous opening page of the Beethoven's second sonata from Op. 10 unfolds, we encounter another significant instance of *rinforzando*. Many performers deliver a strong crescendo to *forte* in measures 15 and 16:

EXAMPLE 3.5. L. van Beethoven: Sonata in F Major, Op. 10, No. 2, I. Allegro, mm. 1–22.

A crescendo from the *piano* implied in measure 15 to the *forte* in measure 16 would have a very limited time to operate, perhaps justifying why many interpretations propose a *forte subito* for the two chords affected by the *rinforzando*. It may have been this restricted space that led Schnabel to make that same interpretive choice, as his recording of 1933 bears out. Plausible as it may be in light of the marking's customary dynamic role, this solution seems to compromise the theatrical effect that would generate from a sudden dynamic change beginning from the second half of measure 16. Here again, as in the first sonata of Op. 10, the *rinforzando* may allude to agogic coordinates: it could be read as a ritenuto to the ensuing *forte*, or as a progressive rallentando through measures 15–18 to introduce the second thematic group, which starts with the anacrusis of measure 19. Following these observations, I realized that it was the presence of *rinforzando* between two diametrically opposite dynamic indications that may have led theorists and performers to assign a dynamic connotation to the marking. Yet this approach would exclude a priori the possibility of a sudden dynamic change, of the kind we observed in the preceding example. Treating this *rinforzando* as a gradual increase in volume would also outline an inconsistent use of interpretive instructions: the marking *crescendo* is profusely used throughout the sonata, and is quite consistently applied to two-bar periods. Had Beethoven intended a crescendo in measures 15 and 16, it seems to me that he would have probably indicated it.

Observing this active agogic involvement of *rinforzando* in the early works of Beethoven made me realize that the appearance of the marking in the Sonata in G Major, Op. 14, No. 2 may refer to a unique interpretive aspect—an extended rallentando that engages the concluding measures of the first movement:

EXAMPLE 3.6. L. van Beethoven: Sonata in G Major, Op. 14, No. 2, I. Allegro, mm. 187–200.

This reading would allow the *rinforzando* to apply agogically to the entire episode, rather than expressing a redundancy with the crescendo in measure 188, which would in any case come to a close with the introduction of the sudden *piano* in measure 191.

Examples 3.1 and 3.3–3.6 suggest that *rinforzando* held a prominent place in Beethoven's first period, and that he used the marking to indicate what many composers in the nineteenth century would often have expressed in their later years with a ritenuto or rallentando. In the first of the Trios, Op. 1, Beethoven had introduced a ritardando, spreading its four syllables over several measures and indicating what Haydn and Mozart had attempted a decade or so earlier with terms such as *perdendosi, mancando*, and *sempre più Adagio*. On the other hand this *ritardando* is found not within a section, but at the end of a movement (the Scherzo). As a strategy, it did not immediately set a precedent: its employment was a relatively rare occurrence in Beethoven's music until the turn of the nineteenth century, when he consistently began to mark a decrease in speed and a return to the original tempo within a passage by using *ritardando—a tempo*. Over time, the use of this new indication probably made *rinforzando* less purposeful in passages that prescribed an extended reduction in speed, such as the one I illustrated in example 3.6.

As *rinforzando* would have been commonly employed to signal a momentary gradual decrease in speed within a phrase, indicating when its effect should come to a close was not necessarily a concern because its context would have been intuitively apprehended from case to case. Still some questions might arise about the placement of the marking in Beethoven's original manuscripts; the printing process in Beethoven's time was rather flawed, and the reproduction of interpretive details within a piece was rarely devoid of errors. The editorial mistakes that abounded in those days must have been quite aggravating to the composer. As the British musicologist and pianist Donald Francis Tovey (1875–1940) pointed out, during Beethoven's lifetime his music in print was the subject of some appalling blunders. *Sforzando* had a particularly regrettable history: Beethoven, who did not possess Haydn's self-effacing humor, must have been incensed upon discovering that several of the *sforzandi* in the treacherously complex counterpoint of "Et vitam venturi" from his *Missa Solemnis*, Op. 123, fresh from the press, were turned into *scherzando* ("playful").[4] *Rinforzando* had a similar destiny: in Variation XV from his Thirty-two Variations in C Minor, WoO 80, the term had mutated into *risoluto*,[5] producing an effect rather distant from what Beethoven had most likely desired.

Tovey also claimed that Czerny was responsible for the inclusion of many of the *rinforzandi* found in Beethoven's scores. After 1805, Beethoven entrusted the fifteen-year-old Czerny—who had been under his tutelage for five years—with the proofreading of his pieces. Terrified by the idea of bothering the irascible master with questions, Czerny allegedly added *rinforzandi* and other markings without the composer's consent. Tovey expressed disapproval of these incorporations, claiming that they were a detriment to the music and that Beethoven would have never authorized them. The sources consulted to gather these conclusions were not specified, and I began to suspect that Tovey's censure derived from his basic misunderstanding of the role of *rinforzando*, which he may have deemed exclusively a dynamic indication. Moreover, it is hard to believe that Beethoven would have not noticed illegitimate additions in the printed version of the works in question. We can safely assume that these *rinforzandi* are authentic, or that Czerny obtained full permission to add them as interpretive elements to the music of his mentor.

— ◆►• —

While I was evaluating *rinforzando* as one of several ways in which Beethoven had indicated rallentando or ritenuto, I returned to the *Katechismus* and wondered whether the notion of "a strong emphasis" to which Knecht alluded was meant to be of the agogic kind. If musicians in the early nineteenth century relied on his description, how did they interpret a marking that he enjoined them to apply exclusively "to a group of several notes," considering that in printed music its placement generally seemed to govern individual pitches or chords? In the case of the Trio in C Minor that we viewed in examples 3.3a and 3.3b, the fact that *rinforzando* seems to belong to specific notes or chords does not exclude the possibility that it may have been "interpreted" for us. In other words, Beethoven may have not marked the *rinforzandi* underneath particular pitches in any of the string or piano parts the way they appear in modern editions, but as belonging to the flow of the passage, so to speak. To verify the composer's intent, we would have to refer to his original manuscripts—a task that is often challenged by the absence of these original sources, or that would be rendered arduous by the degree of approximation that was a prominent characteristic of Beethoven's handwriting.

— ◆►• —

The awareness that *rinforzando* was one of the markings that Beethoven used to indicate a decrease in speed stimulated me to investigate the works of Mozart to verify whether he had employed similar directions. I had previously noticed the *mancando* in the Sonata in C Minor, K. 457, of 1784, but this type of indication was far from being consistent in his vocabulary. Mozart did introduce the term *rallentando,* and the earliest traceable examples emerge in 1785 in pieces such as the Fantasie in C Minor, K. 475 and in the String Quartet in E-flat Major, K. 428, at the onset of the composer's experimental phase with new notational symbols. Before that time, Mozart had trusted that a performer would have presumed from the context whether a decrease in speed was appropriate, but eventually he became more specific in instances in which his intentions might have been unlikely to be deduced. For example, in the Rondo from the String Quartet in E-flat Major, K. 428, the *rallentando* that is indicated before the last return of the main theme would probably not be instinctively executed as such. Or in the Fantasie in C Minor, K. 475, the transitional material that bridges the Più Allegro and the recapitulation, marked *Adagio*—may not support a reduction in speed without the *rallentando* that specifies it as an interpretive element.

Occasionally, Mozart wrote a sequence of progressively larger rhythmic values in the context of a patterned melodic figuration—a particular notation that may suggest a rallentando. The end of the cadenza from the Fantasie in D Minor, K. 397 is an occurrence familiar to many:

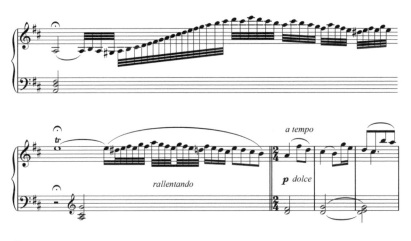

EXAMPLE 3.7. W. A. Mozart: Fantasie in D Minor, K. 397, mm. 86–89.

All the interpretations that I have heard, from the earliest recordings of the piece to renditions by some of the great pianists of our time, feature a rather strict adherence to the rhythmic groups of thirty-second-, sixteenth- and eighth-notes, with a decrease in speed superimposed on this careful subdivision by the *rallentando*. Mozart may have desired a literal reading of values, I thought at first, because the *rallentando* already expresses an agogic coordinate. But similar rhythmic progressions occur, for example, in the cadenza of the Rondo from the Sonata in B-flat Major, K. 333 and in the cadenzas or cadenza-like passages from some of the Concerti for Piano and Orchestra. This led me to an idea that I can only infer: It is generally believed that the Fantasie in D Minor was written in about 1782;

we have seen that the first instances of *rallentando* in Mozart's hand can be traced to 1785; a cursory view of Mozart's works showed that a written-out rallentando in which the rhythmic values become progressively larger disappeared as a practice after 1784 to 1785; the original manuscript of the fantasie has not been located, and its earliest source available is the first edition of 1804, completed by August Eberhard Müller (1767–1817). Is it possible that the *rallentando* near the end of measure 86 of the fantasie is not Mozart's, but was added posthumously by the well-intentioned Müller, and that the passage's progressive rhythmic diminution served the purpose of a rallentando before the marking came into use?

Observing this evolutionary stage in Mozart substantiated an earlier intimation: If a simple cadential passage in his Fantasie in D Minor was indicative of the notational flexibility on which composers relied in the eighteenth century, perhaps my adherence to the inflexible, metronomic playing that often informs the music making of what we modernly define as the classical era needed to be reconsidered. I mentioned earlier that, as romanticism is historically viewed as a response to the emphasis on form, proportion, balance, and restraint that classicism had proposed, musicians today seem keen on the notion that music written in the second part of the eighteenth century should portray that more contained attitude. But I realized this was not quite the case when I began to take to heart what Carl Philipp Emanuel Bach had to say about expression in his *Essay on the True Art of Playing Keyboard Instruments*. The great care he devoted to the description of sentiments and their portrayal in performance through correct inflection, character, and speeds had a lasting influence on the musicians of the second half of the eighteenth and the first half of the nineteenth centuries. Carl Philipp Emanuel lived through a time of great changes in which composers parted with the complexities of polyphony, preferring a style in which melody and accompaniment became predominant, and in which harmony served a greater purpose by outlining the tonal structure of a work. But if this transformation supposedly determined the manner in which affections were conveyed through music, I wondered why the principles exposed in Carl Philipp Emanuel's *Essay* did not similarly mutate through the decades. I understood that the expression of human feelings did not have to diminish by default simply because the focus shifted from intricate contrapuntal exchanges to more linear homophony, and that it is the writing of a piece that informs its intensity of expression and freedom of pulse, rather than the era in which it was written.

I recently came across what I consider an extraordinary recording—an 1891 wax cylinder that features the Fantasie in C Minor, K. 396 by Mozart, performed by Sergei Taneyev (1856–1915). It is believed to be one of the earliest sounds of a piano ever captured. Taneyev's reading is stunning: his grand improvisatory manner, which emphasizes dissonances and harmonic shifts along with the overwhelming absence of a linear organization of bar lines, displays a degree of freedom that no modern piano school would accept. As I exchanged opinions with friends and colleagues about Taneyev's recording, I noticed a basic contradiction in their responses: most of them identified freedom as a compelling aspect of the recording, but viewed it as an exaggerated manifestation of sentiments should it become an integral part of a modern pianist's performance. This reaction held true for other historical recordings with which I was acquainted prior to my encounter with Taneyev's cylinder: Raoul Koczalski's 1938 account of Chopin's Nocturne in E-flat Major, Op. 9, No. 2, which still surprises many; or Józef Hofmann's astounding live performance of Chopin's F Minor Ballade, also from 1938; or some of Chopin's etudes from the late 1920s in Ignaz Friedman's renditions, which sound as if they were dignified salon pieces, such is his degree of textual liberty.

The music of Czech pianist and composer Jan Ladislav Dussek (1760–1812)[6] shows that the marking *rinforzando* had appeared as early as the late 1770s—a time in which composers began to introduce a variety of dynamic and agogic notations in their scores. Dussek is reported to have appeared at the illustrious Salomon concerts in London in 1791 and 1794 alongside Haydn, who expressed great admiration for his performing skills and his equally brilliant musicianship. A mutual esteem probably led the two composers to share their respective ideas on notation. It is possible that Dussek introduced Haydn to the use of *rinforzando* during these exchanges, and that in 1791, upon his return to Vienna from his successful first trip to the English capital, Haydn may have shared its associations with Beethoven. Throughout his works, Dussek showed a frequent employment of the marking, in print often abbreviated as *rf*, as in the Sonata in A-flat Major, C.V. 43, written in 1788:

EXAMPLE 3.8. J. L. Dussek: Sonata in A-flat Major, C.V. 43, I. Allegro, mm. 81–82.

Taking into account the material involved in the measures that follow this *rinforzando*, I could not see how the marking would be musically purposeful as a *ritenuto* or a *rallentando*. A better solution, it seemed, would be its application as a slight agogic emphasis, which would support the vocal inflection of the octave leap (c^2 to c^3). Finally it occurred to me that the *rinforzando* may refer to the tenor voice, which introduces a melodic element to an otherwise unadorned, dry accompaniment of the left hand. This interpretation might further be supported by the presence of a slur above the ascending chromatic line. I was also reminded by the irregular placement of *rinforzando* in the Minuet from Beethoven's Trio in C Minor (example 3.3b) that the original designation of a marking may have been misconstrued in modern printed versions. In the passage from Dussek's Sonata in A-flat Major, the placement of *rinforzando* in the middle of the system lent an ambiguity to its meaning at first, visually encouraging me to apply its effect to both hands. But might Dussek have originally placed the marking closer to the tenor line to indicate the dynamic prominence of a voice in the context of a multilayered texture? "Strengthening" seemed to apply perfectly to such a designation.

In the opening page of the same sonata, two *rinforzandi* notated in close proximity indisputably refer to the tenor voice, which may corroborate my conjecture that the *rf* shown in example 3.8 had a similar goal of outlining an active exchange between the tenor voice and the melody in the right hand:

EXAMPLE 3.9. J. L. Dussek: Sonata in A-flat Major, C.V. 43, I. Allegro, mm. 11–13.

It was the *rinforzando* in measure 15 of the Theme and Variations in E-flat Major on "Partant pour la Syrie" (a French song that achieved great popularity in the early 1800s) that led me to consider the flexibility with which Dussek may have applied the marking. Placed in reference possibly to more than one voice, this instance seemed to have no precise designation in outlining dynamic prominence for any one line:

EXAMPLE 3.10. J. L. Dussek: Theme and Variations on "Partant pour la Syrie", Variation I, mm. 14–16.

The folklike implications of the Variations, I thought, may have justified a predominant dynamic role for the ascending bass line in measure 15, whether or not one might deem its melodic profile particularly appealing or significant. Without dismissing this possibility, I retraced my steps and considered an agogic connotation: could this *rinforzando* propose a slight ritenuto? I began to suspect that Dussek had used *rinforzando* to indicate a range of interpretive aspects, which had to be contextualized to be intelligible.

After learning that Dussek had met Haydn in London, I found the idea that he might have introduced the Austrian composer to *rinforzando* believable, because Haydn began to employ the marking directly after their first contacts in 1791. Example 3.2 showed how, only months before the first of the Salomon concerts, Haydn featured the term *forzando* as a way of implying a ritenuto, applying the agogic validity of *fz* by stretching the symbol over several notes. After 1791 he continued to use *fz* as well, as I illustrated in chapter 2 while investigating the *sforzandi* found in the Sonatas in C Major, Hob. XVI:50 and E-flat Major, Hob. XVI:52, both written between 1794 and 1795. Haydn never included the term *rinforzando* in his keyboard works to intend the prevalence of a specific voice, probably because he had begun to indicate such instances with hairpins (in this respect, the first two movements from the Sonata in E-flat Major, Hob. XVI:52 offer quite a few occurrences). After his first trip to London, he employed the marking in his more mature string quartets, where the multivoiced texture is more open to this kind of notation. For example, in the fourth movement of his String Quartet in D Major, Op. 71, No. 2, written in 1793, the last return of the A section is emphasized by a *rinforzando* on the two-note anacrusis of the first violin, in measure 46:

EXAMPLE 3.11a. F. J. Haydn: String Quartet in D Major, Op. 71, No. 2, IV. Allegretto, mm. 41–49.

Initially I had the impression that this *rinforzando* intended an agogic emphasis to introduce the return of the principal theme—an approach that seemed to make sense because it followed the customary practice of broadening the pulse in the process of introducing a new section, beginning in measure 47. The inappropriate role of a sudden crescendo on the anacrusis in measure 46 after such a long decrease in dynamic intensity prompted this solution as reflexive response. Still, I felt perplexed by the reservation of *rinforzando* to the first violin, while the three other parts were marked *piano*:

EXAMPLE 3.11b. F. J. Haydn: String Quartet in D Major, Op. 71, No. 2, IV. Allegretto, mm. 41–49.

Might this *rinforzando* indicate that the first violin should play not with a crescendo, but louder, in the moment, than the other three instruments because—to put it simply—it has the theme? In the much-used library score that I consulted to reproduce examples 3.11a and 3.11b, this *rinforzando* was crossed out—the irrational placement of what was thought to be the equivalent of a crescendo having created a source of puzzlement or frustration. In some revised editions from the second half of the nineteenth and the early part of the twentieth century, the marking vanished or was replaced by others, such as *mezza voce*. After considering its role in this passage and how revised editions as well as performers decided to ignore its dynamic validity, an important element surfaced in my analysis: in addition to its common reference to "force," *rinforzando* might have developed a misleading connotation that generally refers to an *increase* in volume because the term is expressed in its gerundive form—"reinforcing."

In the second half of the eighteenth and in the first half of the nineteenth century, as I mentioned in chapter 1, newer keyboard instruments offered greater span and dynamic range. It now had become evident to me how significant this evolution was for notation, which could be all the more purposeful. Indeed, notational symbols to indicate voicing could have developed only with the abandonment of the constraints that had been dictated by the harpsichord's homogeneous lack of dynamic variation. The indication of voicing emerged at a time when notation was still at a germinal stage: although the latest instruments made it possible for performers to implement the vision of composers with greater accuracy, it is still feasible that a symbol could have been used with various intentions. We saw, for example, that *rinforzando* for Beethoven may have meant agogic flexibility, and that Dussek and Haydn used it to signal the dynamic relevance of a line within a multivoiced texture. Yet for composers, the new practicality of indicating the prevalence of a particular line over a thicker texture must have been a truly remarkable addition to the already florid notation that addressed agogic and dynamic aspects of interpretation.

In chapter 1 as well, I hypothesized the response of a nineteenth-century musician to the introduction of new notation in printed music. Although composers used symbols with a purpose in mind, a performer might not have known how to contextualize them in the score. Understanding what role should have been attributed to a symbol was generally left to the performer to discern. In most instances, the interpretation of certain symbols must have relied on guesswork. Unless a direct affiliation allowed a performer to familiarize himself with the composer's intentions, it is probable that a small percentage of those who purchased a recently published composition would have known the original intention of a new symbol (the inclusion of footnotes or performing instructions as part of a preface or score was an innovation of modern scholarship). We can surmise that only a portion of the musicians who purchased the music of Dussek or Beethoven would have been acquainted with the scope of *rinforzando*—even more likely if we consider that the marking could have had several attributions and applications, and that these meanings varied greatly from one composer to another.

Rinforzando appeared in the music of some of the composers who operated in Austria, Germany and, peripherally, in England and Eastern Europe at the turn of the nineteenth century. This may indicate the degree of authority that figures of the caliber of Dussek and Haydn exerted on the musical life of their time. Uses similar to ones employed by Haydn and Beethoven are featured in the works of musicians who were directly or indirectly affiliated with the two composers. Johann Baptist Cramer (1771–1858),[7] for example, had ties to Vienna through his friendship with Beethoven, and his active life as a performer, composer, and publisher in London made him acquainted with both Haydn and Dussek. To exemplify the manner in which he employed *rinforzando,* I chose the concluding measures of his Etude in E Minor, published in 1804:

EXAMPLE **3.12.** J. B. Cramer: Etude in E Minor, mm. 25–34.

🔽 EXAMPLE 3.12 (*continued*)

The symbol *rfz* in measure 29 is conventionally viewed as a dynamic emphasis, but it could apply as a progressive rallentando to the end of the piece. In print, the marking may have been attributed by default to the downbeat of this measure, either as an approximation of its original placement or as an arbitrary interpretation of its role. Although *rfz* is found in the original first edition, some later revisions, like the one made in the 1880s by Hans von Bülow, changed it into *sf*.

During the time in which Cramer published his etudes and Knecht's *Katechismus* was enjoying success in Germany, *rinforzando* nearly disappeared in Beethoven scores. This phenomenon may have been determined by his increasing use of *ritardando* (or *rallentando*)—*a tempo*, the first occurrence of which (marked as *rallentando*—*Tempo I*) is found in the closing page of the Sonata in C Major, Op. 2, No. 3. Beethoven successfully experimented with an agogic indication that specified the resuming of the original speed after a momentary suspension of the original tempo. It took the composer several years to adopt this expedient consistently: it is in his Sonata in E-flat Major, Op. 31, No. 3, written in about 1802, that we find the first examples of what would become a habitual practice.

After this substantial development in the codification of agogic flexibility, the rare appearances of *rinforzando* in Beethoven occur almost exclusively in melodic contexts and indicate that the purpose of the marking during the first decade of the nineteenth century seems to have shifted away from a purely agogic connotation. I recently observed the role of the two *rinforzandi* in the opening measures of the Adagio molto from the Sonata in C Major, Op. 53 (1804), which may have a rather different meaning than the dynamic swells commonly heard in performance:

EXAMPLE 3.13. L. van Beethoven: Sonata in C Major, Op. 53, II. Adagio molto, mm. 7–14.

This passage evokes the exchanges between a solo instrument and the orchestra in the slow movement of a concerto. Let us imagine it as an excerpt from an adagio for bassoon and orchestra: The string section plays a few introductory measures, then the soloist enters with two melodic fragments (measures 10 and 12 and their respective anacruses), which alternate with brief interpolating replies by the winds (measures 11 and 13). The *rinforzandi* seem to signal the dynamic relevance of the soloist's lines, as distinguished from the accompanying material. In other words, they indicate not progressive increases in volume, as is commonly believed, but a prominence, by means of a somewhat louder volume, that sets apart the solo portions from their surrounding context. Further, as the responses of the envisioned wind instruments are absent after measure 14, the *rinforzandi* that signaled the presence of the soloist amid the thicker texture are no longer needed, justifying their inclusion exclusively in measures 10 and 12.

I found an interesting correlation between the function of these *rinforzandi* and the occasional appearances of the marking *poco forte* in the works of Johann Sebastian Bach. The context is that of a solo instrument whose prescribed dynamic is *poco forte*, and is supported by an orchestral accompaniment whose dynamic level is *piano*. Examples can be recognized in the oboe part of the duet "Gott du hast es wohl gefüget" from the Weimar Christmas Cantata, BWV 63, and in the first movement of the Concerto for Three Harpsichords and Orchestra in C Major, BWV 1064. Much like *rinforzando*, *poco forte* is conventionally interpreted as expressing loudness without necessarily a regard for context—an approach that is elicited by the inclusion of the term *forte*. This oversight may be especially unfavorable in the music of Brahms, whose *poco forte*, I believe, often seems to suggest a warm, projecting sound in the context of *piano*. It is the case in the opening measures of the Trio for Violin, Cello, and Piano in C Major, Op. 87, where an imposing enunciation of the main theme would not only compromise the scope of the entire first phrase and the tenderness expressed by the thematic material, but would also hinder the function of the heroic *forte* as the outcome of the crescendo that begins in measure 16:

EXAMPLE 3.14. J. Brahms: Trio for Violin, Cello and Piano in C Major, Op. 87, I. Allegro, mm. 1–16.

The excerpt from Beethoven's Sonata in C Major, Op. 53 that we analyzed in example 3.13 reflects changing views toward notation. In its new role in signaling the dynamic prominence of an event, *rinforzando* may have been supplanted by more convenient alternatives to indicate agogic fluctuations, such as *ritardando—a tempo*. Yet in the first part of the nineteenth century Beethoven may have still used the earlier marking to signal a slight decrease in speed. One case that may be interpreted in this way because of its unlikely implications as a device to signal voicing is found in the final movement of the Sonata in F Minor, Op. 57 (1804–05):

🔊 EXAMPLE 3.15. L. van Beethoven: Sonata in F Minor, Op. 57, III. Allegro ma non troppo, mm. 224–229.

Is this occurrence proposing a slight ritenuto to introduce the first return of the A section? Did Beethoven resort to using *rinforzando* because *ritardando—a tempo* would have been an excessive agogic imposition in such a restrained space? A slight decrease in speed to round off the phrase and announce the return of the main thematic material seemed to be a reasonable musical solution, and I noticed that a number of performers apply this coordinate instinctively. Still, in these interpretations the *rinforzando* is superimposed as a dynamic increase on the agogic solution, and is often placed prematurely. A likely explanation is that the limited space before the closing hairpin in measure 227 is conventionally understood as a decrease in volume, in reaction to the crescendo that the *rinforzando* is believed to represent. Yet the hairpin could clarify metric order—the tied octave in the right hand possibly being responsible for a misleading displacement of the strong beats. The challenge posed by this *rinforzando* does not end with my hypothesis: the marking appeared in the manuscript, then was replaced by a *rallentando* in the first printed edition of the sonata—perhaps a misreading on the part of the engraver[8] and, coincidentally, what Beethoven may have intended in meaning all along.

In Beethoven's late works, *rinforzando* appears sporadically and seems to return to its agogic designation. *Ritardando—a tempo* had emerged as a well-established and much more practical manner of notating what *rinforzando* by itself was unable to specify: the length of its application. In a few cases, if the conclusion of a section or movement was supposed to slow down progressively, Beethoven seemed inclined to use *ritardando*, stretching it over that episode. The coda of the first movement of the Sonata in A Major, Op. 101 (1816) provides an example similar to the one I mentioned in regard to the Trio in E-flat Major, Op. 1, No. 1, which the composer had published nearly a quarter of a century earlier. As we observed in example 3.15, *rinforzando* as an agogic concession was perhaps reserved to particular instances in which a *ritardando* would represent an excessive agogic imposition, especially where it did not coincide with the end of an episode.

The decline in the use of *rinforzando* in Beethoven's last decade is well exemplified by the three last piano sonatas, Opp. 109–111 (1820–22), written more or less concurrently, where the marking appears only twice, the first time in measure 42 of the second movement from the Sonata in E Major, Op. 109:

EXAMPLE 3.16. L. van Beethoven: Sonata in E Major, Op. 109, II. Prestissimo, mm. 37–44

This *rinforzando* is found in the manuscript but did not appear in the first edition of the sonata—possibly an inadvertent omission, but reinstated, or at least suggested, in authoritative modern revisions. As an increase in dynamic intensity, it would simply determine a redundancy with the *sempre più cresc.* three measures earlier. Rather, it seems to me, this *rinforzando* would make sense as a slight agogic concession, given the sudden modulation that occurs with the *piano* in measure 43.

The second instance appears in the first movement of the Sonata in C Minor, Op. 111:

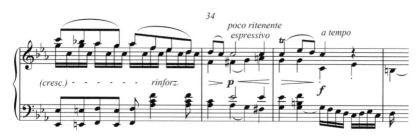

EXAMPLE 3.17. L. van Beethoven: Sonata in C Minor, Op. 111, I. Maestoso, Allegro con brio ed appassionato, mm. 33–36.

Given the *crescendo* that precedes it, I immediately excluded a dynamic connotation for this *rinforzando*. But the *poco ritenente—a tempo* marked in measures 34 and 35 made me doubt its agogic implications as well. Perhaps it was addressing the dynamic prevalence of a specific voice: for instance, the alto line that begins with the top note of the left-hand chords (F) in measure 33 could be voiced with the purpose of interacting with the soprano. This solution seemed plausible until a recent exchange with a friend concerning the role of *ritenuto* and *rallentando* in the music of Chopin inadvertently clarified the role of *ritenente* in Beethoven's Sonata Op. 111: its purpose is not to indicate a gradual decrease in speed, as is normally intended, but a sudden change to a slower tempo,[9] protracted until a new marking interrupts its application. The *rinforzando* in the example could indicate a slight ritenuto to introduce this transitional slower section; the hairpin on the downbeat of measure 34 seems to clarify the metric organization of strong and weak beats, which could be misconstrued because of the emphasis on the second beat of the same measure; and the opening and closing hairpins spread between measures 34 and 35 could refer to agogic fluctuation within this slower cadential episode. Another consideration stems from an analysis that may support my theory concerning agogic rather than dynamic intention: were *rinforzando* and hairpins considered all from a dynamic standpoint in this passage, the three measures shown in example 3.16 would feature no less than seven different markings that indicate dynamic variations—a notational specification that would be truly exceptional in any piece written by any composer during that period.

We saw at the beginning of this chapter that the wording Justin Heinrich Knecht used to describe *rinforzando* in his *Katechismus* might not express a particular designation and is thus bound to interpretation; but coeval methods did not fail to assign to the marking an explicit dynamic role. The *Klavier- und Fortepiano Schule* by August Eberhard Müller, compiled in 1804,[10] supported this connotation with a surprising, original viewpoint:

> *Rinforzando* and *sforzato* are different less in the degree than in the kind of strength with which the note is delivered: the former signifies a gradual strengthening of one and the same note, the latter a sudden accentuation of it. Most composers, however, do not make a sufficiently precise distinction in their writing.[11]

The "gradual strengthening of one and the same note" that Müller described is controversial: increasing the intensity on a note is easily achieved by the human voice or in string and wind playing, but the same effect cannot be rendered by the naturally decaying sound of the piano. Müller's literal translation of the term would be justified if applied to any instrument other than the piano—a paradoxical situation, considering that his description appeared in a Klavier-Schule. This account of *rinforzando* was formulated in a period in which certain symbols seem to have been progressively divested of their early connotations in favor of a more individualistic use. Over the years, composers seem to have reassessed the various functions of *rinforzando* and resolved to employ exclusively one of its original meanings or introduce completely new designations. In the keyboard literature, its reference to voicing probably superseded other roles, but for Beethoven, as we have seen, the marking may have continued to signal a slight decrease in speed even during his more mature years. Its modern accepted meaning may be the consequence of the literal translation "reinforcing," which upstaged its former agogic and dynamic attributes. As the marking was used preeminently by composers who lived in German-speaking countries and whose principal language was not Italian, it is realistic to consider that they may have developed a range of ideas concerning its meaning. If we acknowledge the literal application of the gerundive form of the verb *rinforzare*, a dynamic function of the marking might have more plausibly supported the idea of a *gradual* increase in volume.

The generation of composers born around the turn of the nineteenth century did not seem particularly interested in using *rinforzando*, perhaps because its implications were by then well represented by signs that offered greater precision. Schubert never used it, nor did Chopin. Schumann used it very sparingly. As we saw in chapter 1, Schubert also used the term *diminuendo* to indicate a gradual decrease in speed, and an opening hairpin frequently indicated a slight ritenuto to place the arrival of a new section. Some composers used *rallentando* and *ritardando* interchangeably, either by themselves or with accompanying dashes to specify the span of their duration. For Chopin and most of his contemporaries, *ritenuto* seems to have replaced quite appropriately the agogic function of *rinforzando* in affecting either the transition between two phrases or the end of a piece. *Rallentando* instead exerted a more substantial change of pulse; generally, rather than indicating a brief slackening of tempo, it shaped the conclusion of a major episode. After these considerations, I perceived that there could have been a parallel between *ritenente* and *sostenuto:* for Beethoven, *ritenente* might have intended a temporarily slower speed, whose effect was interrupted by the appearance of the marking *a tempo;* for Chopin and other nineteenth-century composers, *sostenuto* seems to have achieved the same effect.

Unlike most composers of his generation, Franz Liszt displayed a consistent use of *rinforzandi*, which appear in many fashions—alone or followed by dashes, and in either case having reference to long or short episodes. Its application often refers to cadential elements, and many instances show that he used it to emphasize agogically the function of crucial sections within a piece. Two important moments in his most extended piano work, the Sonata in B Minor, aptly support our analysis. The first one concerns the arrival of the first theme in measure 32:

🔊 EXAMPLE 3.18. F. Liszt: Sonata in B Minor, mm. 27–34.

I clearly remember my inability, in my late teenage years, to come to terms with the dual presence of an opening hairpin and a *rinforzando,* both indicating a dynamic increase, I was instructed, from the *fortissimo* of a few measures earlier . . . to the *forte* in measure 32. I resolved to disregard the meaning of both markings and executed a crescendo, trusting that my musical instinct perhaps would have provided a convincing reading. Years later, as I returned to the sonata, I realized that the opening hairpin may signal the melodic importance of the inner line played by the right thumb (E-sharp–E), whereas the *rinforzando* in measure 30 may indicate a ritenuto that underlines the perfect cadence to the key of B minor (measures 31–32), stated at last after an introductory section that features extreme harmonic instability.

The second occasion chosen is the *rinforzando assai* that appears in measure 392, at the onset of what some would consider the golden section of the composition. Here, the marking prepares the arrival of the *fff* with an ideal *molto sostenuto*:

🔊 **EXAMPLE 3.19.** F. Liszt: Sonata in B Minor, mm. 389–396.

These two episodes render unnecessary to specify a return to the original speed, because the circumstances are dictated by the harmonic and melodic content, and are quite self-explanatory.

Examples 3.18 and 3.19 illustrate significant structural moments in the context of a large-scale work, but Liszt frequently used *rinforzandi* in less conspicuous passages, which in many cases engage small groups of beats or indicate the lingering of individual pitches. These localized applications appear consistently in pieces whose idioms derive from folk traditions. In them, a greater oscillation of pulse within phrases is recognized and accepted because a degree of improvisational nuance is required to convey their character. It is perhaps in the Hungarian Rhapsodies that we find the most convincing models. The rustic *Presto giocoso assai* section in the Rhapsody No. 8 in F-sharp Minor (1852), for example, features a sequence of *rinforzandi* that briefly affect the timing of each successive four-measure group:

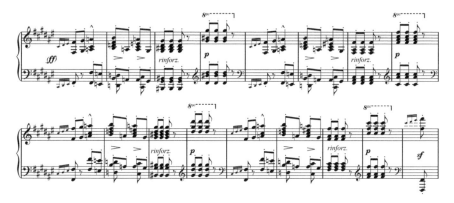

EXAMPLE 3.20. F. Liszt: Hungarian Rhapsody No. 8 in F-sharp Minor, mm. 156–172.

In a more isolated instance, *rinforzando* seems to express inflective freedom for the beginning of the descending arpeggiated figuration in the opening measure of *Prelude*, the first of Liszt's Transcendental Etudes:

EXAMPLE 3.21. F. Liszt: Transcendental Etude No. 1 in C Major, *Prelude*, mm. 1–2.

The fermata in the left hand may validate free reign for the cascade of notes in the right hand. The hairpin that follows the *rinforzando* may indicate a return to the regular speed as the fourth beat of the first measure approaches.

Rinforzando is frequently mistaken for an intensification of a crescendo because the two markings are often found in close proximity. The return of the second thematic block in the Transcendental Etude No. 8, *Wilde Jagd*, shows such an instance:

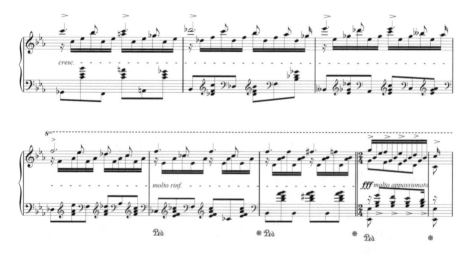

EXAMPLE 3.22. F. Liszt: Transcendental Etude No. 8 in C Minor, *Wilde Jagd*, mm. 110–117.

The dashes that follow the *crescendo* extend to the end of the episode, visually suggesting that the *molto rinforzando* is an extension of the dynamic coordinate; yet this second marking, placed in measure 114, may determine a *molto ritenuto* that precedes the new exhilarating appearance of the second theme, adapted in 2/4, in measure 116.

In the late 1830s, Liszt formulated a highly unusual system of agogic markings while re-elaborating parts of his *Années de pèlerinage* and composing the first ambitious version of the Transcendental Etudes. By using his own symbols, he found that he was able to indicate the flexibility of rubato with greater precision, be the context small or large:

═══════ indicated a slight suspension, shorter than a fermata, on a note or rest

▭▭▭ indicated an accelerando

────── indicated a rallentando

These notational devices might find an antecedent in the *Clavierschule* by Daniel Gottlob Türk (1789), in which combinations of lines were used to specify aspects of agogic flexibility (see chapter 1, page 12). Liszt's symbols did not set a precedent for other composers, or for himself; he abandoned them within a few years, having resolved to employ a simpler, more standard notation. In this transitional phase, his works show that he drastically reduced his use of *rinforzando,* possibly proving that the marking indeed affected the music agogically.

<hr />

We know that Brahms never expressed great admiration for the music of Liszt. Rather, he turned to Beethoven as a model of perfection, following the ideals expressed by the German music critic and writer Eduard Hanslick (1825–1904). Hanslick strenuously opposed composers such as Berlioz, Liszt, and Wagner, whose programmatic depictions deviated from the purely classical forms developed by Beethoven and Mozart. The epic magnitude of Beethoven's "Hammerklavier" fascinated the young composer to such an extent that he deliberately used its incipit in the first movement of his Piano Sonata in C Major—the first piece that he chose to publish, soon after he turned twenty in 1853. Markings found frequently in the music of Beethoven entered Brahms's vocabulary at an early stage, but the use of *rinforzando* was more economical and did not affect extended passages in the way we saw in Beethoven's early works. Instead, its validity seems confined to individual pitches or groups of notes. In the Sonata in F Minor, Op. 5, for example, Brahms employed *rinforzandi* in very rare circumstances— exclusively in melodic contexts offered by the nocturnelike second movement, and in the grand waltz portrayed by the Scherzo. The flexible lyrical material in which they are used might suggest an agogic designation, but a contextual analysis reveals that some of them may refer to voicing. In a passage from the opening page of the Andante, *rinforzando* seems to outline the bass line in contrary motion to the soprano, an aspect that is also emphasized by the kinesthetic element proposed by the *staccato* markings under the slur in the lower register in measure 17. The *rinforzando* is perhaps used here to signal voicing in a less emphatic way than the right-hand accents in measures 17–18, which carry the melody:

EXAMPLE 3.23. J. Brahms: Sonata in F Minor, Op. 5, II. Andante cantabile, mm. 14–20.

Instances found in the Scherzo (measures 173, 175, and 177) may signal that the upper line should prevail against the more active contour of the bass:

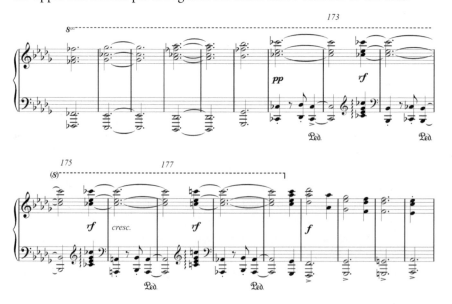

EXAMPLE 3.24. J. Brahms: Sonata in F Minor, Op. 5, III. Scherzo, Allegro energico, mm. 166–183.

Another case in the Andante, this time involving the closing measures, might appear to indicate an increase in volume, were it to be considered as bridging between the *pianissimo* and the *forte*:

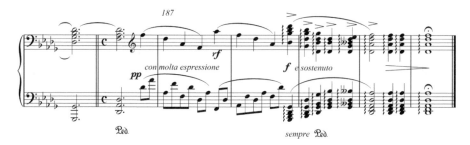

EXAMPLE 3.25. J. Brahms: Sonata in F Minor, Op. 5, II. Andante cantabile, mm. 185–191.

Yet Brahms seems to have been more likely to specify such increases with the marking *crescendo.* I returned to the possibility that this *rinforzando,* on the last beat of measure 187, may indicate a progressive decrease in speed to the sostenuto of the final measures: I could not exclude the possibility that the placement of the *rinforzando* in print may have been erroneously assigned by the engraver or the editor and that, as a result, it affected an individual beat rather than the entire passage.

A few cases singled out in the context of the Sonata in F Minor, whose length approximates to thirty-five minutes, seem to offer very little material for an evaluation of Brahms's entire canon; yet they may be essential for understanding how the composer used *rinforzando* and how it relates to other markings. I mentioned in chapter 2 that a homogenization of symbols was introduced in the 1870s and 1880s in the newly printed scores of most nineteenth-century composers who had used *fz*, such as Chopin and Schubert, and that in some revisions or reprints of older editions *fz* became *sf.* In regard to Brahms, some confusion may stem especially from his use, in his early years, of both *sf* and *fz*, perhaps with the intention of emphasizing the agogic implication of the latter. I would like to suggest some conclusions concerning certain symbols in the early works of Brahms, which in modern practice fall into the same broad category of dynamic emphases:

1. *sf* is used to indicate a dynamic emphasis

2. *fz* determines brief localized agogic lingering or fluctuation

3. *rf,* in its sporadic appearances, is meant to outline voicing or signal a decrease in speed

Over the years, Brahms also began to provide more explicit indications of agogic intent by using markings such as *sostenuto* and *tenuto,* the latter generally on a single pitch. These specifications conveniently usurped the role of *fz,* thereby justifying a substantial decrease in the use of *rinforzando.* In any case the marking had grown more infrequent in his middle period, possibly because the composer initiated a process of notational simplification. This refinement of means could be considered an inevitable course of events: we witness it in all the great composers, from Beethoven to Brahms, from Chopin to Liszt. In the case of Brahms, much of the detailed notation that characterized his early works gradually disappeared, leaving room for a more distilled writing.

Despite his more economical employment of notational tools in his mature years, Brahms returned to *rinforzando,* and he probably was the last composer to use it as the nineteenth century came to a close. At this stage, its presence seems to refer exclusively to voicing, and signal rather specific occurrences, such as the dynamic predominance of an event in the context of a multi-textured writing. An instance in the return of the second thematic group in the Intermezzo in B-flat Minor, Op. 117, No. 2 (1892) evokes a similar use in the Adagio from Beethoven's Sonata in C Major, Op. 53, which we saw in example 3.13:

EXAMPLE 3.26. J. Brahms: Intermezzo in B-flat Minor, Op. 117, No. 2, mm. 72–77.

The *rinforzando* in measure 74 indicates the continuation of a strong dynamic intensity for the chordal writing, intending a steady voicing for the theme that starts in measure 72. The arpeggiated figurations that interpolate with the more substantial body of the theme are purely ornamental, and rely on extended sustained pedals. Their role is specified by the presence of *dolce* and *p.*

In the celebrated Intermezzo in A Major, Op. 118, No. 2, the role of *rinforzando* seems not to have as clear a designation:

EXAMPLE 3.27. J. Brahms: Intermezzo in A Major, Op. 118, No. 2, mm. 77–82.

In this last reiteration of the opening theme, the marking might suggest a prominence for the alto voice against the soprano, emphasizing the melodic modification of the main thematic material (the only occurrence in which it is presented as a descending gesture). An agogic connotation as a slight lingering on that beat might suit this passage as well. Yet, when encouraged to take time on that chord rather than stress it dynamically, a student in a master class that I taught several years ago unexpectedly played it softer, creating a change of color that was rather appealing. It was this unforeseen reading that made me realize one important issue in regard to the way we read musical notation: today's understanding of *rinforzando* may be affected by its shortened specification—in all editions, the letter *f* as part of *rf* presents a bolder character than the *r* that precedes it, generating the assumption that a loud dynamic is implied. This notion may be true of any marking including *f*, such as *fz* and *sf*.

Why has the reading of music changed so radically? Was it an inevitable evolution that affected our perception of Art, or did we unconsciously suffer a *devolution* of the musical language? Perhaps the modern reading of musical notation hinders our comprehension of the freedom that we find appealing in the recordings of the Golden Age of piano playing—a freedom that may have been conventional for Haydn, Beethoven, or Liszt. We recognize its immense worth, yet we are reticent to regard it as a fundamental interpretive point of reference. Is it not we who are inevitably drifting further from the aesthetics of the composers of the eighteenth and nineteenth centuries?

FOUR

...OF PEDALS

I would like to paint the way birds sing.

— CLAUDE MONET

The rare, elusive accounts that illustrate the use of pedals in Chopin's time may leave the inquisitive modern pianist with a sense of dissatisfaction. Their content often praises the artful effects of pedaling or denigrates its excesses and abuses, but it does not allow for a full understanding of how the foot pedals were actually used. One of them, however, intrigued me in its perplexing proclamations— an anecdotal account in Anton Schindler's *Biographie von Ludwig van Beethoven*, written in 1842. Albert Sowiński's translation of Schindler's narrative, published more than two decades later, is quoted in Jean-Jacques Eigeldinger's extraordinary volume *Chopin: Pianist and Teacher as Seen by His Pupils*:

> So Czerny abused this [damper] pedal from the beginning, employing it too often in *fortes*, while it is more advantageous in *piano* passages, particularly when it is tempered by the soft pedal, which, quietening the sound, allows one to prolong it by raising the dampers at the beginning of each bar. This was Chopin's own procedure in his poetic compositions [Mazurkas].[1]

Were I able to travel in time, I wondered, would I find the pedaling of performers from that era inadequate? Although Sowiński's version is an interpretation rather than an accurate rendition of the original, was it possible that the concept of pedaling in the early 1840s was so unremarkable, and that Chopin employed the pedal so ordinarily? If applied literally, in some cases the approach described by Schindler would cause discordant pitches and harmonies to blur together. For decades, piano teachers have instructed their pupils to avoid this lack of transparency, and not only in Chopin's music. Yet, as I investigated this matter, particularly in the more predictable patterned pedal markings found in Chopin's waltzes and mazurkas, I came to the realization that Schindler's observation was not off the mark, and that what he identified as a typical trait of Chopin's pedaling indeed resides as a specific body of instruction within the composer's manuscripts.

In Chopin's time the use of the right pedal (which today we refer to as the "damper" or "sustain" pedal) was spare, and was still firmly rooted in older formulas and archetypes. The general consensus determined that its use be very discreet, limited to supporting—not replacing—legato playing, and occasionally enhancing the coloristic properties of certain passages. This approach remained unvaried for many decades and was espoused by most pedagogues and performers of the time. In the 1830s, a few pianists began to introduce more generous pedaling—a phenomenon that was frequently met with disfavor by the older generation. The German pianist and pedagogue Friedrich Wieck (1785–1873) lashed out at what he considered a deplorable vogue:

> I just returned exhausted and annihilated from a concert, where I have been hearing the piano pounded. [. . .] Time brings into use a great deal that is far from beautiful: does, then, this raging piano revolutionist think it beautiful to bring the pedal into use at every bar? Unhappy delusion.[2]

Nearly eighty years later, Camille Saint-Saëns (1835–1921) lamented that the latest generation of pianists was using an indiscriminate amount of pedal[3]—a practice that, it seems, would have appalled most musicians of the previous century. Yet there seems to be a contradiction between these accounts and Chopin's notation: from the mid-1830s, his manuscripts show that he had begun to introduce the use of the sustain pedal with such profusion that the passages within a piece that benefited from it significantly outnumbered the ones that did not. Chopin's pianism unquestionably prescribed greater amounts of pedal than that of earlier and contemporaneous composers, and the effect produced by certain indications was recognized as unusual—to such a degree that, even decades later, a performer of the caliber of Anton Rubinstein (1829–1894) openly rejected their eccentricity. Not yet twenty years old when Chopin died, Rubinstein may have recognized the composer's effort as an extraordinary enterprise, but may have also perceived that some of his atypical indications were experimental, and that more advanced instruments no longer allowed their intentions to be revealed.

Soon after settling in Paris, Chopin manifested a predilection for Pleyel pianos. With their transparent tone and clear bass register, they offered a richer production of overtones than the instruments of other makers. Their sensitive action appealed to the young composer because it evoked the responsiveness of the Viennese instruments, which he had admired in earlier years. Technology witnessed a remarkable evolution in Chopin's era, and pianos varied significantly in quality and character—even those that were built by the same manufacturer. While experiencing the unique characteristics of historical instruments from the 1820s through the 1840s, I realized how my understanding of original pedal markings was limited by what I heard on modern pianos: not only was a composer influenced by the resonance afforded by the instruments of his time, which determined lengths that might seem undesirable today; I also realized that composers may have not always had the most recently built pianos at their disposal. I was fascinated by the notion that the sound heard by Schubert in his three last sonatas could have plausibly been the same one that inspired Chopin while writing his piano concerti. An even more extreme conjecture arose: Chopin's Scherzo in B Minor, Op. 20, whose impetuous outer sections must have perplexed many at the time of its publication, may have been composed on an instrument that was built at the time in which Beethoven wrote his three last sonatas.

Accuracy seems not to have been one of Chopin's greatest concerns when it came to notating pedal. His manuscripts attest to it: the markings they display vary greatly, depending on their purpose, the available space, the size of his handwriting and the figurations he employed. Chopin used the term *ped* when the pedal was to be depressed; to indicate its release, he wrote a symbol that resembles a cross superimposed on a circle ($\oplus$).[4] To notate subsequent pedal applications, he closely followed the release sign with another *ped*:

EXAMPLE 4.1. F. Chopin: Prelude in D-flat Major, Op. 28, No. 15, mm.24–25 (Catelin Stichvorlage, 1839).

The frequent irregularity displayed by Chopin's release signs has been the object of speculation for decades. For instance, in an article published by the *Journal of Musicological Research*, Sandra Rosenblum suggests that the reason Chopin often left substantial visual separations between release symbols and the next *ped* is that on pianos built between the 1830s and 1840s, the release of the sustain pedal could not immediately eliminate the veiled resonance caused by its application[5]—a reverberation that, in a more limited fashion, was present even without the use of the pedal. Inasmuch as the pianos of that time did produce a slight blurriness after the release of the sustain pedal, as I gathered while experimenting with an 1840 Pleyel, the reverberation would not have overlapped significantly with the next pedal change. More important, I was reminded about the considerable differences among instruments during that period and began to infer that, were Rosenblum correct in her assumption, the specification of each release would have had to vary depending on how each individual piano reacted.

It is Carl Czerny's *Pianoforte School*, Op. 500, published in 1839, that refutes the supposition that the instruments of the time might have required brief interruptions between pedal applications to avoid the overlap of vibrations:

> The release and depression of the pedal shall be realized with extreme rapidity, so as not to leave any void or interstice between the chords; and must take place exactly with the first note of each chord [. . .] as if the pedal were held down without interruption.[6]

Czerny described what we identify today as *syncopated pedal*—a practice that still very much resides at the core of the modern technique of pedaling. This procedure was adopted by all the leading piano schools of the time. As I looked at cases of syncopated pedaling in Chopin's manuscripts, nonetheless, a question remained: why was it so important to mark releases along with a sequence of pedal changes? Would it not have been simpler to notate only when the pedal had to be depressed? Yet Chopin meticulously marked almost every single release—and when he did not, it may have been an oversight that caused the omission, or an instance in which specifying a release could be superfluous, as at the close of a piece.

An important element in understanding the role of these releases has emerged from my analysis of Chopin's manuscripts. I began to notice that the symbols *ped* and ⊕ seem to have been marked only after all the notes of a system found their place on paper. Reasonably conclusive proof that Chopin notated the symbols as a group, rather than intermittently, is his having written them in a straight line, with the exception of instances in which other writing in the lower staff impelled them into a different position. A passage from the first movement of the Sonata in B Minor, Op. 58 shows both these circumstances (see example 4.2a).

Next, a calligraphic analysis of Chopin's continuous employment of the sustaining pedal led me to a surprising insight: when observing the space that Chopin left between a release symbol and the ensuing pedal application, I noticed that this interval was preserved throughout a line. Regardless of the duration of each pedal indication, in other words, Chopin notated the pedal depressions where they should be observed for an entire system at a time, whereas the placement of the release signs was less consequential, as their positioning was intended only to afford enough space to clearly articulate the two different markings. What emerged as a decisive finding from my analysis is that Chopin's primary concern was to offer visual clarity for the marking *ped*, and that the addition of ⊕ merely followed a conventional notational method of the time.

Two excerpts from the Stichvorlage of the first movement from the Sonata in B Minor, Op. 58 illustrate my thesis in regard to Chopin's placement of pedal markings and releases. Midway through measure 161, the symbol ⊕ is positioned beneath the last eighth-note of the left-hand accompaniment to

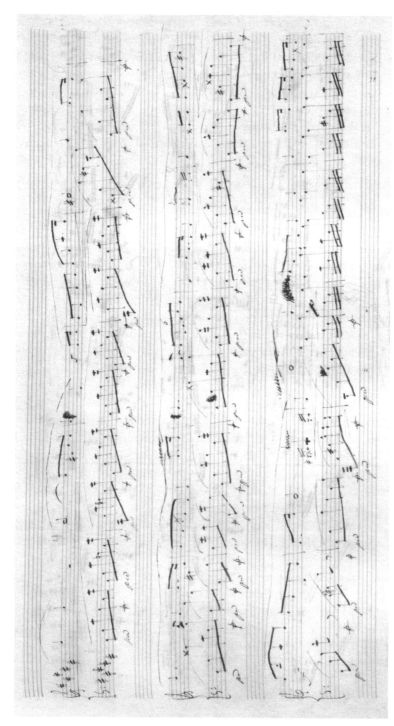

EXAMPLE 4.2a. F. Chopin: Sonata in B Minor, Op. 58, I. Allegro maestoso, mm. 154–168 (Breitkopf & Härtel Stichvorlage, 1844).

permit a reasonable amount of space for the placement of the ensuing *ped*; at the end of the same measure the release symbol is marked after the last eighth-note, because the position of the subsequent depression allows ample space before the bar line:

EXAMPLE 4.2b. F. Chopin: Sonata in B Minor, Op. 58, I. Allegro maestoso, m. 161 (Breitkopf & Härtel Stichvorlage, 1844).

The release near the middle of measure 159 occurs before a left-hand group comes entirely to a close, and the reason is by now evident:

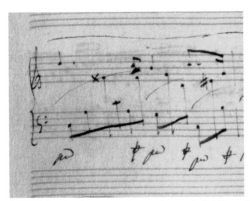

EXAMPLE 4.2c. F. Chopin: Sonata in B Minor, Op. 58, I. Allegro maestoso, m. 159 (Breitkopf & Härtel Stichvorlage, 1844).

When nineteenth- and twentieth-century editors faced decisions about the typographical assignment of the release symbols, they resolved to create an alignment with the notes or chords that were close enough to justify an imposition of verticality. The notation that emerged from this approach often goes against what would have been Chopin's original intentions.

The main obstacle that confronts a performer in regard to the execution of Chopin's release signs is that a decision concerning each instance is usually based on what is shown in print. The way we read pedal indications is a consequence of how editors have understood the original sources for us. In my young years, I believed that the printed version of a work, especially if carried out by an authoritative firm, would feature a faithful reproduction of the composer's markings; as my analysis unfolded, I understood that the interpretation of Chopin's release signs was often premised solely on a calligraphic scrutiny of each symbol as an individual case and not on contextual meaning. I realized that this was not a problem caused exclusively by modern versions, but that it also held true in the case of the early editions. Consider, for example, how the editors at Breitkopf & Härtel, who were following the Stichvorlage just discussed, printed measures 159–66 from the first movement of the Sonata in B Minor, Op. 58, in 1845:

EXAMPLE 4.3. F. Chopin: Sonata in B Minor, Op. 58, I. Allegro maestoso, mm. 159–166 (Breitkopf & Härtel edition, 1845).

In this version, the asterisks are quite systematically placed under the last pitch of each left-hand group of three or six notes (with the exception of measures 164 and 166). The editors at Breitkopf & Härtel may have chosen this alignment in response to the erratic and perplexing placements in the Stichvorlage; yet I wondered why the asterisks were not placed closer to the ensuing *ped* whenever the space permitted it—a solution that would have eliminated any alternative interpretation of the syncopated pedal they propose.

A rather thorny issue concerning inconsistent pedal releases was addressed by Jean-Jacques Eigeldinger, who tried to rationalize the presence of such irregularity in analogous passages in the Stichvorlage of the Prelude in D-flat Major, Op. 28, No. 15. Eigeldinger presumed that these divergences represented a stroke of creativity on Chopin's part:

> The autograph of the Prelude Op. 28/15 indicates the pedal for the whole of bar 1 and its repetitions in bars 5, 20, 24 and 80, but not for the return of the same motif after the second section, bar 76, where the pedal is to be raised on the fourth beat. It is evident there that Chopin intends two different treatments. On an 1840 Pleyel the sound clears more rapidly and the melodic move to Bb colours it without however affecting its clarity, whereas on a modern piano it blurs the harmony. Renewing the pedal just before the fourth beat would effectively negate Chopin's intention of reserving this effect for bar 76; so we are left with the possibility of a half-pedal, more practicable on modern pianos than on old ones.[7]

Here are the two pedal markings in question:

EXAMPLE 4.4a. F. Chopin: Prelude in D-flat Major, op. 28, No. 15, mm. 1–2 (Catelin Stichvorlage, 1839).

EXAMPLE 4.4b. F. Chopin: Prelude in D-flat Major, op. 28, No. 15, mm. 76–77 (Catelin Stichvorlage, 1839).

Chopin's compositional process and the profuse corrections found throughout this Stichvorlage led me to speculate at first that the placement of the release sign under the fourth beat of measure 76 may have been a mistake that was incurred while the composer hastily transcribed the forty complex manuscript pages of the Preludes, Op. 28—a monumental effort that must have taken many hours of work. However, while analyzing the original manuscript of the prelude in question, I noticed a repetition of the kind of pattern identified in example 4.2a: the distance between the release in measure 76 and the *ped* in measure 77 is consistent with the distance between the other releases and *ped* symbols in the same line. The regularity of this spacing would attest to its reference to syncopated pedaling, and would counter the notion that "the same motif," in Eigeldinger's words, would have been subject to a different treatment. Further, if this pedal marking were not extended through the recurring thematic material to the following downbeat, it would be the only such instance in the entire prelude.[8] Had Chopin desired a new pedal application for the fourth beat of measure 76, I thought, he would have probably marked it—as he did a few beats later, still in measure 77:

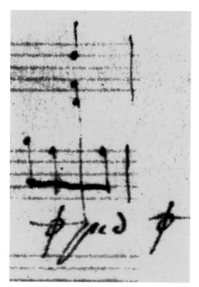

EXAMPLE 4.5. F. Chopin: Prelude in D-flat Major, Op. 28, No. 15, m. 77 (Catelin Stichvorlage, 1839).

Incidentally, the second release in example 4.5 may support my observation in regard to the role of the release symbols: despite the extremely limited space at the end of the system, Chopin still maintained a generous distance between *ped* and ⊕. It was the odd presence of this release symbol beyond the bar line that made me realize one important aspect: I understood that the approximate placement of the asterisks in modern editions incurred flaws that hindered my understanding of Chopin's language, but the idea of relying on the composer's original markings seemed an insurmountable task that would necessitate my gaining access to manuscripts that were disseminated in libraries and private collections around the world. Thankfully, some of Chopin's Stichvorlagen were available in print or online, which facilitated the process of clarification.

The consultation of Chopin's Stichvorlagen helped me resolve a problematic issue in regard to the pedaling that is frequently indicated in mainstream editions of such pieces as mazurkas and waltzes. Their patterned accompanying figures—in most cases three quarter-notes per measure—were the source of a conundrum: the limited amount of space between beats often caused release signs to be placed with some approximation at the end of each measure, close to the next downbeat but not close enough to specify syncopated pedaling with precision. Their ambiguous position led editors to follow an alignment that favored the third quarter-note of each measure, rather than the ensuing downbeat.

This kind of notation has similarly affected our perception of pedaling in structurally more ambitious compositions, such as the ballades. A pedal marking in the first half of measure 116 of the Ballade in A-flat Major, Op. 47, for example, provides a plausible parallel to the Prelude in D-flat Major: as the 1841 Stichvorlage used by Breitkopf & Härtel confirms, the nearness of notes and symbols, combined with the composer's habit of consistent spacing between ⊕ and *ped*, destined the release sign to be placed slightly to the right of the left-hand eighth-note chord E-flat–A-flat–E-flat:

🔊 EXAMPLE 4.6. F. Chopin: Ballade in A-flat Major, Op. 47, mm. 116–117 (Breitkopf & Härtel Stichvorlage, 1841).

This release may visually suggest that an interruption before the following *ped* should apply. Alternatively, the absence of a pedal marking for the same chord leads many to believe that it should be individually pedaled. Foreseeably, most widely used editions report the release as belonging to this very chord, rather than marking it as an uninterrupted application to the next depression.

How did pianists in Chopin's time respond to these shortened pedal applications that appeared in the early editions of the composer's works? Would have they treated them as syncopated pedaling? Would have they left unpedaled the notes or chords notated between the release and the ensuing *ped*? Or would have they subjectively inserted an extra pedal? Ten modern recordings of the Ballade in A-flat Major, Op. 47 used as a test showed that most of the pianists chose the third approach for the pedaling of measure 116, which we just viewed in example 4.6. Had Chopin known what a headache his release markings would prove to be, and had he been acquainted with other ways to indicate syncopated pedaling—such as the more modern brackets under the system (⎣_____⎦)—he might have been delighted to employ these alternatives.

Prolonging pedal applications that are typically shortened in modern editions may occasionally result in the blurring of harmonies or melodic lines. Consider the following episode from the Mazurka in D Major, Op. 33, No. 2 as it appears in the Breitkopf & Härtel edition of 1838:

EXAMPLE 4.7. F. Chopin: Mazurka in D Major, Op. 33, No. 2, mm. 58–67 (Breitkopf & Härtel edition, 1838).

In measure 58, the presence of two G-flats in the right hand blurs the dominant seventh chord of F major; in measure 60, a G-flat in the first beat of the right hand blurs the harmony of D-flat major; and the pitches included in the left-hand motif in measures 62–64 are extraneous to the prevailing harmonies sustained by the extended pedals. In the version published by Schlesinger in 1838, based on a copy made by Julian Fontana, these pedal markings were shortened and placed beneath the third beat of each measure. I thought this could have been a miscalculation on Fontana's part while he was reproducing Chopin's manuscript, but I also could not dismiss the possibility that it was the editor who reproduced his copy erroneously. The French Stichvorlage of this mazurka resides in a private collection in Japan, and it seemed a hopeless prospect to verify whether the shorter markings appear in it. The Stichvorlage that Chopin sent to Breitkopf & Härtel, however, is now in the possession of the Biblioteka Narodowa in Warsaw and accessible to the public. Viewing it confirmed that the engraver at the German firm had followed Chopin's notation faithfully, indicating pedal applications to the end of the measure, with one exception: in the composer's hand, the release in measure 64 extends to the following downbeat, blurring the harmonies of the dominant seventh chord of A-flat major and its tonic D-flat major in the third beat—a solution that any modern pianist would find outrageous. Proposing Schlesinger's shorter indications in some modern editions seems to have been a choice directed to eliminate some of the blurriness that is found so undesirable on modern pianos. Still, these shorter applications in many cases would include some of the overlap of unrelated pitches, and the complete absence of pedal for the third beat of each measure would result in continuous brief interruptions. My experience had taught me that both quandaries would have presented themselves even on the less sophisticated instruments of the 1830s. Further, had Chopin wanted a pedal for the third beat of each measure, I thought, he would probably have specified such an important element in his manuscripts, since he did so in many other instances throughout his works.

It was while researching the location of Julian Fontana's copy of the Mazurka in D Major, locked up in a safe somewhere in Tokyo, that I came to an unforeseen conclusion: if long pedals had been intentionally placed for each measure and in many cases encompassed different harmonies, perhaps their purposes were distant from the necessity of prolonging a single harmony throughout a passage or facilitating the resonance of notes whose intervallic distance would not be reachable by a regular-size hand. Instead, these indications may disclose a specific aesthetic of sound to which we have not been exposed—an experimental stage in Chopin's evolution that broke ground for the new coloristic possibilities he explored in later years in the evocative arpeggios of the opening page of the Polonaise-Fantaisie or in the watercolor-like textures achieved in the second tonal area of the Barcarolle. Put another way, as the effects of these long pedal applications on pianos from the 1830s would have not been too dissimilar to the effects produced on today's instruments, Chopin may have deliberately conceived them as generating blurriness—an outcome that would have been considered unusual during that time, as it is today.

The comparison I had established between original instruments and the modern grand piano, I came to understand, had encouraged the creation of contradictions and double standards in my own playing. Still in the early stages of my explorations, I struggled to accept what on a contemporary instrument seemed an excessive reverberation caused by some of Chopin's original markings, but I also aspired to follow the composer's instructions in ways that represented their outcomes as I imagined them on the pianos he played. This wavering position led me to alter the text by using half pedals, fluttered applications, and interruptions of longer markings so as to reduce the blurriness that the original instruments, I thought at the time, would have not generated. Moreover, I found that certain pedals in Chopin were preimpressionistic, but was willing to apply these instances only when the harmony was agreeable. Should I have become more attuned to these generous pedal applications as particular timbric effects, which seem to be what Chopin had intended for some of his indications? A pianist of the caliber of Anton Rubinstein had come to the conclusion that what appears to be lack of textual logic should be disregarded or modified in favor of each pianist's approximation of the composer's intentions, and that pedaling is bound to vary depending on the instrument, the performance space, and—last but not least— the interpreter's inspiration. I, too, believed that I was altering Chopin's original pedal indications in ways that were allowing me to reproduce the composer's intentions more closely, but in fact my strategy of fluttering, half pedaling and breaking long pedals may have been removing me far from them. As time passed, a greater familiarity with Chopin's manuscripts and early editions made me realize that the presence of unusually long pedal indications was circumscribed to a specific period in Chopin's life—from the mid- to the late 1830s—and that the blurriness that I often tried to modify may have been an intended characteristic of a language in evolution.

———————————— ·◄●►· ————————————

Not so long ago, I had the opportunity to audit a masterclass given by a leading pianist of our time. One of the featured pieces at the much anticipated event was the first movement of Chopin's Sonata in B Minor, Op. 58. The comments that the visiting artist offered focused mainly on the adherence to the pedal markings as they appeared in the edition that the student was using, and which he was not closely observing. For example, here is how that edition notated the episode in measures 61–64:

EXAMPLE 4.8. F. Chopin: Sonata in B Minor, Op. 58, I. Allegro maestoso, mm. 61–65.

"It works perfectly the way Chopin himself marked it, and there is no reason not to follow his original intentions!" was the teacher's peremptory claim. Yet, when I later consulted the Stichvorlage that Chopin prepared for Breitkopf & Härtel, I noticed that the release symbols do not consistently align with the rests in the left hand:

EXAMPLE 4.9. F. Chopin: Sonata in B Minor, Op. 58, I. Allegro maestoso, mm. 61–63 (Breitkopf & Härtel Stichvorlage, 1844).

The release symbols appear with some approximation under the eighth-note rests featured in the left hand, but the even distance between ⊕ and the ensuing *ped* maintained throughout the system support the idea that Chopin intended syncopated pedaling. The gaps between each ⊕ and the following *ped* are more substantial than in other instances throughout the same Stichvorlage (compare the spacing between release symbols and pedal markings in example 4.2 and in this passage from the Breitkopf & Härtel edition), and the inference that the editors seem to have drawn from the generous spacing in these measures was that the composer intended an aural separation with each release. At the same time, some of the silences that would occur coincide with the sixteenth-note rests in the right hand (measures 63 in example 4.9, beats two and four), both creating and justifying the presence of an interruption not just in the left hand but in both hands. The product of this pedaling has been perpetuated as an interpretive tradition, and several authoritative editions have ingrained the belief that this convention is exactly what Chopin intended. Were intuition and, especially, listening to play a larger role in the way we read the printed page, we might object to the continuous interruption of the rich overtones in the texture of this passage, and to the prevention of the left-hand writing from revealing the numerous compound lines that are woven into the thick harmonic fabric. I concluded that the markings we have been considering would make more sense as continuous syncopated pedal, and I realized that their release signs would not be so problematic if pianists were to accept them as indicating nothing more than an uncomplicated prerequisite: before the pedal is depressed again, the right foot has to be lifted. The illustrious pianist trusted that what is generally considered an authoritative edition would never fail to report the original notation correctly, and declared his belief that those rests assuredly represent short suspensions of the pedal. This interpretive choice is evident in his recording of the Sonata in B Minor—a recording that had become very popular years earlier and that, as I remember, had affected the perception of the work in the minds of several young pianists I knew.

The puzzling presence of long pedals over rests is a rather common occurrence in Chopin's writing. Generally, the temporal value of these brief separations is a sixteenth-note. Instances can be highly irregular within a piece, and they do not necessarily set precedents for analogous passages in different keys. I often wondered whether I should have either disregarded the rests entirely or modified the pedal to reproduce those silences faithfully, and in many cases the latter option prevailed.

Eigeldinger's volume may offer insight here as well, in its conveyance of a brief but informative memoir by Chopin's student Anna de Lichocherstoff:

> The *Luft-Pause*... gives the hand the elegance of a wing... The suppleness of the wrist, independent of the forearm, was the virtuoso's prime consideration.[9]

Could the *Luft-Pause*, commonly translated as "breath," be the short hiatus caused by a rest, like the one we have just examined in the passage from the Sonata in B Minor? The significant content of Anna de Lichocherstoff's account is corroborated by a statement made by Jan Kleczyński (1837–1895), who was the first pianist to study Chopin's music with some degree of scholarly effort. Kleczyński recounted that the composer took great care in instilling the concept of wrist flexibility in his teaching, insisting on the notion that the end of a slur should be tapered dynamically and the wrist lifted.[10] A quick annotation written by Chopin himself on a single sheet of paper for inclusion in his unpublished *Méthode* seems to substantiate these two accounts:

The wrist: respiration in voice.[11]

I realized that what Anna de Lichocherstoff described as *Luft-Pause* may not necessarily have been an aural separation, but a gesture indicating a release of the hand—a motion that lies within the realm of the choreography of piano playing. In Chopin's writing, this trait became especially evident in some of the mazurkas of the early 1830s. An excerpt from the Mazurka in C-sharp Minor, Op. 6, No. 2 successfully illustrates the assiduous notation of what should be physically connected under a slur and where the hand should be lifted:

EXAMPLE 4.10. F. Chopin: Mazurka in C-sharp Minor, Op. 6, No. 2, mm. 8–20.

The pedal changes applied at each downbeat make the *Luft-Pausen* in the right hand go completely unnoticed. This detailed articulation was a habitual characteristic of Chopin's early works, including those in which extended melodic lines would suppose a greater involvement of longer slurs (the Nocturnes, Op. 9 come to mind). This notational device, however, changed over the years: as of the mid-1830s the composer began to expand the scope of the slurs to outline primarily the breadth of phrasing. It is with some of the Etudes, Op. 25 and especially with the Nocturne in C-sharp Minor, Op. 27, No. 1 that examples of bel canto lines are marked for the first time with gestures that encompass long episodes. This was a gradual evolution, as we still find short slurs in the Nocturne in D-flat Major, Op. 27, No. 2. But in some of the Preludes, Op. 28 or the Scherzo in B-flat Minor, Op. 31 a propensity for the use of longer gestures is detected (the most extreme case is probably the fifty-seven-measure slur in the opening section of the Scherzo from the Sonata in B Minor, Op. 58). It is traditionally believed that legato should apply to such instances, as a long phrase seems to be intended. Regrettably, this approach could cause the musical material to lack inflection because of the unvaried articulation that derives from it.

The idea that long slurs do not require legato would allow a performer to approach an extended passage with varied articulation. In the introduction of the Mazurka in A-flat Major, Op. 50, No. 2, for example, a lightly detached attack of the quarter-notes would result in a lilting enunciation that is quite appropriate for this Allegretto:

EXAMPLE 4.11. F. Chopin: Mazurka in A-flat Major, Op. 50, No. 2, mm. 1–8.

After the mid-1830s Chopin's writing still featured *Luft-Pausen* over long pedals, though the length of slurs had increased considerably. It was through this more unusual notation that I understood the original intention of the short rests: when the execution of a passage requires the separation of groups whose layout cannot be physically connected, *Luft-Pausen* intervene to facilitate such transitions and the pedal becomes the unifying element that preserves the aural integrity of a line. Measures 25–28 of the Fantaisie in F Minor, Op. 49 illustrate this concept well:

EXAMPLE 4.12. F. Chopin: Fantaisie in F Minor, Op. 49, mm. 25–28.

The group that starts in measure 25 concludes on the downbeat of measure 26. The rest that follows this downbeat marks the beginning of a new group, physically manageable in one gesture until the third beat of measure 27. Here another rest occurs, indicating again the necessity to lift the hand and move to the G/B-flat chord with fingers 1 and 3, setting up a position that is nearly an octave higher. The same concept applies to the next beat, in which the chord G-sharp/B-natural is played by fingers 2 and 4, making it necessary to set up a new position for the octave A–C–A. Long pedals encompass entire half measures and render these breaks inaudible. A similar situation is encountered in the second tonal area of the Nocturne in B Major, Op. 32, No. 1, in which the slurs for the right hand and the pedal markings indicated are self-explanatory. This time the gestures are downward:

EXAMPLE 4.13. F. Chopin: Nocturne in B Major, Op. 32, No. 1, mm. 23–25.

Many performers tend to disregard this purely pianistic element, ignoring Chopin's original pedal markings to highlight the sixteenth-note rests as pronounced separations.

By following two different Stichvorlagen, Schlesinger and Breitkopf & Härtel were able to publish Chopin's Fantaisie in F Minor approximately at the same time (the French publisher in December 1841, the German house in January 1842). The German manuscript was prepared by Chopin, the French one by Fontana. The French Stichvorlage has not been located, but in the first print of the Schlesinger edition the pedal is almost totally absent up to measure 49, which led me to speculate that Fontana did not complete its notation in the first two pages of his manuscript copy.[12] Whatever the cause of the omission, I was prevented from observing possible discrepancies between the two manuscripts. My evaluation of the early prints confirmed that modern editions tend to follow Fontana's deficient copy, with its dryer approach to pedaling. By comparison, the German Stichvorlage, which provides exhaustive pedaling for the entire introduction, creates a sense of unease: despite its authenticity, there is little likelihood that any pianist would instinctively apply the lavish syncopated pedal that Chopin marked in measures 37–40:

♫ EXAMPLE 4.14. F. Chopin: Fantaisie in F Minor, Op. 49, mm. 37–40 (pedal markings as notated in Chopin's hand in the Breitkopf & Härtel Stichvorlage).

As most editions follow the French version, the pedaling generally heard in this passage is very discreet and is limited to the half-notes, since sixteenth-note rests and *staccato* markings visually suggest aural separations. Instead, a long pedal covers the entirety of measure 37 (and, analogously, of measure 39) while two *Luft-Pausen* become aurally undetectable—one before the repeated chord between beats three and four, and one before the downbeat of measures 38, where the right hand would physically need to establish a new position.

◆—◆

Deductive reasoning led me to understand the inconsistently placed release symbols as cases of syncopated pedal, but other instances involving isolated pedal markings proved less easy to discern. It was the case in the Prelude in E-flat Major, Op. 28, No. 19, whose ending is notated as follows:

EXAMPLE 4.15. F. Chopin: Prelude in E-flat Major, Op. 28, No. 19, mm. 65–71.

If observed literally, the last two measures would have to be pedaled independently, each measure featuring a separation to do justice to the rests . . . or, as I once heard it, with no pedal at all! This manner of placing the release, I began to speculate, may have been a convention that implied an extended pedal to the end of the piece. Perhaps Chopin deemed this an intuitive solution because the writing throughout the prelude prescribes the continuous use of the sustain pedal, and because this happens to be the last pedal indication of the piece. A performance that favors separations between each one of the last three measures may be the result of a mechanical response to the rests indicated, but my impression is that Chopin intended them as *Luft-Pausen*, because it would be unfeasible to connect the three measures physically. Further, this ending comprises the same harmony, and a long pedal would generate full overtones by including a broad range of registers otherwise excluded. In the Wessel edition, based on the French edition but revised by Ignaz Moscheles, the last chord was marked with an independent pedal—puzzled by the length of the last pedal indication, he might have tried to justify the void it created.

A parallel to the concluding measures of the Prelude in E-flat Major is encountered in the first French edition of the Scherzo in C-sharp Minor, Op. 39:

EXAMPLE 4.16. F. Chopin: Scherzo in C-sharp Minor, Op. 39, mm. 629–649 (Troupenas & Cie., 1840).

EXAMPLE 4.16 (*continued*)

The idea expressed in the previous example perfectly applies to this ending: one long pedal for the last three chords would reveal the radiance and the broad range of registers covered. The dates of publication of the three different versions of this Scherzo between October 1840 (German and English editions) and December of the same year (French edition), along with the numerous discrepancies between these sources, confirm that three different Stichvorlagen were used. It is the first English edition, published by Wessel in London, which supports the idea of a long pedal application as I had imagined it:

EXAMPLE 4.17. F. Chopin: Scherzo in C-sharp Minor, Op. 39, mm. 643–649 (Wessel, 1840).

I initially contemplated that either Chopin or the editor forgot to include a release sign. Although this possibility could not be completely excluded, I was also aware that the absence of a release was not so unusual in Chopin, and in most cases involved the concluding measures of a piece. Similar cases are found in many of the Preludes, Op. 28; the Nocturne in E-flat Major, Op. 55, No. 2 (example 5.14); the Impromptu in G-flat Major, Op. 51; the Mazurka in B Major, Op. 56, No. 1; or the French edition of the Etude in C Major, Op. 10, No. 7,[13] to mention a few.

The passages that we just observed from the Prelude in E-flat Major and the Scherzo in C-sharp Minor are rare occurrences in their implications for pedaling, yet they provided me with a possible interpretive criterion for other unsuspected instances whose execution is not always intuitive. Many cases in Chopin's Stichvorlagen show releases that I would define as "placed in midair"—inexplicable instances that fail to align with any beat or note. Why would a release be notated between two pitches? No pianist would ever conceive of such a solution as a reasonable interpretive principle. Moreover, whether or not these release signs were meant to align with a specific pitch or chord, it is their contextual placement that seems irrational, because they often do not make particular sonic sense if applied where they are indicated. The opening measure of the Barcarolle, Op. 60 shows one such case:

EXAMPLE 4.18. F. Chopin: Barcarolle in F-sharp Major, Op. 60, m. 1 (Brandus Stichvorlage, 1845). Biblioteka Jagiellońska, Kraków.

In the first French edition published by Brandus, which was based on the Stichvorlage shown in example 4.18, the release was assigned by the editor to the G-sharp in the left hand—slightly to the left of how Chopin had marked it. This is not the only release in the Brandus edition of the Barcarolle to be intentionally displaced, and certainly not an unusual occurrence in the way Chopin's manuscripts were interpreted by his publishers. Subjective readings were perhaps necessary on their part, as Chopin's intentions were not always intelligible. As we have seen, the proofreading process was frequently carried out by some of the composer's associates or by musicians of repute. More recently, these only relatively accurate versions were the object of further revision by editors, scholars and experts—new layers of information that have generated strong interpretive positions, which most pianists today deem indisputable.

In a lively conversation I had with pianist, author, and pedagogue Seymour Bernstein, he proclaimed that this first pedal indication in the Barcarolle should extend until the new *ped* in measure 2, representing a case of syncopated pedal— an approach that he has eloquently described in his book *Chopin: Interpreting His Notational Symbols*:

Example 4.19. F. Chopin: Barcarolle in F-sharp Major, Op. 60, mm. 1–3 (Seymour Bernstein's interpretation of Chopin's pedaling).

At first I found Bernstein's solution debatable, but over time was persuaded by it and resolved to apply it to my own interpretation. Shortly after my conversation with Bernstein, I was fortunate enough to experiment with the resources of two Pleyel pianos from the 1840s: on those instruments, prolonging this pedal marking produced a slight blurriness, a veiled resonance that nicely matched the one created by the syncopated pedal in measures 2 and 3. Experiencing some of the works of Chopin on those two marvelous Pleyels made me comprehend one fundamental aspect of his art: a musical idea and the manipulation of sound that was necessary to produce it were inevitably affected by the unique resources and limitations of the pianos that the composer had at his disposal. But I also understood that the meaning of these mysterious release symbols apparently in midair would have remained completely unknown to me unless I was willing to abandon their mechanical reproduction.

A rather different issue, this time in the Prelude in B-flat Minor, Op. 28, No. 16, has been the object of innumerable discussions among pianists. In fact, long pedals over three-measure groups find many of them in disagreement:

EXAMPLE 4.20. F. Chopin: Prelude in B-flat Minor, Op. 28, No. 16, mm. 2–11.

The three-measure pattern in measures 2–4 and 5–7 switches to a one-measure application for the entirety of measure 8, and to half-measure applications after it. Chopin's pedaling is based on the harmonic changes provided by the left-hand accompaniment. In an attempt to resolve what they considered an excessive resonance, the editors of the Paderewski edition altered the original notation: the long pedals in measures 2–7 were shortened to a pattern of half measures, following the example provided by measures 9–11. The critical notes do not explain why this unjustifiable modification was introduced. The first three measures of the manuscript that Chopin sent to Breitkopf & Härtel in 1839 show that the composer had begun to mark pedal changes for each half measure. But measures 5–7 show an extended pedal, which proves that the indications originally applied to measures 2–4 might have comprised an error that occurred in the haste of notating the opening measures, or an early conception that was soon dismissed, or just a change that fell short—one that Chopin started to notate after finishing the piece and then dismissed soon after. Reducing the pedal to half-measure applications would undoubtedly create more transparency in all the registers, but Chopin's original instructions refer to the coloristic approach to harmony often found in his compositions from the mid-to-late 1830s.[14] While considering possible solutions on modern instruments, I had tried to achieve what I thought was a reasonable effect by adopting a half-pedal or fluttered-pedal treatment. Nevertheless, an element that I had not initially considered in the Prelude in B-flat Minor was *balance*. The left hand was much too loud to do justice to the dynamic level indicated: I attacked the opening measures with a *fortissimo*, whereas I noticed that a lighter left hand would do justice to the texture prescribed and still produce the *forte* marked at the beginning of the piece. My illuminating experience with historical instruments confirmed that the blurriness would have been excessive even on 1830s pianos, unless I properly evaluated the rapport between the pianistically demanding left hand and the virtuosic figurations in the right hand. Chopin's generous notation of the sustain pedal planted the seed for a new conception of sound, yet these long applications might come to life in their original purpose only if balance were properly evaluated. This approach seems to have been a necessary prerequisite on Chopin's beloved Pleyels, and its absence on the resonant modern instruments might cause the texture to sound simply overwhelming.

It is often suggested that when the pedal is not indicated at all in his music, Chopin expected the performer to base its use on personal intuition. In such passages, it is said, pedaling (or abstaining from it) is then bound to adapt to harmony, to the character, or to a pattern whose indication would have been superfluous. In the Prelude in C Minor, Op. 28, No. 20, whose chordal writing features no pedal markings, no modern pianist would dispense with the sustain pedal:

EXAMPLE 4.21. F. Chopin: Prelude in C Minor, Op. 28, No. 20.

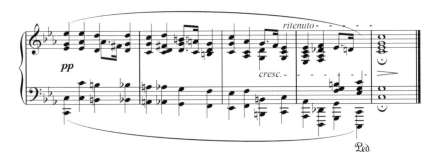

EXAMPLE **4.21** (*continued*)

The only pedal notated is found at the end of the Prelude—an application that would not be intuitive, because it encompasses two chords, and that Chopin chose to indicate without a release sign. As the pedaling seems to be self-explanatory, writing a pedal change for each chord would have indicated the obvious. Many are the instances in which this rule would hold true—for example, the chorale-like middle section of the Nocturne in G Minor, Op. 37, No. 1, written contemporaneously with the Prelude in C Minor and whose material might have been originated from the same compositional idea; or the celebrated Waltz in A Minor, Op. 34, No. 2, whose opening section and its reoccurrences during the piece display a complete absence of pedal indications; or the first ten measures of the Etude in C-sharp Minor, Op. 25, No. 7, in which the complex textures created by the duet in the baritone/tenor and soprano registers in opposition to the accompanying material I always deemed unthinkable without the support of the pedal. In passages that feature tight, active contrapuntal exchanges between voices, the lack of pedal markings could have ideally implied very frequent or detailed pedal changes whose notation would have been too arduous to implement. Chopin seemingly trusted that the performer, knowing how to interpret such moments, would use the appropriate amount of pedal. The opening measures of the development in the first movement of the Sonata in B Minor, Op. 58 offer a good example:

EXAMPLE **4.22.** F. Chopin: Sonata in B Minor, Op. 58, I. Allegro maestoso, mm. 92–96.

The polyphonic intricacy of this passage is such that, had Chopin imagined the use of the sustain pedal here, its painstaking notation would have been virtually impossible. Chopin might have intended for the texture to rely on finger legato, with the pedal perhaps intervening when the writing becomes too cumbersome to be physically sustained. Today, most performances of this passage feature pedaling that relies predictably on patterned changes at every beat, while some display such sparing use of the pedal that the entire passage is essentially unaffected by it.

At the turn of the twentieth century, Camille Saint-Saëns stated that contrapuntal writing was made more successful by relying exclusively on finger legato. Kleczyński, two years his junior, concurred with this position and reported that many instances in Chopin's works should be played without the use of the sustain pedal[15]—an approach that would be considered inconceivable today. After reading Kleczyński's account, I immediately envisioned playing the opening ten measures of the Etude, Op. 25, No. 7 and imagined how challenging it would be to produce the legato, the dynamic shape, and the voicing necessary to carry out such a task on a modern instrument. But what about the almost imperceptible resonance that was present even without the use of the pedal, which modern pianos do not feature? Did Chopin truly play these passages by relying only on finger legato, given that the release of a key would have still entailed a slight blurriness that could not be immediately eliminated? One example cited by Kleczyński concerns the opening page of the Nocturne in F Major, Op. 15, No. 1:

EXAMPLE 4.23. F. Chopin: Nocturne in F Major, Op. 15, No. 1, mm. 1–24.

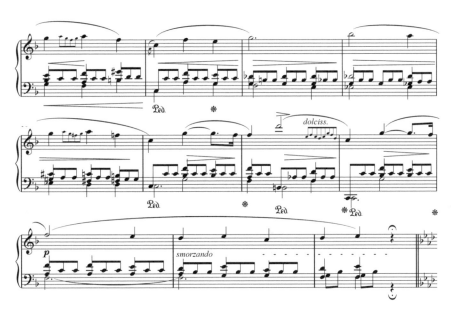

EXAMPLE 4.23. (*continued*)

At first I thought that the advice given by Saint-Saëns and Kleczyński could have possibly revealed a personal preference for not using the pedal to replace legato playing,[16] but as I was inspecting the opening page of the Nocturne in F Major I began to notice a curious set of circumstances: the *sempre legato* was indicated by Chopin below the system, hence referring to the left hand; the writing in the left hand allows much of the accompanying figurations to be played with very small adjustments to one basic hand position; the writing presents separate stemming, alluding to different durations for each of the three lines; and pedal markings make their appearance only when it is not feasible for the left hand to hold or reach the chords prescribed, guaranteeing a continuity of legato. That same day, as I was discussing a group of Chopin mazurkas with one of my students, I noticed that this formula is presented in diametrically opposite cases: when broad accompanying figurations supported by extensive pedal indications are briefly interrupted by writing that permits the implementation of finger legato, in these latter instances the use of the pedal is discontinued and the marking *legato* is often indicated. It is the case in the opening measures of the Mazurka in F-sharp Minor, Op. 6, No. 1:

EXAMPLE 4.24. F. Chopin: Mazurka in F-sharp Minor, Op. 6, No. 1, mm. 1–9.

In another mazurka, the one in D-flat Major, Op. 30, No. 3, I observed that the absence of pedal indications is reserved exclusively to these instances:

1. The left hand features a sequence of chords that are confined to one basic hand position, hence facilitating finger legato.

2. The writing implies intervals limited to an octave, easily allowing finger legato without excessive stretches.

3. A bass note features a double stem, which extends its duration into the following beat(s).

4. The writing prescribes a *staccato* articulation.

After observing these strategies in the Mazurka in D-flat Major, I began to detect identical situations in many other works of Chopin. Pedal markings were featured only when the writing did not prescribe finger legato, but especially when it would not permit it. Chopin may have played these passages without the sustain pedal, but the emergence of increasingly longer pedal indications in his music over the years went hand in hand with the evolution of the instrument: a decreasing reliance on finger legato must have been directly proportional to the development of brilliance and richness of tone that new pianos featured. Technique was changing, and Chopin transformed Biedermeier stereotypes into a sophisticated language that inspired the following generation of composers and that made Impressionism possible.

When I first understood that Chopin may have intended the omission of pedal markings as moments to be taken literally, I envisioned a fairly comical performance of his Etude in F Minor, Op. 25, No. 2 in which the infrequent pedals indicated in the Stichvorlage were religiously observed. With few exceptions, these pedal markings, which appear in twenty-seven of the sixty-nine measures, encompass one full measure at a time, or two overlapping half measures. My analysis suggested that Chopin probably intended to reserve the pedal exclusively for those measures, rather than specifying its use outside of predictable patterned changes. But in thinking about Chopin's intentions for the remaining measures, I noticed that much of the left hand's harmonic structure can be supported by what we call *finger pedaling*—a technique that prescribes holding certain notes to simulate the effect of the pedal. The procedure would allow a performer to dispense with the pedal, or to change it more frequently while preserving the duration of one or more fundamental notes that otherwise would be lost completely or blurred by two or more superimposed harmonies. Although in the Etude in F Minor this strategy is reserved for hands with a span of at least a tenth from white key to white key (e.g., c^1 to e^2), in many instances it represents a manageable and resourceful tool. A combination of both elements in this etude would do justice to the writing, eliminating the excessive and often unwanted blurriness that the continuous use of the sustain pedal would create, while generating greater consistency with the beats that are affected by the marked pedals.

We know that Chopin employed this technique in his own playing because we find examples of written-out finger pedaling in his works. In the Largo from his Sonata in B Minor, Op. 58, for instance, the opening of the middle section shows that he painstakingly notated the duration of the pitches that should be physically held in the right hand. The pedal intervenes exclusively when the left hand would be unable to hold the fifth in the bass (E–B) while reaching the melody in the tenor register (last beat of measure 28 and first beat of measure 29):

🔊 **EXAMPLE 4.25.** F. Chopin: Sonata in B Minor, Op. 58, III. Largo, mm. 28–30 (Breitkopf & Härtel Stichvorlage, 1844).

As we saw, a similar combination of finger legato and spare use of the pedal was intended in the Nocturne in F Major, written more than a decade earlier, but Chopin had limited himself to indicating *sempre legato* beneath the lower register, probably proposing that the left hand should adequately prolong all the pitches. In example 4.25 it is the right hand that is principally in charge of the harmonic backdrop, and indicating *legato* perhaps would have not sufficed to imply the use of finger pedaling. In this case, Chopin designated that the notes to be held should be exclusively the ones that are pertinent to the harmony.[17] No pianist today would strictly observe these indications, as the outcome would sound contrived on modern instruments, and awkward to most pianistic ears. We may also attribute this inobservance to the evolution of a pianistic sound that was based on the experience acquired from the second half of the nineteenth century and the entirety of the twentieth century. The coloristic effects introduced by impressionistic composers such as Debussy and Ravel probably led us to legitimate this passage from the Largo as "pre-impressionistic," whereas the finger pedaling indicated by Chopin would eliminate the pitches and the overtones that are responsible for creating the atmosphere to which we have grown accustomed in this middle section. Is it possible that we have adapted to something that is not *Chopin*?

Other passages from the same movement would however benefit from the use of finger pedaling combined with regular use of the right pedal, even if not notated as such. Were this technique not considered, the pedaling indicated would produce interruptions in the bass register and hinder its support to the treble:

⊕ EXAMPLE 4.26a. F. Chopin: Sonata in B Minor, Op. 58, III. Largo, mm. 38–41.

Finger pedaling the relevant harmony in measures 38 and 40 would give the impression of an extended pedal throughout the measure:

⚓ **EXAMPLE 4.26b.** F. Chopin: Sonata in B Minor, Op. 58, III. Largo, mm. 38–41.

Did Chopin take it for granted that such passages would be finger pedaled because it may have been the lower register that was conventionally subject to that treatment? Would this explain why he went to the extent of notating it for the right hand in the passage illustrated in example 4.25? Antoine François Marmontel wrote that "with most modern virtuosos, excessive, continuous use of the pedal is a capital defect, producing sonorities eventually tiring and irritating to the delicate ear. Chopin, on the contrary, while making constant use of the pedal, obtained ravishing harmonies, melodic whispers that charmed and astonished."[18] Did finger pedaling contribute to the illusion of Chopin's constant use of the pedal, even when the sustain pedal was used with parsimony? Was this device one of the elements that prompted Marmontel to state that Chopin's pedaling had reached a degree of virtuosity that other pianists of the time did not possess?

As I arrived at these conclusions about Chopin's writing, I noticed that the works of other composers feature passages in which the use of finger pedaling may have been overlooked. Consider the opening measures of Beethoven's Sonata in E Major, Op. 109:

EXAMPLE 4.27. L. van Beethoven: Sonata in E Major, Op. 109, I. Vivace, ma non troppo, mm. 1–4.

In an attempt to justify the presence of the double stems in the right hand, some performers identify the quarter-notes as indicating voicing. But if that had been what Beethoven intended, why would the second sixteenth-note of each quadruplet need to be prolonged as a dotted eighth-note? Is it reasonable to believe that this way of indicating different durations represents finger pedaling? Beethoven is reported to have used the sustain pedal abundantly, yet it is possible that he imagined this opening and other analogous passages in the movement as relying on this surrogate way of prolonging sounds.

An opportunity to use finger pedaling is offered by the opening page of Chopin's Barcarolle in F-sharp Major, Op. 60. I first thought that the releases indicated would refer to syncopated pedaling, but a close analysis of the two extant Stichvorlagen revealed Chopin's precision in marking a release for the end of beats one and three throughout passages that feature this kind of writing:

EXAMPLE 4.28. F. Chopin: Barcarolle in F-sharp Major, Op. 60, mm. 4–5 (Brandus & Co. Stichvorlage, 1845). Biblioteka Jagiellońska, Kraków.

In my conversation with Seymour Bernstein about the Barcarolle, he suggested that this passage be treated with both sustain and finger pedal—a solution that would dramatically obviate the awkward voids created by the absence of pedal for the sixteenth-note figurations in the left hand:

EXAMPLE 4.29. F. Chopin: Barcarolle in F-sharp Major, Op. 60, mm. 4–5 showing possible finger pedaling as suggested by Seymour Bernstein (slurs denote holding of the pitch; note the finger substitution on C-sharp[3]).

Despite their unique resonance, 1840s Pleyels would still have exposed the voids caused by the absence of sustain pedal on the transitional sixteenth-notes. Were these separations intentional? And if so, was the adoption of finger pedaling in the accompanying motif for the opening theme of the Barcarolle a miscalculation?

Example 4.28 shows that the pedal markings propose releases that seemingly align with specific notes. Each release sign is carefully placed beneath the G-sharp of each patterned group. Analogous passages in the same Stichvorlage show equal care in indicating exact releases—a precision that Chopin introduced progressively in the 1840s, but that was not yet featured in works such as the Sonata in B Minor, published shortly before the genesis of the Barcarolle. Sadly, we are prevented from confirming an evolution in that direction: Chopin's decline in health did not allow him to write much after 1847, and we are only left wondering to what degree of refinement he would have brought the notation of releases.

It is indeed a challenge to rationalize every occurrence of pedaling in Chopin's music, even with manuscripts and early editions on hand. Chopin was by nature inconsistent: some of his manuscripts show enigmatic idiosyncrasies, occasionally proposing different pedaling in analogous passages within the same piece. One such instance is found in the Prelude in E-flat Major, Op. 28, No. 19. The following examples show measures 57–58 and 59–60 as they appear in the first print of the Breitkopf & Härtel edition:

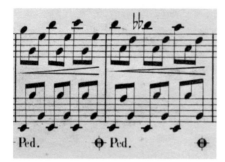

EXAMPLE 4.30a. F. Chopin: Prelude in E-flat Major, Op. 28, No. 19, mm. 51–52 (Breitkopf & Härtel edition, 1839).

EXAMPLE 4.30b. F. Chopin: Prelude in E-flat Major, Op. 28, No. 19, mm. 59–60 (Breitkopf & Härtel edition, 1839).

There is no evidently plausible explanation for Chopin's having marked these two identical instances with slightly different pedaling.[19] Further, the outcome offered by the two applications barely offers grounds for a noticeable contrast. Could the distinction have been simply an oversight on the part of Julian Fontana as he prepared the Stichvorlage that was sent to the German publisher? The Henle edition, which typically follows the first version published by Breitkopf & Härtel, adopted the pedaling of measure 52 in both instances—a version that was proposed by the Catelin edition of 1839. In the recent *New Critical Edition* of Chopin's works, Jean-Jacques Eigeldinger chose the same avenue in his revision of the preludes and refrained from mentioning this curious alternative in the critical notes.

Over time, I realized that the venture of disclosing the meaning of each pedal marking contained layers of complexity beyond any power of analysis to deduce: while composing at his Pleyel, Chopin may have been affected not only by the characteristics of the instrument itself, but also by particular sonic perspectives and necessities. The Polish pianist Carl Tausig observed that Chopin's Barcarolle should be played only in front of a single listener,[20] suggesting indirectly that at least from an emotional standpoint, perhaps even Chopin's larger forms should have not left the intimate, introspective setting of a candlelit parlor. I realized that if in my interpretation a marking adapted to what I thought might have been Chopin's aesthetic ideals, the result was inescapably affected by the concept of sound production that has been developed by modern piano schools, which focuses on the brilliance, power, and strong rhetorical diction that are needed to project satisfactorily in large concert halls. The music critic Ludwig Rellstab remarked that Chopin's sound did not possess the declamatory qualities required to make him an itinerant virtuoso. Other accounts followed: Anton Schindler reported that Chopin's style would not suit the hordes of listeners who wanted to be stupefied rather than seduced.[21] Chopin's limited sound capacity has often been ascribed to his weak constitution: he was about five feet six inches tall and in 1848 weighed about ninety-five pounds. In his last years his ill health steadily worsened, and the German pianist Stephen Heller remarked that his sound was barely audible.[22] If Chopin's sound did not have the requisite incisiveness to suit the growing demand for performances in large spaces on his beloved Pleyels, and if his works were inevitably informed by the intimate ambience that he seemed to prefer, how should I have understood them on modern instruments while playing in modern concert halls?

"[Thalberg] gets his *piano* by the pedal, not the hand",[23] Chopin reported with a touch of contempt to his friend Jas Matuszyński in a letter dated December 25, 1830. This brief description is the only account left by the composer about the left pedal, and the tone in which it was declared tells us something significant: Chopin disapproved of the habit of relying on it to produce soft sonorities. Rather, the left pedal may have been used to obtain special effects, such as the outlining of unique colors in particular passages. As Kleczyński confirms,

> Chopin frequently passed, and without transition, from the open to the soft pedal, especially in enharmonic modulation. These passages had an altogether particular charm, especially when played on Pleyel's pianofortes.[24]

Chopin made ample use of the left pedal without ever marking the then common *una corda* in his scores.[25] As he may have deemed its use largely subjective, we may assume that its implementation was a decision left to the interpreter's discretion. This approach was prevalent before Chopin's time, although Beethoven had specified the notation of the left pedal in works such as the Sonata in A-flat Major, Op. 110, which shows an unusual amount of interpretive instructions, doubled in Italian and German. The instrument that Beethoven had used in 1820 to 1821 to write this sonata was probably the piano with which the Broadwood firm gifted him in 1817. It was a triple-stringed instrument that allowed the composer to achieve different levels of sonority with the use of the left pedal. It was then that he indicated *tre corde*, three strings; *due corde*, two strings; and *una corda*, one string. As the instruments of the time were constantly evolving, this notation became obsolete within a few years, but the marking *una corda* remained to indicate the depression of the left pedal. A series of improvements enhanced sound strength and mechanical accuracy in the soft pedal, and by the 1830s on most pianos it operated essentially the way it does today. Still, the pace of change in piano manufacture was such that each performer would have probably responded differently to the use of the left pedal, depending on the instrument in question. I thought this could have been another reason why Chopin never indicated the soft pedal in his music: given the substantial differences in the way pianos reacted to its use, he may have found that marking subtle nuances with exacting notation would have created boundaries in the expressive potential of the instrument and the interpreter.

In the 1830s, Chopin introduced the markings *mezza voce* (a bel canto term that indicates a subdued tone) and *sotto voce* ("whispering" or "under one's breath"), often abbreviated as *m. v.* and *s. v.* in manuscripts and in early editions. I had overlooked the meanings of these markings, and had grown accustomed to considering them a way of indicating the presence of a particular color in the context of a soft sonority, until it occurred to me that these special sounds are usually prescribed in association with a substantial character change, regardless of the dynamic indications involved. A most vivid instance may be found in the Scherzo in B-flat Minor, Op. 31, with its drastic change of scenery from brilliant passagework to hymnlike chorale as the Trio opens:

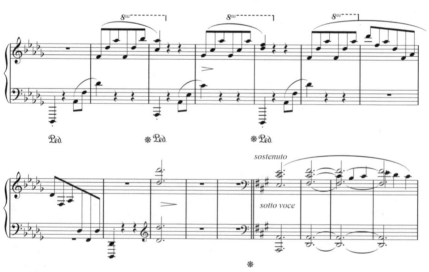

⊟ EXAMPLE 4.31. F. Chopin: Scherzo in B-flat Minor, Op. 31, mm. 253–268.

Sotto voce or *mezza voce* appears without complementary dynamic markings, and each is frequently placed in the context of a *piano* or after a diminuendo. In several mazurkas and nocturnes, their presence is often concomitant with the beginning of a new episode. In the Mazurka in A-flat Major, Op. 59, No. 2, for instance, the opening lyrical theme, marked *piano*, is exposed in a more orchestral fashion some twenty or so measures later, doubled in strength via chords in the right hand and supported by a healthy *forte*. As this second period comes to a close, a diminuendo drastically reduces the volume to a *sotto voce*, which begins the new episode. In the Nocturne in G Minor, Op. 15, no. 3, an extensive phrase of twenty-four measures is repeated almost literally. A *forte* placed at the onset of the last third of each one of the two phrases vanishes, via a diminuendo, into an implied *piano*. The second diminuendo is accompanied by an additional diminuendo for the final three measures, and concludes in a *sotto voce* that introduces a highly unstable harmonic progression which, twenty-six measures later, culminates in the dynamic climax of the nocturne.

The soft pedal creating an effect that depended largely on the colors that each individual instrument would have been able to achieve, the manner in which Chopin used it rested upon his uncommon sensitivity and inspiration, as Kleczyński's account seems to suggest. Passing from the open to the soft pedal without transition to change timbre, especially in enharmonic modulations, would have depended mostly on his extemporaneous adaptation to sound, yet I wondered whether Chopin may have hinted at this passing to the left pedal when using *sotto voce* or *mezza voce*, rather than requesting a further reduction in volume obtained with the fingers.

Instances in which one of the two markings appears at the beginning of a piece as the only dynamic indication similarly suggested a possible role for the left pedal: *mezza voce*, for example, is found in the opening measure of the Ballade in A-flat Major, Op. 47, whose evocative ascending and descending lines and captivating polyphony could be well served by this coloristic tool:

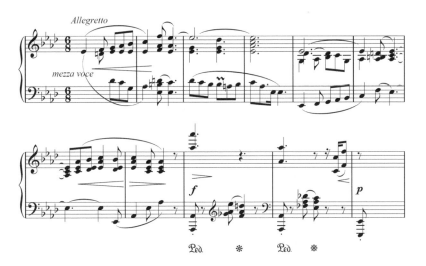

EXAMPLE 4.32. F. Chopin: Ballade in A-flat Major, Op. 47, mm. 1–11.

As I explored the opportunity of shading these passages, I was left with a question: were I to use the soft pedal, when should I release it? Chopin never marked when the effect of *mezza voce* or *sotto voce* should cease, possibly implying that in these instances the left pedal should apply to an entire phrase, or an entire section, or until a dynamic change occurs. In the Ballade in A-flat Major its release would probably coincide with the *forte* in measure 9.

It is perhaps speculative, but the marking *dolce* in Chopin's music may have also alluded to the use of the left pedal. In the second thematic group of the Ballade in F minor, Op. 52, for example, a color change obtained with the left pedal would quite aptly serve the *dolce* in measure 84, as a *piano* applies to the entire section:

EXAMPLE 4.33. F. Chopin: Ballade in F Minor, Op. 52, mm. 80–92.

The impact created by the soft pedal on Chopin's beloved Pleyels generated an unusual shift in sound quality. It was a silvery, magical resonance quite unlike anything our pianos can produce. Although this may explain why Chopin found it unacceptable that Thalberg should use the device prosaically, we are left wondering how this attitude should affect the way we use it on our modern instruments. If the effect provided by the *una corda* pedal on Chopin's pianos does not correspond to any practical application on today's instruments, should we dismiss these ideas entirely? Or should we let them guide us toward a broader vocabulary of sounds—an inventory that is enriched and expanded in its scope, and that encourages us to explore and develop refined and evocative *pianissimi*?

Many of the issues discussed in this chapter made me aware of an aspect that I now deem fundamental: the importance of referring to the original manuscripts, whenever available, to establish the veracity of what is provided in print—even in the latest scholarly editions. In many cases, viewing a passage the way the composer notated it disclosed a broad variety of nuances, from slight adjustments caused by reinterpretations to striking discrepancies generated from subjective analyses. The veiled resonance that I experienced while pedaling on 1840s Pleyels persuaded me to find a comparable effect on modern pianos; and while trying to imitate the precursory sound, I became acquainted with elements that would not otherwise have become part of my pianistic vocabulary. As the evolution of the piano and its potential show dramatic changes that inevitably affected quality, quantity and production of sound, I embraced the notion that the variables presented by modern instruments and the spaces in which we perform dictate minor adjustments—changes that we cannot entirely dismiss for the sake of an accurate reading of the score. What should prevail, ultimately, is good judgment combined with instinct and the profits of listening. Without these criteria, our reading of pedal markings can only lead to half truths.

FIVE

...OF STRETTI

*I love music passionately. And because I love it
I try to free it from barren traditions that stifle it.*

— CLAUDE DEBUSSY

Rather accidentally, the subject of this chapter took shape as I was comparing pedal markings in different editions of Chopin's Preludes, Op. 28. Open before me was the third page of the sixteenth prelude with its perilous runs, when for the first time I noticed a startling anomaly: a four-measure section marked *stretto* precedes the *sempre più animato* that leads to the inexorable ending. It is conventionally accepted that an increase in speed be applied at the sight of both signs, and that *stretto* has a more circumscribed intent; and though some performers claim that *stretto* should prescribe a purely expressive connotation— passion, agitation, rage—these are attributes that, ultimately, might incite an acceleration and lead to a similar, undifferentiated outcome.

As I eventually noticed, this curious instance is not isolated in the works of Chopin. I had grown accustomed to his sometimes idiosyncratic instructions, yet I thought the idea peculiar that a composer for whom writing was an open-ended process that involved constant revision would have blatantly overlooked a set of conspicuous redundancies in regard to tempo. Here is the passage in question:

EXAMPLE 5.1. F. Chopin: Prelude in B-flat Minor, Op. 28, No. 16, mm. 28–35.

Just as I had previously parted with the traditional reading of hairpins, I wondered whether I should have temporarily broadened the purpose of *stretto* or *sempre più animato* in the prelude by imagining that one marking or the other might refer to something other than an agogic coordinate. I began my investigation when I stumbled upon a letter that Felix Mendelssohn-Bartholdy wrote to Robert Schumann on January 10, 1835—not long before Chopin wrote the Prelude in B-flat Minor. Mendelssohn expressed his dissatisfaction about a performance of his overture *The Hebrides*, which Schumann had described unfavorably:

> It surprises me much to hear of my Overture in B minor being taken faster at the end than at the beginning. I suppose you mean after the *animato*? If so, I shall certainly adopt Sebastian Bach's practice, who hardly ever marked a *piano* or *forte* on his music. I thought a *più stretto* would hardly do well, as I referred rather to an increase of spirit, which I did not know how to indicate except by *animato*.[1]

I sensed that Mendelssohn's response to the misattribution of the term *animato* was not to be taken lightly. It supports the assertion that certain markings had begun to lose their intended connotation—to such extent that the composer, perhaps facetiously, was contemplating to return to a complete absence of interpretive directions in the score. Markings that had been chosen for their descriptive nature were becoming the subject of ambiguous interpretation. As symbols were still proliferating and composers were still wavering about their use, a consensus on their standardized meaning would not emerge for decades. The letter provided me with precious information: for Mendelssohn, the marking *stretto* conveyed an increase in speed, whereas *animato* indicated a heightened excitement in the musical material that pertains more to character than agogics. Was the *sempre più animato* in Chopin's B-flat Minor Prelude also intended to evoke an increase of spirit? And if that had been the case, should we assume that Chopin meant for *stretto* to indicate a temporary acceleration, and that what ensues should return to the original speed? Or should the extensive coda be performed at a faster pace as a result of that acceleration?

The Italian adjective *stretto* means "tight," "narrow," "drawn closer." In musical terms, specifically in reference to a fugue, *stretto* is used as a noun to define a contrapuntal device in which the subject is played against itself in a canonlike fashion. Often spaced one beat apart, successive statements of the subject are temporally offset yet intentionally overlap. At various stages in the composition, this phenomenon enhances structural climaxes by thickening their texture and underscoring their dramatic intensity. In a fugue the term fulfills its literal meaning, as the entrances are tighter, drawn closer, producing imitations that in many cases eliminate bar lines as points of reference. Johann Sebastian Bach's Fugue in C minor, BWV 871 from the second volume of the *Well-Tempered Clavier* provides an example. Here is the short subject and its tonal answer as the piece opens:

EXAMPLE 5.2a. J. S. Bach: Subject of the Fugue in C Minor, BWV 871, *Well-Tempered Clavier*, Book II, mm. 1–3.

The subject is then presented in two virtuosic *stretti*. Here is the second instance, which occurs just before the concluding measures of the piece; the different entrances are introduced one beat apart, and generally involve two interacting voices:

EXAMPLE 5.2b. J. S. Bach: Stretto in mm. 23–27 of the Fugue in C Minor, BWV 871, *Well-Tempered Clavier*, Book II, showing overlapping entrances of the subject (marked with brackets).

Material that derives from the subject is introduced by the tenor voice in measure 24 and by the soprano and alto voices in measure 26, creating the illusion of a third imitating entrance. At the height of contrapuntal intricacy, in measure 26, the subject is heard at the bass in its inverted form, its rhythmic and melodic profile slightly modified.

Stretti were commonly found in fugues written by composers who lived in the first half of the eighteenth century. Only several decades later, a musical term that shares the same etymological root and nearly the same spelling came into use: *stretta*. As a compositional tool, *stretta* was used typically to indicate a faster speed, and produced great effect at the end of an act or a significant episode in an opera. Mozart had employed this device as early as the 1780s in *Le nozze di Figaro*, and examples can be found in nineteenth-century operas as well. *Strette* are also used in orchestral works, and the last pages of Beethoven's Fifth Symphony provide an excellent illustration. In the piano literature, the concluding page of Liszt's Transcendental Etude No. 10 in F Minor is marked *stretta*, perfectly conveying the idea of the driving impetus of a radical acceleration, which brings the piece to a close.

My first conjecture in reading Mendelssohn's letter to Schumann was that the attribution of acceleration to the marking *stretto* had derived from its erroneous association with the term *stretta*. But how could that have happened? Mendelssohn must have been acquainted with the meaning of both markings and their rather different purposes. Yet, as I had speculated in regard to notations we considered in earlier chapters, it seemed to me plausible that a lack of familiarity with the nuances of the Italian language may have led German-speaking composers to apply the terms *stretto* and *stretta* arbitrarily as well. Then again Mendelssohn, who was devoted to the music of Johann Sebastian Bach and who had become versatile in counterpoint at an early age, must have understood the role of *stretti* in baroque fugues. Did composers of the first half of the nineteenth century view the two markings as interchangeable, or did *stretto* have a dual connotation?

By the time Chopin left Warsaw, at the age of twenty, the marking *stretto* was becoming a common occurrence in printed music. It was perhaps through the works of Johann Nepomuk Hummel that the young composer became acquainted with the relatively new agogic indication. Substantial parallels between Chopin's Concerti for Piano and Orchestra and Hummel's Concerti in A Minor, Op. 85 and in B Minor, Op. 89—two pieces that Chopin taught and kept in his repertoire even during his Parisian days—have been frequently drawn, and attest to the influence of the older musician. Hummel might have been the first composer to use the marking *stretto* with the purpose of indicating an increase in speed. In his Sonata in F-sharp Minor, Op. 81, written in 1819, *stretto* ostensibly brings the episodes marked *Lento* back to *Allegro*—the original, faster tempo—indicating what composers in the following decade would have most likely specified with the marking *accelerando*:

EXAMPLE 5.3. J. N. Hummel: Sonata in F-sharp Minor, Op. 81, I. Allegro, mm. 144–149.

That in Chopin's early years *stretto* expressed different degrees of agogic fluctuation is corroborated by the marking's customary appearance with other interpretive instructions such as *ritardando* or *a tempo*, placed as a reaction to the forward thrust that *stretto* was meant to produce. Consider an excerpt from the Variations in B-flat Major, Op. 12, written shortly after the composer arrived in Paris. In the second variation, the concluding measures feature a *poco stretto*, followed by a *ritenuto*:

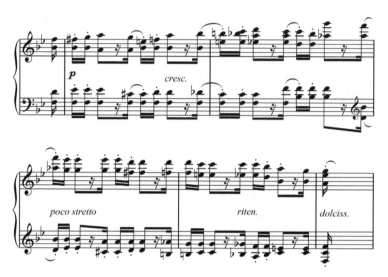

EXAMPLE 5.4. F. Chopin: Variations Brillantes sur "Je vends des Scapulaires de Ludovic," Op. 12, mm. 108–113.

Other works published by Chopin in the same period are just as rich with interpretive indications and consistently employ *stretto* to signal an acceleration. An unusual occurrence in the Mazurka in F minor, Op. 7, No. 3 shows that the marking, in measures 25 and 33, was followed by opening hairpins, perhaps indicating an agogic response to the acceleration set off by the *stretti*:

EXAMPLE 5.5. F. Chopin: Mazurka in F Minor, Op. 7, No. 3, mm. 24–40.

EXAMPLE **5.5** (*continued*)

In the second thematic group of the first movement of the Concerto in E Minor, Op. 11—written in 1829 but published in 1833 only several months after the Mazurkas, Op. 7 and three months before the Variations, Op. 12—some of the *stretti* may also be convincing as indicating an increase in speed, especially in light of the intensely lyrical material. In this passage, the musical context seems to be responsible for dictating the extent of its application, as no other markings intervene to counteract or intrude on its function:

EXAMPLE **5.6.** F. Chopin: Concerto in E Minor, Op. 11, I. Allegro maestoso, mm. 252–257.

Other interpretive instructions within the same section seem to suggest comparable intentions: *poco agitato, appassionato, con anima*, and *con fuoco* all allude to emotions that may be successfully evoked with degrees of agogic nuance in addition to varied dynamic levels.

These considerations notwithstanding, equating *stretto* with an *accelerando* did not always seem to provide an appropriate and persuasive solution as I tried to interpret the function of the marking in the works of Chopin. Its acknowledged meaning as an increase in speed in some cases appeared to be inorganic and to contradict instinctive musical sense. In the few measures that precede the recapitulation in the Mazurka in E Minor, Op. 17, No. 2, for instance, I would have applied a broadening of the material:

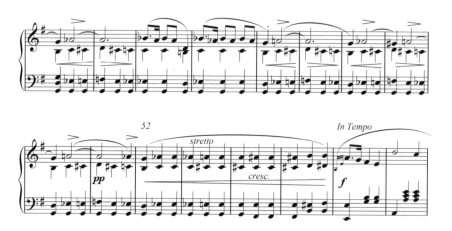

EXAMPLE 5.7. F. Chopin: Mazurka in E Minor, Op. 17, No. 2, mm. 42–57.

I felt that the opening hairpin[2] in measures 52–55 may in fact suggest a ritenuto to outline the onset of this important structural moment—an interpretive element that would contradict the idea of an acceleration. I thought it to be a curious circumstance that, if Chopin had uniformly intended for *stretto* to indicate an increase in speed, it was often prescribed in passages in which I tended to apply a decrease. One such case is found in measure 16 of the Prelude in E Minor, Op. 28, No. 4, as the climax nears:

EXAMPLE 5.8. F. Chopin: Prelude in E Minor, Op. 28, No. 4, mm. 13–21.

I always thought that the accelerando generally proposed in this passage is incompatible with the narrative of the prelude. Instead, I felt the necessity to apply a ritenuto leading to the downbeat of measure 17: doing so seemed to enhance the climax and the placement of the octave B in the bass—a strong point of reference that, I thought, had to be agogically prepared in view of its harmonic and emotional content. Mendelssohn's inclination to follow Bach's practice in providing scarce interpretive instructions came to mind as I considered the *stretto* in the Prelude in E Minor. An increase in speed seemed to invite a contradiction: most pianists bring the acceleration to an abrupt extreme for the very reason that, were no *stretto* indicated, the passage itself would probably lead to a decrease in speed. I began to suspect that perhaps the general acceptance of *stretto* as an *accelerando* may be misconstrued in these instances, and that the designation of the marking *stretta* may have affected the notion that composers and performers developed in regard to its twin marking. Is it really possible that the term has been intended erroneously in the music of Chopin for nearly two centuries? Is implementing an accelerando at the sight of the marking the result of our bending to decades of widespread traditions and conventions? Do we simply submit to the notion that Chopin must have had a reason to prescribe an acceleration whether or not it opposes musical logic?

———————— ◆▶ ————————

It was while contemplating possible meanings for the *stretto* in the Mazurka in E Minor, Op. 17, No. 2 that I observed a curious fact: the long peroration on the pedal point of G that precedes the recapitulation is perceived as originating from a metric system of two-measure patterns; then, as the marking *stretto* makes its appearance, a temporary diminution to more urgent one-measure units takes place:

⊕ **EXAMPLE 5.9.** F. Chopin: Mazurka in E Minor, Op. 17, No. 2, mm. 39–54.

🔊 EXAMPLE 5.9 (*continued*)

My observation stemmed from the more rapid harmonic shifts that accompany the measures affected by *stretto*, but also from the placement of the marking above what would have been the second measure of a two-measure group. I resolved to label this solution with the term *foreshortening*, as Chopin seems to have desired a distinct metric diminution. Eliminating the agogic coordinate for *stretto* allowed me to view the hairpin in measures 52–55 as a progressive ritenuto, which would end with the appearance of the marking *In Tempo* in measure 56. It did not take me long to identify another intriguing detail, and this one emerged as fundamental in my understanding of *stretti*. While consulting the first French edition of the Mazurka in E Minor, which was published by Pleyel in 1834 and served as the basis for the German and English editions, I noticed that the term *stretto* was placed above the second beat of measure 53, not the first beat, as it appears in some mainstream editions today. Rather than denoting a straightforward metric diminution, the marking seemed to signal a displacement of the downbeats—already announced in measures 39–40 and 43, 45, and 47—by introducing harmonic shifts that begin on the second beat of each measure:

🔊 EXAMPLE 5.10. F. Chopin: Mazurka in E Minor, Op. 17, No. 2, mm. 49–54 (metric shift outlined by dotted lines).

I immediately sensed that this discovery could have resolved the perplexity caused by passages in which *stretto* did not seem to make sense as an agogic indication. The occurrence in the Mazurka in E Minor impelled me to verify whether Chopin used the same formulas in the passage from the Prelude in B-flat Minor from Op. 28, which had prompted me to research the marking. Was the harmonic layout tightened? Was the metric system displaced? The writing confirmed it:

EXAMPLE 5.11. F. Chopin: Prelude in B-flat Minor, Op. 28, No. 16, mm. 28–35.

With the appearance of *stretto* in measure 30, the rolled chords in the left hand outline a switch from a two-beat to a one-beat unit—a diminution that is clearly demarcated by the rapid harmonic changes in the left-hand rolled chords, in opposition to the more static two-beat groups previously displayed. As the *stretto* comes to an end, measure 34 brings back the two-beat harmonic pattern. Further, beginning in measure 30, the groups of four sixteenth-notes in the right hand would better organize in patterns if shifted by half a beat (see the dotted lines above the system and the restemming of the right-hand sixteenth-notes). The long accent placed in the middle of the system on the second beat of measure 32 seems to reestablish the metric order while the diminution is still in effect.

It seems plausible that the Mazurka in E Minor was the first composition in which Chopin fully adopted this strategy, since he was writing the Mazurkas, Op. 17 while awaiting the publication of works such as the Variations, Op. 12 or the Mazurka in F Minor, Op. 7, No. 3, in which *stretti* closely identify with an *accelerando*. It is possible that Chopin had begun to consider an alternative to the agogic utilization of *stretto*, but that its new designation may have not found an immediate purpose. The placement of *stretto* in the Mazurka in E Minor, though, suggested to me that Chopin employed the marking at crucial structural moments of a piece—among them, episodes that culminate in the trio, the coda, or the recapitulation. At first I thought these convergences to be coincidental, but I later understood that the effect exerted by more rapid harmonic shifts could have been a successful compositional device for enhancing the onset of a structurally relevant section—or, as in the case of the Prelude in E Minor, for emphasizing the emotionally overwhelming climax.

Earlier in the chapter we saw that *stretto* was used in a fugue to affect the metric order of a passage. How would this application be analogous with the two cases of *stretti* that we just encountered in the Prelude in B-flat Minor and the Mazurka in E Minor? Just as the entrances of the subject in a fugue are drawn closer to one another, heightening the tension of the musical material, the use of the marking in these works seems to indicate an increase in excitement created by a greater harmonic conciseness, along with the displacement of predictable metric points of reference. In Bach's Fugue in C Minor, which we analyzed in examples 5.2a and 5.2b, the perception of metric order comprises two-beat units. This outline narrows to single beats once the *stretto* is introduced, each entrance drawing the listener's attention to a design that departs from the expected metric pattern. This finds a remarkable resonance in Chopin's Mazurka in E Minor and Prelude in B-flat Minor. Although a change in the metric perception does not exclude the possibility of an increase in speed, my impression is that Chopin would have indicated an agogic coordinate with different markings, such as *accelerando* or *stringendo*. In the case of the B-flat Minor Prelude, perhaps a prolongation of the *sempre più animato* as an agogic indication starting four measures earlier would have sufficed.

•─────•◆▸•─────•

Written between 1836 and 1837, the Scherzo in B-flat Minor, Op. 31 displays a *stretto* that visibly represents Chopin's obsessive quest for metric, harmonic, and structural perfection. The marking affects the eight measures 740–47 in the vigorous coda, whose central organization relies on groups of four measures and their two-measure subgroups:

🔊 **EXAMPLE 5.12.** F. Chopin: Scherzo in B-flat Minor, Op. 31, mm. 724–755.

The appearance of the *stretto* signals a tighter harmonic organization in two-measure groups and a transitory metric shift—both successfully enhancing the onset of the energy-driven closing section, in which the regular metric pattern of four measures resumes.

In note 9 of chapter 2 (pages 241–242), I mention the presence of dynamic and agogic accents and their function in the context of metric order. A dynamic accent is a louder sound applied to a note or chord; an agogic accent is a stress that prolongs its duration. Both kinds of accents greatly inform our approach to pulse, rhythm and speed, prominently affecting our interpretations. Expounding on their role at this point seems pertinent, as metric organization and the possible deviations from its regularity within a passage can rely on both kinds of accents. While listening to a piece, we identify its meter by aurally perceiving critical stresses that are assigned to specific beats. For example, we understand that the meter being used is 2/4 because a special emphasis is given to the first of each group of two beats. Likewise, 3/4 or 3/8 will be clarified by a stress on the first of each group of three beats. By necessity, a shift in metric order relies heavily on dynamic or agogic emphasis, or both, since the only way to make new points of reference intelligible is through their accentuation. In the passage illustrated in example 5.12, the metric shift caused by the *stretto* will succeed only if the performer accentuates the downbeat of measure 741 and avoids an emphasis on the downbeat of measure 740, giving the illusion that an extra measure was added to the preceding four-measure group. The downbeat of measure 748 will have to be given dynamic precedence over the downbeat of measure 747 if the listener is to recognize the return of the regular metric system.

During the crucial winter of 1838 spent in Majorca, Chopin completed the Ballade in F Major, Op. 38 and the Scherzo in C-sharp Minor, Op. 39—two major works whose *stretti* reveal a metric organization that strongly resembles the one in the Scherzo in B-flat Minor. The *stretto* placed shortly before the recapitulation of the Scherzo, Op. 39 is followed by an *accelerando*:

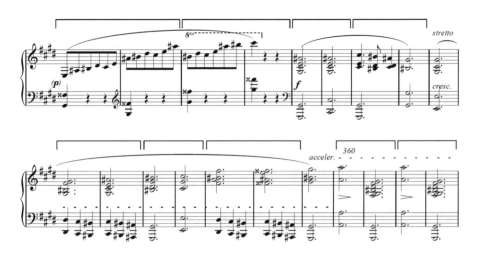

⊕ **EXAMPLE 5.13.** F. Chopin: Scherzo in C-sharp Minor, Op. 39, mm. 344–373.

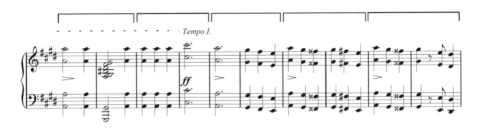

🔊 EXAMPLE 5.13 *(continued)*

In measure 360, as the accelerando has already begun to take effect, the accents placed in the middle of the system seem to specify the return of the original pattern. One significant element, which I had not noticed when I first began to study the scherzo, convinced me of the metric validity of this *stretto*: had Chopin intended for the marking to represent an increase in speed, why would it have been necessary to overlap its ending with the beginning of the accelerando in measure 359?

The *stretti* encountered in the Ballade in F Major, Op. 38 similarly present a circumstance that, in my mind, confirms their metric legitimacy: sudden changes of mood in measures 108 and 133 are signaled by the marking *stretto, più mosso*. Example 5.14 shows the one that begins in measure 133:

🔊 EXAMPLE **5.14.** F. Chopin: Ballade in F Major, Op. 38, mm. 130–137.

The writing quickly switches from a rocking siciliana to an imperious call. The *stretto* shifts the metric organization, temporarily reallocating the beginning of the one-measure patterns to the second beat of each measure. As in the Prelude in B-flat Minor or the Scherzo in C-sharp Minor, this *stretto* is unusual, because it appears next to a relevant interpretive instruction—*più mosso*. Were both markings read agogically, they would not necessarily express a redundancy, as different coordinates are implied—the *più mosso* indicates a sudden faster speed; and the *stretto* an increase in speed. Yet many performers do not accelerate at all but instinctively broaden the end of this passage before the *fortissimo* in measure 136. The *stretto* is often ignored, perhaps because an *accelerando* in addition to a faster speed is perceived as an unreasonable interpretive direction. In some cases, it is the *più mosso* to be disregarded, and the only coordinate considered is a progressive acceleration. An ingenious adaptation of the passage is found in one of the overly edited versions from the turn of the twentieth century, in which the marking *stretto* was moved to the previous measure to imply a brief accelerando to the *più mosso*.

In the interest of clarity, I have presented instances in which *stretto* seems to indicate a metric irregularity that finds its logic by negotiating the organizational system within strong and weak beats of a measure, or within patterned groups of measures. Such a plan would not seem completely intuitive in the section that precedes the coda of the Ballade in F minor, Op. 52, in which the highly chromatic content features quick, unpredictable harmonic shifts:

EXAMPLE 5.15. F. Chopin: Ballade in F Minor, Op. 52, mm. 195–202.

That this *stretto* does not represent an agogic direction is perhaps confirmed by the position of the marking, notated above the last eighth-note of measure 198. Had Chopin intended an acceleration, I thought, it seemed unlikely that he would have needed to be so specific; rather, it was apparent that relying on the availability of a certain number of beats, beginning from the anacrusis of measure 198, was a vital element in reorganizing the metric system. At first, I identified a possible role for this *stretto* in the abandonment of strong and weak beats—a layout that would not design any specific new metric system. But in time I noticed that a binary subdivision from duple meter (6/8) to triple meter (3/4) would outline a hemiola, successfully contributing to a sense of disorientation and emotionally reinforcing the arrival of C major at the end of the progression:

EXAMPLE 5.16. F. Chopin: Ballade in F Minor, Op. 52, mm. 195–202 (the brackets outline the hemiola caused by the stretto).

Perhaps not coincidentally, this modification[3] almost consistently underlines the ascending and descending minor seconds in the left hand, following the basic intervallic motif of the main theme of the ballade.

I have always resisted the idea of the accelerando conventionally heard in this episode. In the hands of some performers, an excessive increase in speed at times may compromise an otherwise convincing interpretation. I realized that reconsidering the role of *stretto* in this passage did not imply that agogic flexibility should have been completely dismissed. Were an acceleration felt as a necessary interpretive element, however, the sense of acceleration that is determined by the hemiola could suffice—the stability of the duple meter that outlines the entire composition being for the first time interrupted, its narrative attributes violently truncated. At the same time, were the *stretto* observed strictly as affecting the metric distribution of these measures, broadening the entire passage may be considered a plausible solution—an approach that would probably enhance its climactic importance more than an abrupt acceleration would, but that might also leave quite a few pianists perplexed.

From the late 1830s, Chopin consistently began to employ *stretto* in the context of carefully planned metric schemes that followed patterns based on multiples of two or four measures. This approach to phrase structure had been illustrated decades earlier by theorists such as Joseph Riepel (1709–1782), an Austrian composer and violinist. His five chapters of the *Anfangsgruende zur musikalische Setzkunst* (Fundamentals of Musical Composition), published between 1752 and 1768 in the form of dialogues between a teacher and his pupil, had become a highly popular essay on composition in the second half of the eighteenth century. The appearance of its first volume coincided with the treatises on performance by Johann Joachim Quantz, Carl Philipp Emanuel Bach, and Leopold Mozart, all published between 1752 and 1756. Riepel codified what theorists of the nineteenth and twentieth centuries would eventually label as *Taktordnung* (loosely translated, "systematic metric organization")—a term that describes the metro-rhythmic order of phrases, which are to be organized in groups of four measures. According to these theorists, among them Hugo Riemann, a phrase should never be shorter than this established order. This structure was also subject to its harmonic content: according to Riepel, each group had to be outlined by a strong concluding cadence. It is in the music of Mozart that we find perfect representations of this principle. Long phrases are often organized in two subphrases, the first one of which is expressed in the form of two smaller subdivisions. The main theme from his Fantasie in D Minor, K. 397 aptly demonstrates it:

EXAMPLE 5.17. W. A. Mozart: Fantasie in D Minor, K. 397, mm.12–19.

EXAMPLE 5.17 (*continued*)

This *Ordnung* was most likely instilled in Mozart at an early age by his father, Leopold, who displayed a certain formal rigidity in regard to phrasing and its harmonic implications. Chopin undeniably longed to achieve Mozart's admirable sense of architecture and displayed a comparable preoccupation in matters of proportion and length of phrases. Early in his life, Chopin had attested to his interest in Mozart when he used the duet "Là ci darem la mano" from *Don Giovanni* as a theme for his Variations, Op. 2. Indeed, Chopin expressed the desire to have Mozart's Requiem in D Minor, K. 626 performed at his funeral, so close was the composer to his heart. Too close, perhaps, considering that Chopin never assigned Mozart's works to his own pupils. Some have speculated that it was a means of preventing them from compromising the beauty of the master's compositions. Kleczyński recounts that in his teaching, Chopin imposed basic rules for phrasing, claiming, for instance, that a phrase should never be less than four measures long, especially in fast-paced movements.[4] With some reasonable exceptions in which the composer introduced surprising irregularity, the metric organization of phrases in his writing faithfully follows the simplicity of that rigorous system. I wondered whether the strong emotional bond that he felt toward traditional Polish dances such as the mazur and the polonaise, whose metro-rhythmic systems by necessity adhere to the same design, unconsciously affected this intrinsic characteristic as well. Consider the opening phrase of the first mazurka that Chopin published:

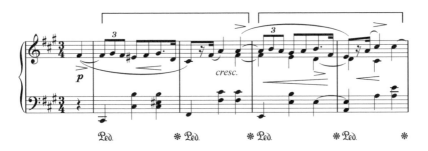

EXAMPLE 5.18. F. Chopin: Mazurka in F-sharp Minor, Op. 6, No. 1, mm. 1–9.

EXAMPLE 5.18 (*continued*)

Chopin's punctilious craftsmanship in structural matters is epitomized by the final measures of the Nocturne in E-flat Major, Op. 55, No. 2. Here, Chopin prolonged the chord in measure 66 by tying it to the downbeat of the following measure—an expedient, I believe, that was used to preserve the four-measure periods of the metric layout:

EXAMPLE 5.19. F. Chopin: Nocturne in E-flat Major, Op. 55, No. 2, mm. 62–67.

Had metric consistency not been a concern, Chopin could easily have placed a fermata over the chord in measure 66, instead of extending its value.

I soon realized that the influence exerted on his compositional process by this sense of proportion became increasingly prominent as Chopin developed an affinity for the preludes and fugues of Bach's *Well-Tempered Clavier*—a cycle that played an essential role in his life. Reportedly, on his journey to Majorca, this was the only score that the composer cared to bring with him, along with some staff paper and manuscripts of his own unfinished works.[5] Chopin professed a sense of great devotion toward Johann Sebastian Bach, a love that probably had been instilled in his youth by his early mentor Adalbert Žiwny. A Czech musician (violinist, pianist, and composer), Žiwny displayed an immense respect for the master and taught in the German tradition, most likely following the precepts elaborated by Bach's son Carl Philipp Emanuel. Chopin knew all forty-eight preludes and fugues of Bach's *Well-Tempered Clavier* from memory: we learn from her correspondence that Friedericke Müller witnessed him perform fourteen of them after one of her morning lessons[6]—a feat that only a few pianists of the time would have felt compelled to accomplish or been able to achieve.

In Majorca, Chopin spent weeks in isolation, the *Well-Tempered Clavier* being the most available musical solace on the inhospitable island. A piano, provided by Pleyel, was scheduled to be delivered after his arrival, but the plan did not unfold as expected. The long lead in the shipment caused a delay, and the strict island customs literally held the piano hostage, forcing Chopin to rent a small, unreliable instrument that compromised his ability to write. Only several weeks before returning to France did Chopin finally receive his piano—a small consolation, considering the amount of music that must have occupied his mind. In the absence of a good instrument on which to compose, Chopin had the company of the *Well-Tempered Clavier*. A detailed study of it away from the piano might have corroborated, among other things, the primary role of metric organization within phrases and how *stretti* affected it. Although this concept had been instilled in Chopin in the early stages of his training, it must have taken hold with even more tenacity after he so closely explored the perfectly crafted language of Bach's preludes and fugues.

Perhaps not coincidentally, upon returning from Majorca in 1839, Chopin embarked on an exhaustive study of Luigi Cherubini's *Course de contrepoint et de fugue* and Jean-Georges Kastner's *Théorie abregée de contrepoint et de la fugue*, published in Paris in 1835 and 1839, respectively. An incomplete Canon in F Minor and a Fugue in A Minor remain from his exercises in these forms. That his compositional procedure was affected by Cherubini's and Kastner's treatises after that time is confirmed by the extensive employment of canons and fugal elements in pieces such as the Mazurka in C-sharp Minor, Op. 50, No. 3; the Ballade in F Minor, Op. 52; the Sonata in B Minor, Op. 58; the Mazurka in C-sharp Minor, Op. 63, No. 3; and the Sonata in G Minor for Cello and Piano, Op. 65. Cherubini and Kastner did not reveal anything entirely innovative to Chopin, yet substantiated an intimation, most likely gathered at an earlier stage—that adopting linear counterpoint would eliminate harmonic tensions.

We saw that Chopin at first had used *stretto* to indicate acceleration, following the manner in which Hummel and other composers of the time employed it. The *stretti* encountered in the music written during his Warsaw years or at the beginning of his experience in Paris strongly seem to suggest that. Still in the early 1830s, Chopin wavered between the marking's agogic and metric application. Earlier, I illustrated a case in the first movement of the Concerto for Piano and Orchestra in

E Minor, Op. 11 in which *stretto* may have had agogic validity (example 5.6). The idea of foreshortening that I described earlier was in its primordial stages, perhaps not completely codified. In time, a more careful analysis led me to notice that the marking as Chopin used it in this movement may have indicated a germinal form of diminution of the metric system. The second thematic block shows some cases in which this logical operation was perfectly observed:

EXAMPLE 5.20. F. Chopin: Concerto in E Minor, Op. 11, I. Allegro maestoso, mm. 245–257.

In other cases, the mathematical proportions were not completely respected, the phrases being suddenly shortened and subjected to irregular subgroups. The measures that follow immediately the ones just illustrated show this asymmetry:

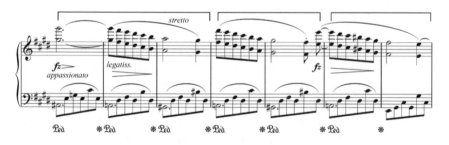

EXAMPLE 5.21. F. Chopin: Concerto in E Minor, Op. 11, I. Allegro maestoso, mm. 258–264.

This second theme ends a few measures later with a foreshortening of the already diminished meter, switching from two- to one-measure groups:

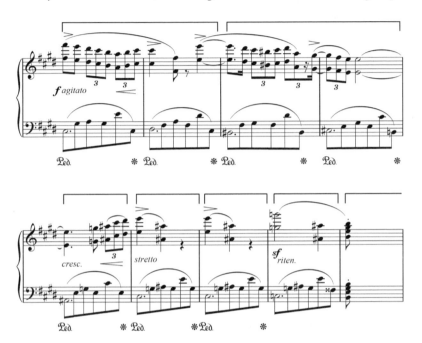

EXAMPLE 5.22. F. Chopin: Concerto in E Minor, Op. 11, I. Allegro maestoso, mm. 267–275.

In the mid-1830s, Chopin continued to employ the marking in accordance with this open approach. Nonetheless, while in Majorca, the composer must have come to a resolution concerning the proper use of the term *stretto*. Over the years, markings such as *accelerando* (usually abbreviated as *accel.*) had been introduced to refer explicitly to an increase in speed. Although *accelerando* had a univocal meaning, *stretto* possibly remained the object of ambiguous interpretations, because of its similarity to the term *stretta* and because of its agogic attribution in the works of contemporaneous composers. As I previously mentioned, after Chopin arrived in Paris his writing began to advocate a more economical use of notation, thus eliminating symbols and indications that he had previously believed to be essential contributions to the performer's interpretation. Not coincidentally, this reconsideration of his notation—which involved agogic, inflective and articulatory markings—started after the composer came to the realization of the demand for his works on the European market. *Stretto* may have fallen into the extended process of refinement of notational tools, and the trip to Majorca seems to have determined a rupture with the tradition brought to prominence by Hummel in the second decade of the nineteenth century. The influence that Bach exerted on Chopin resulted in his concluding that *stretto* should exclusively have metric designation.

Born in 1843—the year in which Chopin published the Nocturnes, Op. 55 and the Mazurkas, Op. 56 and was writing the Berceuse, Op. 57 and the Sonata in B minor, Op 58—Edvard Grieg gained wide recognition in his mid twenties through his Concerto for Piano and Orchestra in A Minor, Op. 16, which achieved iconic status as one of the most popular piano concerti of all times. Yet Grieg's career as a composer for the piano was dominated by small-scale compositions that belonged to the legacy of the miniature, initiated by Chopin and perpetuated by most composers during the second half of the nineteenth century. At his best in this form, over the span of more than three decades Grieg wrote dozens of short works titled *Lyric Pieces*. Some of these beautifully conceived pages feature passages in which *stretto* ostensibly indicates an increase in speed. In *Melodie*, from the fourth cycle, Op. 47, the writing (undoubtedly inspired by the opening section of Chopin's Ballade in F Major, Op. 38) continues unperturbed in its patterned figuration when a *stretto* makes its appearance in measure 21, following the *più mosso* of measure 17:

EXAMPLE 5.23. E. Grieg: *Melodie* in A Minor, Op. 47, No. 3, mm. 13–24.

As no difference in the writing was adopted in this passage and analogous ones, we can reasonably assume that the *stretto* refers to an agogic thrust—an increase in emotional intensity that leads to a vehement climax a few measures later.

Earlier examples in Grieg's music point to a different approach. In the first movement of the Piano Concerto in A Minor, Op. 16, we encounter *stretti* that seem to suggest a modification of the metric system:

EXAMPLE 5.24. E. Grieg: Concerto in A Minor, Op. 16, I. Allegro molto moderato, mm. 62–70.

Although agogic flexibility is only to be expected in such a passionate moment in the piece, pianists accelerate these measures to such extremes that one is left to wonder whether Grieg really intended for this passage to be subject to such displays of virtuosity, which often disfigure its melodic profile. The idea of a metric displacement, from triplets to hemiolas that comprise two-note gestures (hence outlining the chromatic groups), seems to me musically more coherent than a sudden rush. In confirmation of this approach, the opening hairpin in measure 65 might indicate a broadening of tempo to the highest note of the ascending and descending gesture. Is it coincidental that the *stretto* in this early work by Grieg is so closely reminiscent of Chopin's treatment? Or was the term used with a different connotation, interchangeably with *stringendo* or, as we saw earlier, with *stretta*, because of a shared etymological root?

In the second half of the nineteenth century, Chopin received worldwide recognition. Along with Beethoven, he was the most featured composer in recital programs. It does not come as a surprise that composers such as Grieg were affected by his vocabulary. Yet, among nineteenth-century composers, Chopin was undoubtedly alone in using *stretto* with the intention of designing a temporary diminution and displacement of the metric system. Was the absence of a consistent legacy for this innovation perhaps the cause of its reinterpretation? If so, it would explain why composers in the second half of the nineteenth century borrowed the marking but possibly confused it with similar terms such as *stretta* or *stringendo*, elaborating individual approaches to its use, oblivious to its nuances. Chopin might have been the most original composer of his time: not only did his harmonic invention affect his contemporaries and future generations of composers; his pioneering conceptions of sound and technique were also fundamental contributions to the development of a pianistic language that broke with old traditions and opened new perspectives. And yet all these revolutionary elements were firmly grounded in the past, finding strength in compositional principles that were deemed essential in the eighteenth century. The truth about Chopin's *stretti* may lie in the notions imparted by his venerated predecessors, Bach and Mozart.

SIX

...OF RHYTHMIC VALUES

This morning I took out a comma
and this afternoon I put it back in again.

— OSCAR WILDE

The substantial corpus of recordings that Artur Rubinstein made in the 1930s secured his reputation as one of the most admired Chopin interpreters—a status that remained virtually unchallenged for decades. Rubinstein captured the major works of the Polish composer on record several times, and it is intriguing to observe the evolution of an artist whose life spanned the first use of wax cylinders and the introduction of modern recording technologies. The difference between two of his recordings of the Polonaise-Fantaisie, Op. 61, made thirty years apart, in 1934 and 1964, is indeed remarkable: the easy virtuosity of earlier years transmuted into a more contemplative reading that emphasized textural and melodic richness. As a teenager, ever since my first experience with both recordings and their distinctive approaches, I was nonetheless perplexed by the way Rubinstein resolved the rhythmic intricacies presented by the demanding pages that conclude the piece. The labored sketches and Stichvorlagen that led to the final version of this closing section consistently show that Chopin aligned the sixteenth-notes with the third note of each triplet:

EXAMPLE **6.1.** F. Chopin: Polonaise-Fantaisie in A-flat Major, Op. 61, mm. 242–245
(Breitkopf & Härtel Stichvorlage, 1846).

Despite Rubinstein's great interpretive conviction, his reading is in opposition
to the unmistakable configuration in the Stichvorlage. In some cases, he placed
the sixteenth-note after the third note of the triplet:

EXAMPLE **6.2a.** F. Chopin: Polonaise-Fantaisie in A-flat Major, Op. 61, m. 244, beat 3 as it appears
in the Breitkopf & Härtel Stichvorlage (left) and as it is interpreted by Artur Rubinstein (right).

At other times, when the left hand displays dotted eighth-notes, the triplets in
the right hand lose their definition and become syncopated sixteenth-/eighth-/
sixteenth-note figurations:

EXAMPLE **6.2b.** F. Chopin: Polonaise-Fantaisie in A-flat Major, Op. 61, m. 264 as it appears
in the Breitkopf & Härtel Stichvorlage (left) and as it is interpreted by Artur Rubinstein (right).

The misalignment between the sixteenth-note and the third note of the triplet is a consistent feature in the first edition of the Polonaise-Fantaisie that was published by Breitkopf & Härtel in 1846. This version remained in fashion well into the twentieth century. I assume that Rubinstein used the Breitkopf & Härtel edition, which possibly explains his effort to desynchronize the two rhythms:

EXAMPLE 6.3. F. Chopin: Polonaise-Fantaisie in A-flat Major, Op. 61, mm. 242–250 (Breitkopf & Härtel edition, 1846).

That Breitkopf & Härtel did not strictly follow Chopin's Stichvorlage is a rather puzzling circumstance, I thought, as the editors employed by the German firm during the 1840s generally reproduced the composer's Stichvorlagen with unprecedented accuracy. What I found even more unusual is that Rubinstein adopted these displacements exclusively where the distribution of values is pianistically feasible or, as in example 6.2b, when the writing could be construed as rhythmically ambiguous. "Rubinstein was a performer, not an academic," some will contend. Much as I appreciated his immense contribution as an artist, on the other hand I could not dismiss a number of publications that began to appear in the first half of the twentieth century and that contained testimonials by Chopin's associates and pupils. The essays provided an insight into basic principles of performance practice and, by clear inference, illuminated the intentions of the composer. With the commemoration of the hundredth anniversary of Chopin's death in 1949, the Paderewski edition launched a project that for the first time would include his complete works, with critical notes that highlighted the numerous discrepancies found in the first editions—though at times in a slightly selective and arbitrary way. In the case of the Polonaise-Fantaisie the Paderewski edition followed Chopin's manuscripts and showed the correct alignment between figurations, but I presumed that Rubinstein may have never been exposed to these publications—or that he was simply indifferent to scholarly readings.

•◄●►•

The interaction of dotted rhythms and triplets was discussed in the late seventeenth century by composers and theoreticians, starting presumably with Nicolas Gigault (1627–1707), who devoted attention to this interpretive element in his *Livre de musique dedié à la Très Sainte Vierge* (1683) and the *Livre de musique pour l'orgue* (1685). During this time, dotted rhythms offered manifold possibilities without imposing rigid exactness, as the dot entailed an increase in value of unspecified length, generally dictated by the context. Since a performer was responsible for identifying the character of a piece or section, dotted figurations would have been inflected with varied emphases. The value of the dotted note could have been increased (overdotting) or decreased (underdotting). If the character was solemn, as in the French style, overdotting would have been implemented (the notation of the double dot had not yet been introduced, and a dotted note out of necessity assumed its role). If a passage prescribed a tender temperament, underdotting would have reduced the value of otherwise excessively pronounced rhythmic emphases. Underdotting was frequently used in the context of a quick tempo that employed a patterned figuration of triplets, and the smaller value of the dotted figuration would have been assimilated with the third note of the triplet—an occurrence not uncommon in the music of eighteenth-century composers.

In his third revised version of his *Essay on the True Art of Playing Keyboard Instruments*, published in 1787, Carl Philipp Emanuel Bach observed:

> Now that triplets have come increasingly into use in common time or 4/4 time, as well as in 2/4 and 3/4, many pieces have made their appearance, which could with greater convenience be notated 12/8, 9/8 or 6/8.[1]

Added to the *Essay* nearly four decades after the death of Carl Philipp Emanuel's father, Johann Sebastian, this excerpt allowed me to gather illuminating details and expound on the role of dotted figurations throughout the eighteenth century, as follows:

1. Eighth-note triplets were progressively being introduced as a regular feature in time signatures such as 2/4, 3/4 or 4/4, and were already common in compound meters such as 3/8, 6/8, 9/8, or 12/8 because each beat normally prescribed three subdivisions.

2. A dotted figuration was employed in the context of a compound meter to indicate a time ratio of 2 + 1, because dotted figurations afforded that flexibility.

3. Despite the increasing use of triplets in regular meters, a quarter-/eighth-note figuration had not yet been introduced in those time signatures: dotted figurations were already providing a valid alternative, hence making the quarter-/eighth-note notation superfluous.

For these reasons, if the writing required frequent dotted figurations (what we read today as quarter-/eighth-note figurations), regular time signatures were more conveniently used to entail compound meters. In the Gigue from Johann Sebastian Bach's French Suite in D Minor, BWV 812, for example, the much-used dotted eighth-/sixteenth-note figuration refers to a quarter-/eighth-note triplet that informs the fundamental motif of this fuguelike movement:

EXAMPLE 6.4a. J. S. Bach: Subject of the Gigue from the French Suite in D Minor, BWV 812, mm. 1–2, in Bach's original notation.

A performer would have deduced such transformation of the rhythmic material, because a gigue generally prescribed the use of a compound meter. In other words, the performer would have intuitively underdotted and reconfigured the original values in 12/8 to represent faithfully the character of the dance:

EXAMPLE **6.4b.** J. S. Bach: Subject of the Gigue from the French Suite in D Minor, BWV
812, mm. 1–2, as it would be rhythmically interpreted according to Carl Philipp Emanuel
Bach's instruction.

Further, if two notes were to be played against a triplet, rather than creating
a cross-rhythm between the two, the performer would have been responsible for
assimilating the second note with the one of the remaining two in the triplet that
provided a consonance. A passage familiar to many, and which might be plausibly
affected by this notion, is found in Johann Sebastian Bach's Fugue in D Minor
from the second volume of the *Well-Tempered Clavier*:

EXAMPLE **6.5a.** J. S. Bach: Beats three and four, measure 9, from the Fugue in D Minor,
BWV 875, *Well-Tempered Clavier*, Book II, as it was notated by the composer.

This principle by no means applies to music after the baroque era, yet in the
Fugue in D Minor modern interpreters do not normally follow the reconfiguration,
which would conceivably turn the third beat of measure 9—and possibly, by
contextual association, the fourth beat—into triplets. Although the Fugue in
D Minor is conventionally assigned a somber character, this simple rule could
transform it into a gigue:[2]

🔊 **EXAMPLE 6.5b.** J. S. Bach: Beats three and four, measure 9, from the Fugue in D Minor, *Well-Tempered Clavier*, Book II, as they would be rhythmically interpreted according to Carl Philipp Emanuel Bach's instruction.

Carl Philipp Emanuel Bach illustrated these basic practices in his *Essay* with a diagram that provides indisputable evidence concerning the object of our discussion in this chapter—the assimilation of different figurations:

EXAMPLE 6.6. Carl Philipp Emanuel Bach's illustration of how two notes against three should be executed, as found in his *Essay on the True Art of Playing Keyboard Instruments*.

These notions seemed to apply perfectly in works such as Johann Sebastian Bach's Menuet from the Partita in D Major, BWV 828; the Tempo di Gavotta from the Partita in E Minor, BWV 830; and the Fuga from the Toccata in G Minor, BWV 915. If Johann Sebastian had used these notational expedients in the 1720s, and if his son Carl Philipp Emanuel confirmed that the practice was still in use in 1787, when the third edition of his *Essay* was published, I gathered that the music that was written throughout the eighteenth century would have generally conformed to the same rules. Consider, for example, the convenience provided by this notation in the first movement of Franz Joseph Haydn's Sonata in C Major, Hob. XVI:35, composed in 1779:

EXAMPLE 6.7. F. J. Haydn: Sonata in C Major, Hob. XVI:35, I. Allegro con brio, mm. 26–28.

Occurrences in the works of Haydn, Salieri, Mozart, Clementi, and other composers of the time confirm that the process of using the values that best approximate an alignment—in case there are no exact values to create one—was a universally accepted aspect of their musical language. Composers such as Beethoven, Weber, and Schubert absorbed and employed rhythmic homogenization as the only notational device that could specify quarter-/eighth-note or eighth-/sixteenth-note figurations against patterned triplets in regular meters. The character of a piece or its fundamental pulse did not seem to set any particular limitation: underdotting was used equally in fast-paced movements, as the excerpt from Haydn's Sonata illustrates in example 6.7, and in slow movements such as the Adagio cantabile from Beethoven's Sonata in C Minor, Op. 13 (1798) or the Andante from Weber's Sonata in A-flat Major, Op. 39 (1816). In 1828, only a few months before his premature death, Schubert was still applying this strategy in the final movement of the Sonata in B-flat Major, D. 960:

EXAMPLE 6.8. F. Schubert: Sonata in B-flat Major, D. 960, IV. Allegro, ma non troppo, mm. 185–193.

Even taking into account the expediency of a dotted eighth-/sixteenth-note against a triplet figure in the context of a binary subdivision, witnessing the practice in Chopin's Polonaise-Fantaisie—nearly a century after the death of Johann Sebastian Bach and about six decades after Carl Philipp Emanuel Bach revised his *Essay*— might come as a surprise. In the mid-1840s, quarter-/eighth-note figurations to imply compound groups in regular meters were still to become a widespread device and were conventionally indicated by using the assimilation of different values. There were exceptions, however: in 1838 Chopin had used eighth-/sixteenth-note figurations as triplets in the opening Prelude from Op. 28:

EXAMPLE 6.9. F. Chopin: Prelude in C Major, Op. 28, No. 1, m.1 (Catelin Stichvorlage, 1838).

This is the only instance in the works of Chopin, yet he was not the first composer to employ the device: the rare instances of quarter-/eighth-notes that indicate triplets in *Norma* (1831) by Vincenzo Bellini (1801–1835) preceded the Prelude in C Major only by several years:

EXAMPLE 6.10. V. Bellini: *Norma*, excerpt from final scene.

An analysis of the first printed version of *Norma* in its reduction for piano revealed that dotted figurations in compound meters were subject to homogenization—an alignment that the engravers of the time often applied systematically. I was interested in knowing why Bellini found it necessary to employ both figurations in the same context. Did marking a distinction between dotted-eighth-/sixteenth-note and quarter-/eighth-note intend to signal an anomaly? Did the dotted figure specify a stronger rhythmic enunciation (a double dot), which could be identified only by recognizing its contextual function when it was placed alongside quarter-/eighth-note figurations? While perusing the score of *Norma*, I realized that Bellini did not use double-dotted figurations in compound meters. Although at a germinal stage, was Bellini's effort symptomatic of a change of attitude in the evolution of rhythmic notation? Was his attempt to eliminate possible misinterpretations partly responsible for modifying a tradition that had been in place for decades?

—————————◄●►—————————

Chopin expressed great admiration for Bellini, whom he met in Paris in 1831. Although the premature death of the Italian composer prevented the two from developing a long-lasting friendship, Chopin always felt drawn to the sheer beauty of Bellini's melodic invention. A fascinating circumstance brought the two composers together, and might be of some relevance in our investigation: In 1837, his celebrity on the rise, Chopin was commissioned by the Princess Christina Belgiojoso-Trivulzio (1808–1871) to write a variation on "Suoni la tromba" from Bellini's last opera, *I puritani*. Franz Liszt, Carl Czerny, Sigismond Thalberg, Johann Peter Pixis, and Henri Herz were challenged with the same task. Liszt ultimately assembled the six variations; composed an Introduction, transitional material and a Finale; and titled the work *Hexaméron*.[3] Here is how Tobias Haslinger published Chopin's variation,[4] which appeared in Vienna in 1839:

EXAMPLE 6.11. F. Chopin: Variation in E Major from *Hexaméron*, mm.1–2 (Haslinger edition, 1839).

Thalberg, Czerny, and Liszt also used 4/4 as a time signature and homogenized the two figurations. Herz chose to notate his variation in 12/8 instead, because of the predominant use of compound groups of six sixteenth-notes. The transitional material that Liszt placed after Chopin's variation (and which he also used earlier, in the Introduction) switches seamlessly between 4/4 to an implied 12/8, showing a rather casual treatment in the interpolation. It was this remarkable degree of notational freedom that led me to the inevitable correlation between the adaptability in the treatment of rhythmic values and the agogic flexibility that I classified in the early chapters of this book—a higher degree of freedom that pertained to the expression of sentiments and that abandoned preconceived notions about appropriateness of style and sound. This freedom, I realized, could be revealed only by reconsidering the literal reproduction of the printed page to which I had been so long accustomed.

——— ‹•›· ———

If homogenizing different rhythmic profiles by underdotting was still the norm during Chopin's lifetime, I speculated whether the first movement from Beethoven's Sonata in C-sharp Minor, Op. 27, No. 2, written some nine years before Chopin's birth, should conceivably imply an assimilation of the two figures:

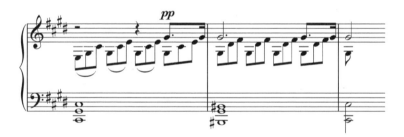

EXAMPLE 6.12. L. van Beethoven: Sonata in C-sharp Minor, Op. 27, No. 2, I. Adagio sostenuto, mm. 5–7.

We are all familiar with the displacement of the sixteenth-notes as the second half of the third note of the triplets in the enunciation of this theme, but after witnessing the many instances of equalization in works that were written well after this sonata, I entertained the thought that Beethoven may have intended an alignment between the two values. While learning the piece in my teenage years, I spelled out the three-against-four cross-rhythm and acquired independence in the execution of a formula that is frequently encountered in the piano repertoire. In time I sensed that my imposition of exactness may have been excessive, but I would have never imagined that the assimilation of the two figures could have been a possibility.

Shortly after considering this unpredictable twist in the opening movement of the "Moonlight" Sonata, I returned to a text that I had not consulted for some time—the *Vollständige theoretisch-practische Pianoforte-Schule* (Complete Theoretical and Practical Piano Forte School), Op. 500 by Carl Czerny. The second volume of this fascinating method comprises brief analyses of some of Beethoven's more substantial piano works, and the paragraph that Czerny devoted to the first movement of the "Moonlight" prescribes the placement of the sixteenth-notes *after* the third note of the triplet[5] by overdotting the thematic element. Czerny seems to have specified this instance as an anomaly that parted from a habitual performance practice, implying that the more conventional alignment had to be avoided. Although not intrinsically wrong, his position on the matter has never been supported by any evidence provided by Beethoven himself.[6] Czerny's *Pianoforte-Schule* was influential throughout Europe during the nineteenth century and likely affected several generations of pianists, but I wondered whether it might be our ever-increasing accuracy in reproducing rhythmic values that is responsible for informing the way we hear this theme today, and whether the visual impact of the way the sixteenth-note is printed in all editions—slightly to the right of the last note of the triplet—affects the way we understand it. In a conversation I had with an illustrious pianist about the possibility of homogenization between the two figures in this movement, he conceded that what I was proposing may have been based on a historically correct assumption, but retorted that he would never align the two notes simply because . . . no one does. As the conversation unfolded, my mind returned to a consideration I had made a few days earlier: it would be of great interest to hear how Chopin interpreted and taught this first movement. It is unlikely that he was acquainted with Czerny's *Piano School*—certainly not before 1840, the year a French translation of the method appeared on the market. Would he have made the sixteenth-note coincide with the last note of the triplet?[7]

In example 6.14, I illustrated how Franz Schubert adopted synchronized rhythms in the final movement of the Sonata in B-flat Major, D. 960. While I was exploring the various ways in which this practice affected his music, "Wasserfluth" from the cycle *Winterreise*, D. 911, written in 1827, supplied intriguing interpretive elements. Throughout the lied, the alignment of the two figurations should be observed:

EXAMPLE 6.13. F. Schubert: "Wasserfluth" from *Winterreise*, D. 911, mm. 1–8.

In June 1963, an animated and entertaining exchange of letters appeared in *The Musical Times* in response to the review of a performance of *Winterreise*, given by Peter Pears and Benjamin Britten. The critic Desmond Shawe-Taylor was attacked for objecting to Britten's alignment of the sixteenth-note with the third note of the triplet throughout the performance of "Wasserfluth." One of the contributors wrote bitterly:

> I don't suppose Mr. Shawe-Taylor would want to hear the dotted bass of Bach's *Jesu, joy of man's desiring* galumphing along after each triplet in the tune? [. . .] Schubert would have certainly written *Wasserfluth* in 9/8 time, obviating all ambiguity, had it not been for the inspired twist back into duplets in bar 12.[8]

A second reader observed that the autograph manuscript of the lied shows without doubt that the two figurations are aligned. Britten's own reply to the correspondence is consistent with that statement: his approach had been instinctive at first, he said, and was eventually supported by the homogenization of the two figures in the sketches that Schubert made for the lied. The letter quoted is particularly significant, because it aptly summarizes the reason Schubert chose 3/4 as a time signature: the momentary appearance of duplets excluded any possible involvement of a compound meter, because a change of time signature at that time was conceived exclusively as a permanent alteration that applied to an extended section.

I had found confirmation in "Wasserfluth" that Schubert prescribed the assimilation of the two figures, but wondered whether double-dotted figurations, which had already become common during the second half of the eighteenth century, would follow the same criterion. Should a thirty-second-note as part of a double-dotted figuration also follow an alignment? Many instances in the works of Schubert seem to point to that solution, and this turbulent section from the Adagio of the late Sonata in C Minor, D. 958, written in 1828, offers an example:

Example 6.14. F. Schubert: Sonata in C Minor, D. 958, II. Adagio, mm. 31–36.

If a sixteenth-note is given the flexibility to align with the third note of an eighth-note triplet, it would be intuitive that in this passage the thirty-second-notes in the right hand be executed simultaneously with the last note of a six-note group in the left hand's accompaniment. Until a few years ago, when performing this sonata, I preferred the more biting enunciation afforded by the displacement of the thirty-second-note. I conceded that the idea may have been incorrect when I viewed the 1838 Stichvorlage of Chopin's Prelude in E Major, Op. 28, No. 9, which he prepared for the French publisher Catelin: the assimilation of triplets alongside dotted figurations is unmistakable—the sixteenth-notes are consistently aligned with the third note of a triplet—and, by inference, a thirty-second-note as part of a double-dotted figuration should be counted as the second half of that third note:

Example 6.15. F. Chopin: Prelude in E Major, Op. 28, No. 9, mm. 1–3 (Catelin Stichvorlage, 1838).

If this held true for Chopin in the late 1830s, I found it reasonable to apply the same subdivision to the Adagio from Schubert's Sonata in C Minor, written a decade earlier. A lack of awareness concerning the synchronization of these figurations in the Prelude in E Major has probably generated from the rhythmic layout of the three first editions, in which the notation that Chopin had so accurately indicated in the Stichvorlage was surprisingly disregarded. Such alignment was strictly observed in print by Tobias Haslinger in the nocturnelike variation[9] included in *Hexaméron* (example 6.11), published only months before the Preludes, Op. 28. Even though no Stichvorlage of the variation has survived, the alignment employed in the first edition of *Hexaméron* might confirm Chopin's original notation, and may be an indication that an identical approach should have been used in the first printed version of the Prelude in E Major.

As I encountered instances of homogenization and their derivations in the form of subdivisions in music written during the nineteenth century, the issue became more complicated than I had anticipated. The presence of certain dotted rhythms amid regular meters seemed inexplicable. How did Robert Schumann play "Von fremden Ländern und Menschen" from *Kinderszenen*, Op. 15, for example?

EXAMPLE 6.16. R. Schumann: "Von fremden Ländern und Menschen" from *Kinderszenen*, Op. 15, mm. 1–5.

Schumann never employed quarter-/eighth-note or eighth-/sixteenth-note figurations to underline triplets, which suggests the possibility of assimilation of dotted rhythms and compound subdivisions in his works. However, as no duplets are engaged at any point during the piece, why would a regular meter be necessary? Why did not Schumann opt for the simpler 6/8, if the synchronization of the two figurations was his goal? At first I struggled to understand his motivation, but eventually realized that his choice stemmed from one notational drawback: a compound meter would have entailed a more laborious notation, featuring irregular values such as quarter-notes tied to sixteenth-notes, and complicating both the writing process of the piece and the ease with which it could be read once it was in print. It also occurred to me that the absence of regular groups such as duplets would have provided a telling piece of information to the performer, who would have been led to guess that the assimilation of dotted figurations and triplets was not intended.

Observing this purely practical aspect of notation in Schumann's opening movement from *Kinderszenen* clarified Chopin's intentions in the notation of his Prelude in E Major. Writing the piece in 12/8 would have visually provided a cumbersome notational layout:

EXAMPLE 6.17. F. Chopin: Prelude in E Major, Op. 28, No. 9, mm. 1–3 (adaptation in 12/8, showing the misalignment of the thirty-second-notes the way Chopin would have notated them had he chosen to write the prelude in compound meter).

Such writing was inconvenient—hence a regular meter sufficed to simplify the notation. In this case, the assimilation of the sixteenth-notes was indispensable for explicating the correct placement of the thirty-second-notes. Perhaps Chopin chose C as a time signature also because 12/8 could have visually deprived the prelude of its solemn inflection—the presence of dotted quarter-notes rather than quarter-notes as solid emphatic pillars may have not fully conveyed its hieratic feel.

In retrospect, Czerny was probably correct in identifying the misalignment of the sixteenth-note with the compound figurations in the first movement of Beethoven's "Moonlight," for the same reason that led Schumann to choose a regular meter for "Von fremden Ländern und Menschen." Had Beethoven chosen a compound meter, the "Moonlight" would have shown a further layer of complexity: the decision to write the Adagio sostenuto in cut time would have forced him to notate it in the atypical time signature of 12/16, utilizing sixteenth-note compound triplets—a visual arrangement that might have obscured the correlation between notation and the poignant stillness of the movement.

The impossibility of freely alternating time signatures compelled composers to rely extensively on compound figurations in regular meters if subgroups of two eighth-notes or four sixteenth-notes were to be used at any point during a composition. The homogenization of figures in the final movement of Chopin's Sonata for Cello and Piano in G Minor, Op. 65, for instance, was caused by this unyielding aspect: had it not been for the regular meter in which the second theme is notated, the movement could have been written in 12/8. At that time, duplets in compound meters were not conventional, and no examples are found in Chopin's works. This was perhaps a choice determined by an aesthetic criterion that extended to the visual aspect of his notational style. I have the impression that, had duplets been customary, he would have probably regarded them as inelegant, intrusive signs. Yet the homogenization intended in this last movement of the cello sonata lies at the base of a common misconception: were a rigid reading imposed on the rhythmic profile of the two figures, the rather perplexing effect would interfere with the tarantelle-like character of the first theme. Many pianists tend to accentuate the discrepancy between figurations in instances such as the opening measures:

EXAMPLE 6.18. F. Chopin: Sonata for Cello and Piano in G Minor, Op. 65, IV. Allegro moderato, mm. 1–5.

The interaction between the two instruments suggests the same approach in the cello part:

EXAMPLE 6.19. F. Chopin: Sonata for Cello and Piano in G Minor, Op. 65, IV. Allegro moderato, mm. 60–65.

Most cellists tend to execute the dotted figures by introducing a double-dotted rhythm to avoid a slackening that would lead to a "triplety" feel . . . which, ironically, is just what Chopin would have liked to hear.

The lack of synchronization of rhythmic figures in the early editions of the works of Chopin or in their later reprints has assisted in perpetuating the belief that the rhythm should not bend, and that a mechanical execution of the values notated is necessary to reveal a faithful reading of the score. The instances illustrated thus far validated what I had earlier begun to suspect: that decades of traditions have been instilling a sense of overexactness in our reading habits—a way of evaluating notation that is remote from how a composer probably imagined it. Although *Hexaméron* is by no means a mainstream piece in the piano repertoire, the issue of homogenization surfaces more prominently in familiar instances such as Chopin's Prelude in E Major, in which the practice of underdotting, chosen by very few performers, is often encountered with disdain. The disregard for Chopin's original intention can be ascribed partly to the displacement found in the earliest printed versions, but also to traditions that have been perpetuated by the recordings of the twentieth century, some of which we all admire but that may reveal historically incorrect approaches. Constantly referring to these recordings might affect our conception of particular interpretive details and result in unconscious imitation—including the reproduction of their accidental flaws.

Numerous works by Chopin feature patterned accompaniments in compound triplets while using regular time signatures, in juxtaposition to melodic material that proposes varied rhythmic profiles. Dotted figurations that imply a time ratio of 2 + 1 are generally overlooked and are enunciated with great emphasis. The lyrical second theme in the first movement of the Sonata in B Minor, Op. 58 is one such instance:

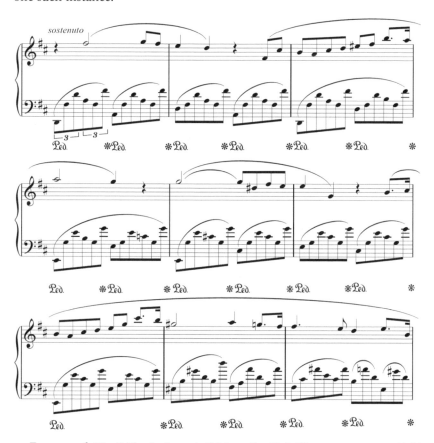

EXAMPLE 6.20. F. Chopin: Sonata in B Minor, Op. 58, I. Allegro maestoso, mm. 41–52.

EXAMPLE 6.20 (*continued*)

In the Stichvorlage of the sonata that Chopin sent to Breitkopf & Härtel, a sense of vertical alignment between the two hands seems to have been intended. In this second thematic idea, that the sixteenth-notes are supposed to coincide with the third notes of the left-hand triplets is discernible in passages such as the one in measures 48–50:

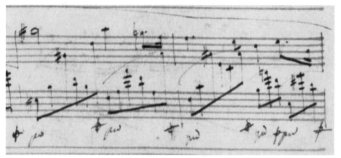

EXAMPLE 6.21a. F. Chopin: Sonata in B Minor, Op. 58, I. Allegro maestoso, mm. 48–49 (Breitkopf & Härtel Stichvorlage, 1844).

EXAMPLE 6.21b. F. Chopin: Sonata in B Minor, Op. 58, I. Allegro maestoso, m. 50 (Breitkopf & Härtel Stichvorlage, 1844).

The same Stichvorlage reveals even more intriguing subtleties: measure 51 shows that there may have been an effort to align the eighth-note in the right hand (E) with the last eighth-note of the left hand's sextuplet (B-flat), which would extend the notion of assimilation throughout the passage:

EXAMPLE 6.22. F. Chopin: Sonata in B Minor, Op. 58, I. Allegro maestoso, m. 51 (Breitkopf & Härtel Stichvorlage, 1844).

My initial thought was that this had been an inadvertent displacement on Chopin's part, especially because the irregular group of five notes that ensues in the right hand fails to be properly aligned. Yet similar situations are presented throughout the Stichvorlage of the sonata—in measure 29 from the Largo, for instance:

EXAMPLE 6.23. F. Chopin: Sonata in B Minor, Op. 58, III. Largo, mm. 28–30 (Breitkopf & Härtel Stichvorlage, 1844).

Consider also a passage from the first movement that shows the synchronization of the last eighth-notes in both hands in measure 183. In this case, the right hand features two triplets against the eighth-note/quarter-note rest/eighth-note figuration in the right hand:

🔊 EXAMPLE 6.24. F. Chopin: Sonata in B Minor, Op. 58, I. Allegro maestoso, mm. 183–184 (Breitkopf & Härtel Stichvorlage, 1844).

The alignment of the last eighth-note in the measure was meticulously reported in the first printed version of the Breitkopf & Härtel edition in 1845. Whereas this placement may be considered a casual indication by Chopin, the Meissonier edition, which used a Stichvorlage prepared concomitantly with the one for Breitkopf & Härtel, offers an alternative rendition of the same measure:

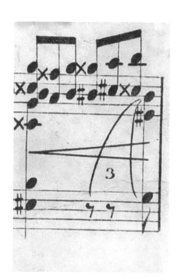

EXAMPLE 6.25. F. Chopin: Sonata in B Minor, Op. 58, I. Allegro maestoso, m. 183 (Meissonier edition, 1845).

Doubtfully an editorial license, this seems to be one of Chopin's capricious discrepancies, simply showing a variation in expressing the same basic idea[10] (notice also how the left-hand chords contain richer textures). Despite the vertical alignment between the two hands in Chopin's manuscripts is not consistently accurate, the deliberate homogenization between eighth-notes and compound groups throughout the Stichvorlage of the Sonata in B Minor is too frequent to be coincidental. This type of notation had been employed for quite some time by other composers (Schubert, for instance, had used it in the 1820s in works such as the Impromptu in C Minor, D. 899, No. 1) as a convenient tool in the absence of exact rhythmic values to specify more complex subdivisions. Such was the flexibility of this rhythmic figure that a couple of measures earlier in the movement shows the use of the same dotted quarter-/eighth-note figuration to indicate a rather different arrangement. Observe how in the last beat of measure 26 the eighth-note in the right hand aligns not with the last note of the left-hand group, but with the preceding pitch (F-sharp)—in my opinion, a configuration that is musically more pleasing than a cross-rhythm or an alignment with the last eighth-note:

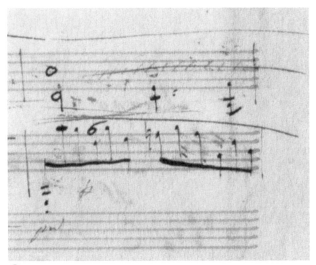

EXAMPLE 6.26. F. Chopin: Sonata in B Minor, Op. 58, III. Largo, m. 26 (Breitkopf & Härtel Stichvorlage, 1844).

These adaptations, which disregarded strict readings of dotted quarter- or dotted eighth-notes, were quite common in the music of nineteenth-century composers. Briefly returning to *Hexaméron*, we see how Liszt notated the main theme:

EXAMPLE 6.27. F. Liszt: Tema from *Hexaméron*, Allegro marziale, mm. 1–2 (Haslinger edition, 1839).

Measure 2 shows that a double-dotted quarter-note/sixteenth-note figuration precisely aligns with the compound writing of the left hand. Yet an analogous case within the same section, melodically derived from these opening measures, features an identical alignment but quite a different layout—a single-dotted quarter-note/eighth-note:

EXAMPLE 6.28. F. Liszt: Tema from *Hexaméron*, Allegro marziale, mm. 17–18 (Haslinger edition, 1839).

We witness the same rhythmic flexibility in the Prelude and Fugue in E Minor by Mendelssohn, published soon after *Hexaméron*. In this case the alignment is unambiguous, because the melody in the alto register is consistently integrated with the accompanying figuration and is outlined with extra stems. This expedient causes an amendment of the cross-rhythm that would otherwise occur:

EXAMPLE 6.29. F. Mendelssohn: Prelude and Fugue in E Minor, WoO 13, Prelude, mm. 42–43.

A composer from the first half of the nineteenth century would not have had a notational device to spell the correct subdivision of a beat in a case such as this. An option would have been to use the meter 12/8 and notate as follows:

or by using this subdivision:

The necessity of employing the regular 4/4 meter within the piece led Mendelssohn to favor compound triplets as the prevailing figuration. Despite the options illustrated above, we cannot deny that the greater visual clarity offered by Mendelssohn's arrangement had its advantages. Moreover, this notation discloses one basic aspect concerning our instinctive approach to reading music: only when a double stem is present to outline a leading voice against the accompaniment do we realize that the eighth-note is meant to coincide with the last note of each six-note accompanying figuration. In print, this kind of writing is not visually consistent, and in most circumstances it suggests a misalignment between the two hands, as shown in instances such as the one in measure 68 of the same prelude:

EXAMPLE 6.30. F. Mendelssohn: Prelude and Fugue in E Minor, WoO 13, Prelude, m. 68.

Performers rarely alter these instances to conform to the prevailing rhythmic inflection of the thematic material.

Johannes Brahms was possibly the first composer to introduce a consistent use of quarter-/eighth-note figures in replacement of dotted rhythms. We see this strategy fully employed in the early "Lied" from *Sechs Gesänge*, Op. 3 and the Scherzo in E-flat Minor, Op. 4, both written around 1854. Although explaining Brahms's evolution is beyond the scope of this chapter, it will suffice to mention that he never radically abandoned the more established notation, even though other composers adopted the new system quite regularly during the second half of the nineteenth century. As late as 1880, in the Rhapsody in G Minor, Op. 79, No. 2, Brahms was still employing that more economical solution. The absence of quarter-/eighth-note figurations might confirm that the dotted rhythms were meant to replace them:

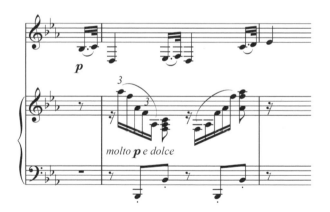

EXAMPLE 6.31. J. Brahms: Rhapsody in G Minor, Op. 79, No. 2, mm. 26–32.

As the years passed, Brahms never truly parted with the older notation, even though its employment seems to have been reserved primarily to passages that prescribed a repeated use of the figuration. In his late works, several instances confirm that the equalization of dotted figures and triplets was still very much at the core of his writing. The concluding movement of the Sonata for Clarinet and Piano in E-flat Major, Op. 120, No. 2 (1894) shows such a treatment:

EXAMPLE 6.32. J. Brahms: Sonata for Clarinet and Piano in E-flat Major, Op. 120, No. 2 III. Andante con moto, mm. 28–30.

Underdotting this passage in the clarinet part might be viewed as a miscalculation because of regular sixteenth-note subdivisions against triplets in the piano part a few measures later. Yet, as the movement unfolds, the two instruments show an exchange that clearly suggests the homogenization of the two rhythms:

EXAMPLE 6.33. J. Brahms: Sonata for Clarinet and Piano in E-flat Major, Op. 120, No. 2 III. Andante con moto, mm. 36–38.

In the same period, the newer notation appears in passages that do not prescribe its patterned use. Measure 3 of the Intermezzo in E Major, Op. 116, No. 4 provides an example:

EXAMPLE 6.34. J. Brahms: Intermezzo in E Major, Op. 116, No. 4, mm. 1–5.

At the turn of the twentieth century, vestiges of the dotted rhythm remained to indicate homogenization, notably in *L'isle joyeuse* by Claude Debussy, written in 1904. In the light dancelike material of the main theme, triplets and dotted-sixteenth-note figurations constantly alternate, improbably specifying two contrasting rhythmic profiles:

EXAMPLE 6.35. C. Debussy: *L'isle joyeuse*, mm. 9–12.

That the dotted figurations in *L'isle joyeuse* are intended to imply equalization is most definitely confirmed by the way Debussy notated the two coexisting rhythms in the last beat of measure 14:

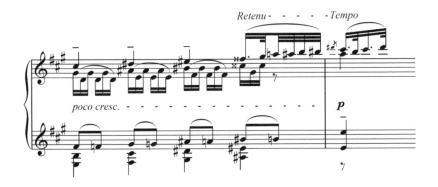

EXAMPLE 6.36. C. Debussy: *L'isle joyeuse*, mm. 14–15.

In a rather different area of the world but in the same epoch, Sergei Prokofiev (1891–1953) used homogenization in works such as his Sonata in A Minor, Op. 28, completed in 1917 but begun ten years earlier. Prokofiev indicated two time signatures—4/4 and, parenthetically, 12/8—thereby having the two alternate without needing to specify when a new meter is introduced. In this sonata, dotted quarter-notes in 12/8 are avoided altogether, and are replaced by regular quarter-notes that imply the 4/4 time signature. Quarter-/eighth-note figurations are employed exclusively when they are independently stemmed from a compound triplet played by the same hand, and dotted eighth-/sixteenth-note figurations are featured regularly against triplets, entailing synchronization:

EXAMPLE 6.37. S. Prokofiev: Sonata in A Minor, op. 28, mm. 14–21.

To my knowledge, no modern performer strictly observes the assimilation of these two rhythms unless the displacement of the two figures becomes unfeasible. Although mixing the two meters might inevitably create some perplexities, an analysis of the score confirms that Prokofiev used dotted eighth-/sixteenth-note figurations exclusively when he employed 4/4, be it for a portion of a measure or for extended episodes. This strategy appears in other compositions of Prokofiev from the same decade, such as the fourth movement of the Sonata in D Minor, Op. 14. The first movement of the Concerto for Piano and Orchestra in G Minor, Op. 16, completed and premiered in 1913 but revised in 1924, also shows the use of dotted figurations in combination with compound subdivisions.

At first in the same environment as Prokofiev's, but immersed in the atmosphere of fin de siècle from which Prokofiev distanced himself, Alexander Scriabin (1872–1915) developed the function of the dotted figure into an emblem of communication. From his early works, which clearly aspired to the language and forms elaborated by Chopin, to those written after 1907, when his idiom began to evolve toward atonality, a short anacrusis en route to a long note assumed a fundamental role—a gesture that symbolized what he described as *zov*, "call." Although it was expressed purely on an intuitive level in his earlier years, it came to assume a more deliberate, explicit meaning, and remained an essential motif in his music throughout the rest of his brief existence.

In Scriabin's early writing we find many cases in which dotted figurations are mixed with triplets, but their interaction proves that the composer treated them as two distinct rhythmic constituents. We know from the piano rolls that Scriabin recorded for Welte-Mignon that the enunciation of what would become the *zov* was invariably pronounced with an overdotted inflection. This approach might have been dictated by the musical emphasis that the motif required, as Scriabin's playing was extremely changeable and improvisatory—a style of performance that was confirmed and perpetuated by pianists close to his circle (his son-in-law Vladimir Sofronitsky, for instance). The rhythmic drive of the *zov* is found in the mature *Poème tragique*, Op. 34, written in 1903 not long after Scriabin had turned thirty, although it was already a characteristic of earlier works such as the celebrated Etude in D-sharp Minor, Op. 8, No. 12 of 1894:

EXAMPLE 6.38. A. Scriabin: Etude in D-sharp Minor, op. 8, No. 12, mm. 1–3.

We are fortunate to have a performance of this etude on a piano roll dated 1912 and played by Scriabin himself. What makes the recording unique, apart from its historical relevance, is the palpable role that the *zov* had acquired over time in Scriabin's own playing. The sixteenth-notes are played rather quickly, and are not any broader than the thirty-seconds found occasionally in the piece, which corroborates that their inflection had a much greater contextual effect than the precision of execution expressed by the score. Several cases of quarter-/eighth-note groups prove that Scriabin may have considered a stronger enunciation for dotted figurations. How did this approach at the early stages of his career as a composer affect the way he viewed cases of homogenization in eighteenth- and early-nineteenth-century music? One can only wonder how he would have played coexisting rhythms in Chopin's music: assimilation may never have occurred to Scriabin, and it is possible that he would have not aligned any of them.

A few months ago I assigned Beethoven's Sonata in D Major, Op. 28 to one of my students, and pointed out that since triplets are a predominant element in the writing of the Andante's middle section, she should have probably homogenized the dotted figurations:

EXAMPLE 6.39. L. van Beethoven: Sonata in D Major, Op. 28, II. Adagio, mm. 27–32.

"I like the idea of homogenization, and would love to apply it,"—said the student in response to my reminding her about the practice of underdotting while working with me on this section of the piece a few weeks later—"were it not for the fact that . . . no one does!"

Notes

Chapter 1

1. Quoted in Charles Rosen, *The Romantic Generation* (Cambridge, MA: Harvard University Press, 1995), 339.

2. Daniel Gottlob Türk, *Clavierschule* (Lincoln, NE: University of Nebraska Press, 1982), 362.

3. Carl Czerny, *Vollständige theoretisch-practische Pianoforte-Schule* (Complete Theoretical and Practical Piano Forte School), Op. 500 (Milan, Italy: Edizioni Ricordi, 1840), 47. Author's translation.

4. In a productive exchange with Jeffrey Kallberg, he presented me with an unforeseen alternative: Chopin himself may have wavered over what the note should be. There is a chance that the now lost German manuscript may have proposed a D instead of the E-flat to which we are accustomed.

5. Paul Badura-Skoda, *Chopin: Etudes, Op. 25 and Trois Nouvelles Etudes* (Vienna, Austria: Wiener Urtext edition, 1973), 67.

6. Rosen, 339.

7. Ludwik Bronarski, Josef Turczynski, *Commentary to the Ballade in F Minor* (New York, NY: Dover Publications, Inc., reproduction of the Paderewski edition, 1949), 200.

8. Paul Badura-Skoda, *Chopin: Etudes, Op. 10* (Vienna, Austria: Wiener Urtext edition, 1973), vi.

9. Eigeldinger, *Chopin: Pianist and Teacher as Seen by His Pupils* (Cambridge, UK: Cambridge University Press, 1967), 68.

10. Example 1.44a shows that Chopin had originally begun to mark these hairpins in the middle of the system but stopped after two such placements, carefully erased them, and proceeded to notate them consistently above the right hand. He may have wished to avoid the confusion that might have generated from a symbol that was invested with various designations. In examples 1.39–1.41, we saw the potential of hairpins placed in the middle of the system to signal voicing and metric order. Yet I had misconstrued them as intending agogic fluctuation. In this case, the hairpins so placed could have been similarly misread.

11. *The Cambridge Companion to Chopin*—Anatole Leikin, The Sonatas (Cambridge, UK: Cambridge University Press, 1992), 167.

12. Original English version, supplied by the author; for the published versions see "*Les Concertos de Chopin et la notation de l'exécution,*" in *Frédéric Chopin, interprétations,* ed. Jean-Jacques Eigeldinger (Geneva: Librairie Droz, 2005), 69–88.

13. Will Crutchfield, *Chopin, the Day After the Opera* (*The New York Times,* June 20, 1999).

14. Manuel Patricio Rodríguez García was born in Zafra, Spain, and died in London at the venerable age of 101. His father was Manuel del Pópulo Vicente García (1775–1832), a Spanish opera singer, composer, and voice teacher. His sisters were Maria Malibran and Pauline Viardot-García (intimate friend of Chopin and George Sand). He was also the teacher of Jenny Lind, Julius Stockhausen, and Mathilde Marchesi, to name a few.

15. Eigeldinger, 148.

16. Wilhelm von Lenz, an amateur pianist and a pupil of Chopin's, reported that "[a] remarkable feature of his playing was the entire freedom with which he treated the rhythm, but which appeared so natural that for years it has never struck me. [. . .] The more remarkable fact was that you received the impression of 3/4 rhythm while listening to common time." Quoted in Eigeldinger, 72.

17. Depending on the edition, the dynamic specified for this passage ranges from an implied *piano* (Wessel) to a *forte* (Breitkopf & Härtel).

18. To understand the extent of authority that this treatise still exerted on interpretation during the early years of the nineteenth century, it is worth knowing that upon offering to teach the ten-year-old Carl Czerny in 1801, Beethoven recommended that the boy's father obtain a copy for the new pupil.

19. Carl Philipp Emanuel Bach, *Versuch über die wahre Art das Clavier zu spielen* (Essay on the True Art of Playing Keyboard Instruments) (New York, NY: W. W. Norton & Co., 1949), 88.

20. Ethel Lillian Voynich and Henryk Opienski, *Chopin's Letters* (Mineola, NY: Dover Publications, 1988), 110.

21. In the preface to his organ piece *Komm, süßer Tod* (Come, Sweet Death) (1894), Riemann's pupil Max Reger (1873–1916) explains that "the hairpins have dynamic and agogic significance" and that "one could [. . .] slightly increase in pace (*stringendo*) where the hairpin opens, and slightly relax in pace (*ritardando*) where the hairpin closes (*Tempo rubato*)"—quite a different situation from the conclusions discussed in this first chapter, and perhaps testimony to how hairpins may have taken on a life of their own, adapting to the specific language of a composer. Reger also used hairpins to indicate dynamic fluctuations via the use of the *Walze*, more

commonly described as "crescendo and diminuendo pedal," and also referred to as "Venetian swell." As not all organs possessed this division, in its absence hairpins would have exclusively had agogic significance on this particular instrument.

22. Hugo Riemann, *Die Elemente der musikalischen Ästhetik* (The Elements of Musical Aesthetic) (Berlin/Stuttgart, Germany, 1900), 76.

Chapter 2

1. Leopold Mozart, *Gründliche Violinschule* (Treatise on Violin Playing, 1756) (London, UK: Oxford University Press, Editha Knocker, trans. 1951), 115.

2. See Carl Philipp Emanuel Bach's description of appoggiaturas from his *Versuch über die wahre Art das Clavier zu spielen*, quoted in chapter 1 on page xxx.

3. *Dizionario della lingua italiana De Mauro* (Turin, Italy: Edizioni Paravia, 1997), 1143.

4. Author's translation.

5. Christa Landon, *Haydn: Sonatas* (Vienna, Austria: Wiener Urtext edition, 1963), 5.

6. While Variation IX is marked *Adagio*, Variation VII does not feature an autonomous tempo indication. Still, it is the only variation in the parallel key of D minor; and when encountered in a set of variations written in a major key, the minor mode may have prescribed a more introspective feel, which was understood to affect tempo as well as expression.

7. Instances such as the one illustrated in example 2.6 would have not accepted the use of fermatas until decades later. In Mozart's time, the symbol was generally placed at the end of a piece or movement to specify its conclusion, functioning also as an indication that a page turn would not be necessary. Cadenzas and cadenza-like instances would have admitted the use of fermatas to denote undetermined lengths well beyond the regular duration of a measure. Early-music specialists tend to concur that in choral writing the symbol does not indicate a prolongation of the value in question, but signals where a breath should be taken.

8. Emily Anderson, *The Letters of Mozart and His Family* (New York, NY: W. W. Norton & Co., 1985), 417.

9. Only rarely did someone advance the position that *sforzando* may also imply a slight agogic placement. This small group showed a prevailing notion according to which music strongly relies on agogic accents. There are two accepted types of accents—dynamic and agogic. The former consists of an intensification in the sound of a

specific note or chord; the latter relies on the lengthening of certain beats within a rhythmic pattern. Agogic accents are a natural part of the musical discourse, as they characterize the intensity of a passage. They are conventionally placed on the downbeat or, alternatively, on the strong beats of a measure. Our perception of rhythm is based on the specification of dynamic and agogic accents. Any deviation from the predictable placement of strong beats must rely on these kinds of accents, used either individually or in combination.

10. In the hands of some performers, Beethoven's *fp* is at times treated as a special effect: in the opening chord of the first movement of the Sonata in C Minor, Op. 13, for instance, some pianists feature a sudden dynamic reduction on the chord itself, obtained by a quick release and a new depression both of fingers and sustain pedal. The idea that *fp* on this chord should indicate this treatment seems to be the result of an approach in which the inventiveness of the analysis may be overdrawn for the sake of resolving this particular case and a minuscule number of analogous ones. In my opinion, such cases simply indicate that the chord should be played *forte*, and that what follows should be played *piano*.

11. Lewis Lockwood and the Juilliard String Quartet, *Inside Beethoven's Quartets* (Cambridge, MA: Harvard University Press, 2008), 45.

Chapter 3

1. Hugo Riemann, *Musik-Lexikon* (Leipzig, Germany: 1882), 772.

2. Justin Heinrich Knecht, *Knechts allgemeiner musikalischer Katechismus* (Biberach, Germany: 1803), 50.

3. In the Italian language, the periodic rising and falling of the oceans and their inlets are respectively described as *crescente* and *calante*. The same terminology is used to illustrate the crescent and gibbous phases of the moon. While Mozart usually employed the marking *calando* with the purpose of expressing exclusively the opposite of *crescendo*, nineteenth-century composers were responsible for developing a modified connotation, generally intending a decrease in both speed and volume. We observed that Schubert used *decrescendo* to indicate a decrease in dynamic level and *diminuendo* to suggest a gradual decrease in speed. For Beethoven *diminuendo* quickly became a common way of expressing a decrease in dynamic intensity, and his usage overshadowed Schubert's separate connotations. It took twentieth-century scholarship to restore Schubert's original intent.

4. Donald Francis Tovey, *Beethoven Sonatas for Pianoforte*, vol. 2 (London, UK: The Associated Board of the Royal Schools of Music, 1931), 13.

5. Ibid., 13.

6. Considered a pianist of great distinction by many of his contemporaries, Dussek was known for his *cantabile* style, but also for his handsome features. He was the first performer to place the piano sideways on stage so that his profile could be better admired—a precedent that remains in effect to this day. Dussek's fame reached every corner of Europe. His music was published in virtually every country of Europe, an achievement that secured him celebrity status during his lifetime.

7. A British pianist, composer, and piano manufacturer of German descent, Cramer was recognized by Beethoven as a musician of great stature. The esteem was mutual, as Cramer was one of Beethoven's most devoted admirers. Cramer studied with Muzio Clementi in London and enjoyed an international reputation. Although his vast output for piano has fallen into oblivion, Cramer is remembered for his etudes, many of which are still used today in the training of young pianists.

8. *Beethoven: Sonaten für Klavier, Band II* (Munich, Germany: G. Henle Verlag, 1980), 155.

9. This conclusion is based on Beethoven's use, in the same movement, of the marking *ritardando*, which conventionally leads to sections marked *Adagio*. In the case of *ritenente*, the marking affects short portions of the music—half a measure, one measure, or two measures. These sections are always transitional and not substantial enough to represent new structural moments within the piece. I believe this to be the underlying reason that in these instances Beethoven used the present participle (*ritenente*) rather than the gerundive form (*ritardando*). Further, the use of *rinforzando* to indicate a decrease in speed may have obviated the predictable confusion that the placement of *ritardando* and *ritenente* in such close proximity would have caused.

10. On page 116, we observed that in the same year, Müller had carried out the revision and completion of Mozart's Fantasie in D Minor, K. 397.

11. August Eberhard Müller, *Klavier- und Fortepiano Schule* (Jena, Germany: 1804), 29.

Chapter 4

1. Quoted in Jean-Jacques Eigeldinger, *Chopin: Pianist and Teacher as Seen by His Pupils* (Cambridge, UK: Cambridge University Press, 1967), 74.

2. John Sullivan Dwight, *Dwight's Journal of Music: A Paper of Art and Literature*, vol. 35 (Boston, MA: Oliver Ditson & Co., 1877), 17.

3. Camille Saint-Saëns, *On the Execution of Music: And Principally of Ancient Music* (San Francisco, CA: The Blair-Murdock Company, 1915), 14.

4. Indicating the depression and release of the sustain pedal was a formula used for the first time around 1793 by Daniel Steibelt (1765–1823)—unless we consider Beethoven's *mit dem Knie*, "with the knee," which appeared in one of his sketches two years or so earlier. Steibelt's praxis had such a fundamental impact as a new notational device that other composers adopted it immediately. Such was his dedication to the subject that Steibelt was also the first composer to write music explicitly devoted to the study of the pedal. In it, ⊕ generally indicated the depression of the pedal, while + indicated its release—an application that was advocated by publishers such as Wessel in London during the first half of the nineteenth century, but to which not every firm adhered. Moreover, composers found it convenient to determine their own set of notational markings: as we just saw, Chopin used ⊕ to indicate the release instead.

5. Sandra Rosenblum, *Journal of Musicological Research*, vol. 16 (1996), 49.

6. Carl Czerny, *Vollständige theoretisch-practische Pianoforte-Schule* (Complete Theoretical and Practical Piano Forte School), Op. 500 (Milan, Italy: Edizioni Ricordi, 1840), 85. Author's translation from Italian.

7. Eigeldinger, 45.

8. It was only after writing this portion of chapter 4 that I learned of an illuminating turn of events: thirty years later, in his position as the editor of Chopin's Preludes, Op. 28 for *The Complete Chopin: A New Critical Edition* published by Peters, Eigeldinger reviewed the stance he had taken in *Chopin: Pianist and Teacher as Seen by His Pupils*, and decided to reject a strict reading of the release in measure 76 by proposing a uniform pedaling for all these instances—an indication that scholarship can always be in evolution.

9. Eigeldinger, 113.

10. Ibid., 113.

11. Ibid., 45.

12. One lonesome *ped* appears in measure 7 of the Schlesinger edition, though without a release sign.

13. The German and English editions of the Twelve Etudes, Op. 10 were prepared from the first impression of the Schlesinger edition, printed in Paris. In both versions, the long pedal marking in the concluding measures of this etude is accompanied by a release symbol—clearly an editorial addition.

14. In that respect, compare the strikingly similar pedaling in the opening of the Sonata, Op. 35—perhaps not coincidentally also in the key of B-flat minor. The Prelude was elaborated and refined during the composer's sojourn in Majorca, whereas the sonata was mostly completed a few months later during the first summer he spent at Nohant.

15. Eigeldinger, 58.

16. Saint-Saëns's rolls for Ampico and Welte-Mignon show a very limited use of the sustain pedal. Should they be regarded as trustworthy sources for evaluating the way he pedaled? Indeed, since pedal applications were usually added after the performance was fixed on paper, we are left to wonder whether they were reported correctly. Notoriously, the results offered by piano rolls frequently disappointed: asked to record for Welte-Mignon, which tempted him with the idea that its recording technique provided up to sixteen different dynamic levels, Artur Schnabel is reported to have initially declined the invitation by humorously claiming that he had seventeen.

17. This notion would not include intended suspensions such as the last eighth-note of measure 29 (A), which is tied to the downbeat of measure 30.

18. Quoted in Eigeldinger, 274.

19. It must be pointed out that in the excerpt from the Breitkopf & Härtel edition illustrated in example 4.30b, a misprint occurred in the first beat of measure 59, left hand: A-flat should read B-flat.

20. Frederick Niecks, *Frederick Chopin: As a Man and Musician* (London, UK: Novello Ewer & Co., 1890), 266.

21. Eigeldinger, 292–93.

22. James Cuthbert Hadden, *Chopin* (London, UK: J. M. Dent & Son, 1903), 190.

23. Ethel Lillian Voynich, Henryk Opienski, *Chopin's letters* (Mineola, NY: Dover Publications, 1988), 133.

24. Quoted in Eigeldinger, 58.

25. The only exception is perhaps the pencil indication *i due ped.* (albeit not in Chopin's hand) that is marked in the Nocturne in F-sharp Major, Op. 15, No. 2 as part of the Jędrzejewicz collection—a group of scores that were the property of Chopin's sister Ludwika and that were purchased in 1936 by the Museum of the Fryderyk Chopin Society in Warsaw. These scores are thought to have been in Chopin's possession, and it is believed that Ludwika took the collection to Poland with her after her brother's death.

Chapter 5

1. Quoted in David Masson, John Morley, Mowbray Morris, George Grove, *Macmillan's Magazine*, 26 (London, UK: MacMillan and Co., 1871), 129.

2. Several modern editions delete the *crescendo* marked alongside the opening hairpin, because of the apparent redundancy of the two markings when viewed dynamically. The marking for *crescendo*, however, is present in all three first editions of the piece.

3. The second half of measure 201 shows a three-note slur, which I would interpret as a momentary departure from the two-note groups established by the *stretto*. The extension of the dashes to the end of the next measure would suggest that the hemiola-like organization continues after the slur. The arousing charge that derives from this arrangement is perceived even more powerfully because of the tonicization of C major (unquestionably an allusion to the role of the same key in measure 7, which concludes the introduction of the ballade).

4. Jean-Jacques Eigeldinger, *Chopin: Pianist and Teacher as Seen by His Pupils* (Cambridge, UK: Cambridge University Press, 1967), 44.

5. Charles Rosen, *The Romantic Generation* (Cambridge, MA: Harvard University Press, 1995), 285.

6. Eigeldinger, 181.

Chapter 6

1. Carl Philipp Emanuel Bach, *Versuch über die wahre Art das Clavier zu spielen* (Essay on the True Art of Playing Keyboard Instruments) (New York, NY: W. W. Norton & Co., 1949), 160.

2. Perhaps not coincidentally, in his revision of the *Well-Tempered Clavier*, Carl Czerny marked this fugue with the tempo indication *Vivace*.

3. The term *Hexaméron* theologically refers to the six days of creation, from the Greek Εξαήμερος—*hexa* (six) and *emera* (day), but in Liszt's title there is an explicit reference to the collaboration of the six pianists who were commissioned to write the variations.

4. Chopin's contribution to *Hexaméron* is the only portion of the piece to propose a transformation of the theme in a lyrical fashion. We gather from a letter written to Liszt by Christina di Belgiojoso that this element was planned in advance in order to create a balance with the other variations, brilliant in character: "No news from M. Chopin, and since I am still proud enough to fear making a nuisance of myself, I do

not dare ask him. You do not run the same risk with him as I, which prompts me to ask if you would find out what is happening with his Adagio, which is not moving quickly at all." Quoted in Alan Walker, *Franz Liszt: The Virtuoso Years, 1811–1847* (Ithaca, NY: Cornell University Press, 1987), 242.

5. Carl Czerny, *Vollständige theoretisch-practische Pianoforte-Schule,* Op. 500, vol. 2 (London, UK: Cocks, 1839), 49.

6. That Czerny occasionally reinterpreted some of Beethoven's intentions is confirmed by instances such as the facilitation of certain trills in his teacher's works, which he suggested in the first volume of the *Pianoforte-Schule,* Op. 500. These instructions are in opposition to Beethoven's own approach in similar instances, which is persuasively illustrated by the composer at the end of the autograph of the Sonata in C Major, Op. 53.

7. I recently came across a 1924 recording of this movement in a transcription for winds performed by the Bellini Ensemble Unique. The approach to the dotted figuration is so radically different each time that the placement of the sixteenth-note seems not to have been a significant concern. In particular, the French horn player wavered between homogenization and a rather pronounced double-dotting, even within the same phrase—as if variety of inflection had been the ultimate goal.

8. Quoted by Desmond Shawe-Taylor in "Schubert as Written and as Performed," *The Musical Times,* 104, no. 1447 (September 1963), 626.

9. Perhaps not coincidentally, this variation and the Prelude in E Major from Op. 28 bear a significant resemblance. They share key signature, underlying triplets, and single- and double-dotted figurations. The striking harmonic shifts featured in the two pieces also display a similar exploration in modulating to remote keys, and may be confirmation that Chopin wrote them concurrently. Further, the material for the Prelude in E Major may have been originated from discarded ideas initially considered for the Variation. It would not have been an unusual occurrence in compositions written during the same period, as the remarkable likeness between material from the Ballade in F Major, Op. 38 and the B section of the Nocturne in G Major, Op. 37, No. 2 confirms—both the result of work done prior to and during the trip to Majorca.

10. We do not know whether this arrangement for the left hand was Chopin's original intention (a Stichvorlage for the Meissonier edition has not been located), but the presence of two eighth-note rests replacing a quarter-note one might confirm that, at least for the French editor, a quarter- /eighth-note figuration to entail a compound subdivision was still not a widespread notational device at the time.

Index of Musical Works

Works with generic titles such as Sonata, Etude, and Fugue are for piano/keyboard solo unless otherwise specified.

Bach, Johann Sebastian
    Concerto for Three Harpsichords
      and Orchestra in C Major, BWV
      1064, 124
    French Suite in D Minor, BWV 812,
      211–212
    Fugue in C Minor, BWV 871, *Well-*
      Tempered Clavier, Book II, 183–
      184, 192
    Fugue in D Minor, BWV 875, *Well-*
      Tempered Clavier, Book II, 212–
      213, 246n2 (chap. 6)
    Partita in D Major, BWV 828, 213
    Partita in E Minor, BWV 830, 213
    Toccata in G Minor, BWV 915, 213
    Weimar Christmas Cantata, BWV 63,
      124
    Well-Tempered Clavier, 200–201

Beethoven, Ludwig van
    Concerto for Piano and Orchestra in
      C Major, Op. 15, 87
    Missa Solemnis, Op. 123, 113
    Piano Trios, Op. 1, 16, 104, 108, 113
    Piano Trio in E-flat Major, Op. 1, No.
      1, 15–16, 126
    Piano Trio in C Minor, Op. 1, No. 3,
      107–109, 118
    Sonatas, Op. 2, 16, 104
    Sonata in F Minor, Op. 2, No. 1,
      53–55, 105–106
    Sonata in C Major, Op. 2, No. 3, 87,
      123

Sonata in E-flat Major, Op. 7, 16–17,
    55
Sonata in C Minor, Op. 10, No. 1,
    109–111
Sonata in F Major, Op. 10, No. 2,
    111–112
Sonata in C Minor, Op. 13, 214,
    242n10
Sonata in G Major, Op. 14, No. 2,
    112–113
Sonata in B-flat Major, Op. 22, 81–82
Sonata in C-sharp Minor, Op. 27, No.
    2, 217–218, 222–223, 247n7
Sonata in D Major, Op. 28, 237–238
Sonata in D Minor, Op. 31, No. 2, 83
Sonata in E-flat Major, Op. 31, No.
    3, 123
Sonata in C Major, Op. 53, 17,
    123–124, 125, 136, 247n6
Sonata in F Major, Op. 54, 17–18
Sonata in F Minor, Op. 57, 126
Sonata in A Major, Op. 101, 85–86,
    88, 126
Sonata in B-flat Major, Op. 106, 134
Sonata in E Major, Op. 109, 84–85,
    127, 171–172
Sonata in A-flat Major, Op. 110, 18,
    127, 175
Sonata in C Minor, Op. 111, 14–15,
    83–84, 127–128, 243n9
Symphony in C Minor, Op. 67, 184
Variations in C Minor, WoO 80,
    113

Bellini, Vincenzo
   I puritani, 216
   Norma, 215

Berg, Alban
   Sonata, Op. 1, 67

Brahms, Johannes
   Intermezzo in E Major, Op. 116, No.
     4, 234
   Intermezzo in B-flat Minor, Op. 117,
     No. 2, 136
   Intermezzo in A Major, Op. 118, No.
     2, 136–137
   Piano Trio in C Major, Op. 87, 125
   Rhapsody in G Minor, Op. 79, no. 2,
     232–233
   Scherzo in E-flat Minor, Op. 4, 232
   Sechs Gesänge, Op. 3, 232
   Sonata in C Major, Op. 1, 133
   Sonata in F Minor, Op. 5, 134–135
   Sonata for Clarinet and Piano in E-flat
     Major, Op. 120, No. 2, 233–234

Chopin, Frédéric
   Ballade in G Minor, Op. 23, 23–24,
     28–29, 43, 65, 92–94, 239n4
   Ballade in F Major, Op. 38, 36, 194,
     195–196, 204, 247n9
   Ballade in A-flat Major, Op. 47, 149–
     150, 177–178
   Ballade in F Minor, Op. 52, 27–28,
     51–53, 117, 178, 196–198, 201,
     246n3 (chap. 5)
   Barcarolle in F-sharp Major, Op. 60,
     3–4, 6–7, 58, 97, 99, 151,
     161–162, 172–173, 174
   Berceuse in D-flat Major, Op. 57, 204
   Canon in F Minor (fragment), 201

Concerto for Piano and Orchestra in
   E Minor, Op. 11, 44, 46–47, 187,
   201–203
Concerto for Piano and Orchestra in
   F Minor, Op. 21, 44
Etude in C Major, Op. 10, No. 1,
   30–31
Etude in C Major, Op. 10, No. 7,
   160, 244n13
Etude in F Major, Op. 10, No. 8, 31
Etude in C Minor, Op. 10, No. 12,
   31–32, 39
Etude in F Minor, Op. 25, No. 2, 169
Etude in C-sharp Minor, Op. 25, No.
   7, 165, 166
Etude in D-flat Major, Op. 25, No. 8,
   25–26
Fantaisie in F Minor, Op. 49,
   156–158, 244n12
Fugue in A Minor, 201
Hexaméron, 216–217, 221, 224,
   229–230, 246n3 (chap. 6), 246n4
   (chap. 6)–247n4, 247n9
Impromptu in G-flat Major, Op. 51,
   160
Mazurka in F-sharp Minor, Op. 6,
   No. 1, 167–168, 199–200
Mazurka in C-sharp Minor, Op. 6,
   No. 2, 155
Mazurkas, Op. 7, 187
Mazurka in F Minor, Op. 7, no. 3,
   186, 189–190, 192
Mazurka in E Minor, Op. 17, no. 2,
   187–188, 189–190, 192, 246n2
   (chap. 5)
Mazurka in G Minor, Op. 24, No. 1,
   36–37, 47–49, 65
Mazurka in C Major, Op. 24, no. 2,
   50–51

Mazurka in D-flat Major, Op. 30, No. 3, 168

Mazurka in G-sharp Minor, Op. 33, No. 1, 24

Mazurka in D Major, Op. 33, No. 2, 150–151

Mazurka in A-flat Major, Op. 50, No. 2, 156

Mazurka in C-sharp Minor, Op. 50, No. 3, 201

Mazurkas, Op. 56, 204

Mazurka in B Major, Op. 56, no. 1, 160

Mazurka in A Minor, Op. 59, No. 1, 35–36

Mazurka in A-flat Major, Op. 59, No. 2, 177

Mazurka in C-sharp Minor, Op. 63, No. 3, 60–61, 201

Nocturnes, Op. 9, 46, 156

Nocturne in E-flat Major, Op. 9, No. 2, 117

Nocturne in F Major, Op. 15, no. 1, 166–167

Nocturne in F-sharp Major, Op. 15, No. 2, 245n25

Nocturne in G Minor, Op. 15, No. 3, 177

Nocturne in C-sharp Minor, Op. 27, No. 1, 91–92, 99–100, 156

Nocturne in D-flat Major, Op. 27, No. 2, 156

Nocturne in B Major, Op. 32, No. 1, 157

Nocturne in G Minor, Op. 37, No. 1, 49, 165, 240n17

Nocturne in G Major, Op. 37, No. 2, 247n9

Nocturne in C Minor, Op. 48, No. 1, 46, 56–57

Nocturnes, Op. 55, 204

Nocturne in E-flat Major, Op. 55, no. 2, 160, 200

Nocturnes, Op. 62, 46

Nocturne in B Major, Op. 62, No. 1, 58

Nouvelle Etude No. 1 in F Minor, 26–27

Polonaise in B-flat Minor, 44

Polonaises, Op. 26, 99

Polonaise in E-flat Minor, Op. 26, No. 2, 98–99

Polonaise in A-flat Major, Op. 53, 97–98

Polonaise-Fantaisie in A-flat Major, Op. 61, 1–3, 38–39, 151, 207–210

Preludes, Op. 28, 148, 156, 160, 181, 221, 244n8

Prelude in C Major, Op. 28, No. 1, 215

Prelude in E Minor, Op. 28, No. 4, 188–190, 192

Prelude in A Major, Op. 28, No. 7, 59–60

Prelude in E Major, Op. 28, No. 9, 220–221, 222, 224, 247n9

Prelude in D-flat Major, Op. 28, No. 15, 142, 147–149, 244n8

Prelude in B-flat Minor, Op. 28, No. 16, 162–164, 181–182, 183, 191, 192, 196, 245n14

Prelude in A-flat Major, Op. 28, No. 17, 100–101

Prelude in E-flat Major, Op. 28, No. 19, 158–159, 161, 173–174, 245n19

Prelude in C Minor, Op. 28, No. 20, 164–165

Rondo à la Mazur in F Major, Op. 5, 92

Scherzo in B Minor, Op. 20, 141

Scherzo in B-flat Minor, Op. 31, 156, 176, 192–193

Scherzo in C-sharp Minor, Op. 39, 159–160, 161, 194–195, 196

Scherzo in E Major, Op. 54, 4–5

Sonata in B-flat Minor, Op. 35, 32–33, 42–43, 94–96, 245n14

Sonata in B Minor, Op. 58, 7, 29–30, 33–34, 40, 41–42, 50, 59, 61–63, 90, 143–146, 152–154, 156, 165–166, 169–171, 201, 204, 225–229, 239n10, 245n17, 247n10

Sonata for Cello and Piano in G Minor, Op. 65, 201, 223–224

Variations in B-flat Major, Op. 12, 185–186, 187, 192

Variations on "Là ci darem la mano" for Piano and Orchestra, Op. 2, 44, 199

Waltz in A Minor, Op. 34, No. 2, 165

Clementi, Muzio
Sonata in G Minor, Op. 34, No. 2, 87
Sonata in A Major, Op. 50, No. 1, 88

Cramer, Johann Baptist
Etude in E Minor, 122–123

Czerny, Carl
Hexaméron, 216–217, 221, 224, 229–230, 246n3 (chap. 6), 246n4 (chap. 6)–247n4, 247n9

Debussy, Claude
L'isle joyeuse, 9, 234–235

Dussek, Jan Ladislav
Sonata in A-flat Major, C.V. 43, 117–118
Theme and Variations in E-flat Major on "Partant pour la Syrie," 118–119

Grieg, Edvard
Concerto for Piano and Orchestra in A Minor, op. 16, 204, 205–206
Lyric Pieces, 204
Melodie in A Minor, Op. 47, No. 3, 204–205

Haydn, Franz Joseph
Sonata in C Minor, Hob. XVI:20, 63
Sonata in C Major, Hob. XVI:35, 213–214
Sonata in G Major, Hob. XVI:40, 14
Sonata in G Minor, Hob. XVI:44, 14
Sonata in C Major, Hob. XVI:48, 13–14
Sonata in E-flat Major, Hob. XVI:49, 14, 70–71, 74, 86, 106–107
Sonata in C Major, Hob. XVI:50, 71–72, 76, 102, 119
Sonata in E-flat Major, Hob. XVI:52, 16, 73, 86, 119
String Quartets, Op. 50 (Hob. III:44–49), 11
String Quartet in D Major, Op. 71, No. 2, 119-121

Herz, Henri
Hexaméron, 216–217, 221, 224, 229–230, 246n3 (chap. 6), 246n4 (chap. 6)–247n4, 247n9

Hummel, Johann Nepomuk
Concerto for Piano and Orchestra in A Minor, Op. 85, 185

Concerto for Piano and Orchestra in B Minor, Op. 89, 185

Sonata in F-sharp Minor, Op. 81, 185

Liszt, Franz
Années de Pèlerinage, 133
Hexaméron, 216–217, 221, 224, 229–230, 246n3 (chap. 6), 246n4 (chap. 6)–247n4, 247n9
Hungarian Rhapsody No. 8 in F-sharp Minor, 131
Sonata in B Minor, 5–6, 130–131
Transcendental Etude No. 1 in C Major, 132
Transcendental Etude No. 8 in C Minor, 132–133
Transcendental Etude No. 10 in F Minor, 184

Mendelssohn-Bartholdy, Felix
Prelude and Fugue in E Minor, WoO 13, 230–232

Mozart, Wolfgang Amadeus
Adagio in B Minor, K. 540, 78, 82, 105
Concerto for Flute, Harp, and Orchestra in C Major, K. 299, 79
Fantasie in C Minor, K. 396, 116–117
Fantasie in D Minor, K. 397, 115–116, 198–199
Fantasie in C Minor, K. 475, 114–115
Idomeneo, Re di Creta, K. 366, 69
Le nozze di Figaro, K. 492, 184
Requiem in D Minor, K. 626, 199
Serenade for Winds in E-flat Major, K. 361, 69
Sonata in D Major, K. 284, 76–77, 241n6
Sonata in B-flat Major, K. 333, 77–78, 115

Sonata in C Minor, K. 457, 14, 114
String Quartet in G Major, K. 387, 69
String Quartet in E-flat Major, K. 428, 114–115

Piani, Giovanni Antonio
XII Sonate a violino solo e violoncello col cimbalo, opera prima (Twelve Sonatas for Violin, Violoncello, and Harpsichord, Opus 1), 11

Pixis, Johann Peter
Hexaméron, 216–217, 221, 224, 229–230, 246n3 (chap. 6), 246n4 (chap. 6)–247n4, 247n9

Prokofiev, Sergei
Sonata in D Minor, Op. 14, 236
Sonata in A Minor, Op. 28, 235–236
Concerto for Piano and Orchestra in G Minor, Op. 16, 236

Rachmaninoff, Sergei
Prelude in D Major, Op. 23, No. 4, 41

Schubert, Franz
Impromptu in C Minor, D. 899, No. 1, 229
Impromptu in E-flat Major, D. 899, No. 2, 20–21
Impromptu in B-flat Major, D. 935, No. 3, 21
Sonata in A Minor, D. 845, 90
Sonata in C Minor, D. 958, 141, 220, 221
Sonata in A Major, D. 959, 5, 19–20, 21, 34, 141
Sonata in B-flat Major, D. 960, 141, 214, 218
Winterreise, D. 911, "Wasserfluth," 218–220

Schumann, Robert
 Kinderszenen, Op. 15, "Von fremden
  Ländern und Menschen," 221,
  222
 Fantasie in C Major, Op. 17,
  40

Scriabin, Alexander
 Etude in D-sharp Minor, Op. 8, no.
  12, 237
 Poème Tragique, Op. 34, 237

Thalberg, Sigismond
 Hexaméron, 216–217, 221, 224,
  229–230, 246n3 (chap. 6), 246n4
  (chap. 6)–247n4, 247n9

Tomášek, Vaclav Jan
 Variationen über ein bekanntes Thema,
  Op. 16, 35

Weber, Carl Maria von
 Sonata in A-flat Major, Op. 39, 214